POSTCARD HISTORY SERIES

Barrington

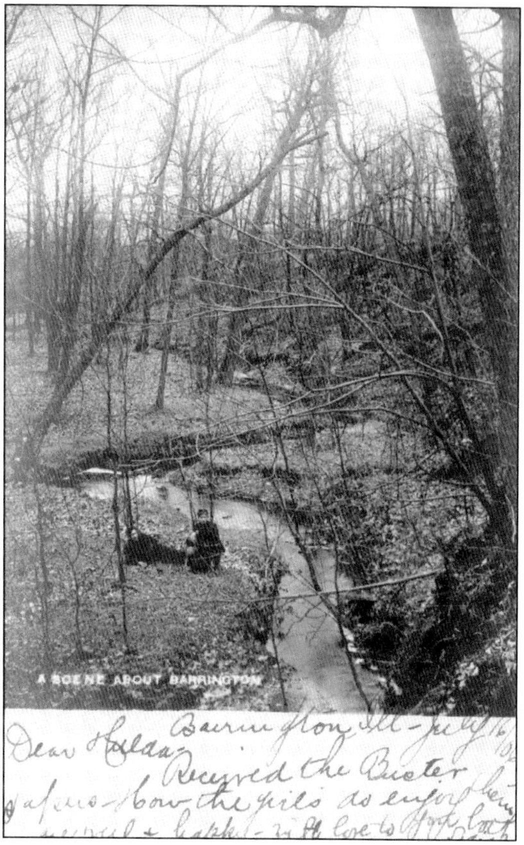

This postcard echoes an early 1872 advertisement promoting the Village of Barrington in the 1870s, stating that, "This beautiful suburban village offers high and rolling ground, many natural attractions commanding in site and an abundance of good water within four miles of the wonderfully charming Lake Zurich, Honey, Grass and Spring Lakes, all abounding in fish and graced with beautiful pleasure boats." (Courtesy author's collection.)

ON THE FRONT COVER: In 1857, a railroad timetable listed two passenger trains a day to and from Barrington and Chicago. Although train rails were made from iron in 1855, by 1865, the railroad industry was using steel rails. In 1887, the local newspaper listed six trains a day scheduled from Barrington to Chicago with a running time of an hour and a half to two hours. In 1895, a railroad timecard showed nine trains from Barrington to Chicago and eight from Chicago to Barrington. (Courtesy author's collection.)

ON THE BACK COVER: After 1889, the local Barrington bank occupied several different locations, including those on East Main Street and South Cook Street. This bank went through a number of name changes, beginning with Dwigging, Starbuck and Co., to the Bank of McIntosh, Sandman & Co., to the Barrington Bank of Sandman & Co., to the Bank of Robertson, Plagge & Co. In 1893, local merchant John C. Plagge, a feed and lumber dealer, rebuilt his store at the southwest corner of Cook and Park Avenues. A corner room in this brick building was used for banking purposes, with a large vault behind the cashier's window. In 1913, another reorganization changed the name to the First State Bank of Barrington (pictured), with capital of $50,000. (Courtesy author's collection.)

POSTCARD HISTORY SERIES

Barrington

Ken Munson

ARCADIA
PUBLISHING

ISBN 978-0-7385-8856-8

Published by Arcadia Publishing
Charleston, South Carolina

Printed in the United States of America

Library of Congress Control Number: 2011937397

For all general information contact Arcadia Publishing at:
Telephone 843-853-2070
Fax 843-853-0044
E-mail sales@arcadiapublishing.com
For customer service and orders:
Toll-Free 1-888-313-2665

Visit us on the Internet at www.arcadiapublishing.com

This book is dedicated to the memory of my parents, Alfred and Ruth Munson, who devoted countless hours to preserving the local history of Barrington through their work with the Barrington Area Historical Society, helping to assemble its archives, as well as their continuing commitment to educational outreach and special projects.

Contents

ACKNOWLEDGMENTS

My special thanks to my wife, Louise, for her continuing support, encouragement, and assistance during the production of this work. In addition, I extend special gratitude to Dee Larson for her valuable friendship and continuing interest and encouragement in preserving Barrington's history. Unless otherwise noted, all of the postcards in this book are from the personal collection of Ken Munson.

Introduction

In 1831, Cook County was organized and named after Daniel P. Cook, a territorial legislator who devoted much time and energy to the formation of a state government. According to the terms of the 1833 Treaty of Chicago, the Potawatomi Indians had relinquished all claims to the lands in northeastern Illinois, and by 1834, the first white settlers arrived in the area that would become Barrington township. William Van Orsdal and Jessie F. Miller settled temporarily on the school section because of the abundant timber. At that time, a school section was a section of public land set apart in a surveyed township by the US government for the maintenance of public schools. When they arrived, there were approximately 500 Potawatomi in the wooded grove. Other early settlers included Henry C. Lawson, Phillip Hawley Sr., William H. Otis, Homer Willmarth, William B. Freeman, Shubuel W. Kingsley, George W. Waterman, Alvah Miller, and Gilbert A. Applebee.

At first, the center of Barrington township was called Miller's Grove because of the many Miller families living there. Later, it was called Barrington Center. Settlers from Berkshire County, Massachusetts, as well as New York State, were drawn to the Barrington area by news of land with rich soil that could be purchased reasonably, and they found the surrounding area to be three-fourths prairie and one-fourth timber. In 1840, the town of Barrington was organized at a meeting in the William Otis log house east of Miller's Grove.

In 1854, the Illinois & Wisconsin Railroad, which soon became the Chicago & North Western Railroad (C&NW), was extended to Deer Grove and on to Cary. The station for this new railroad line was placed in Deer Grove, about two miles east of present-day Barrington. It didn't stay there. Several early settlers objected to selling parts of their farms for a village to be developed there, so Robert C. Campbell, a civil engineer for the railroad, went two miles farther northwest, purchased a 40-acre farm, and proceeded to plat Barrington in blocks and lots. The original village was bounded by Hough Street, County Line Road, a point east of Spring Street, and a line south of Russell Street. The train station, originally located at Deer Grove, was placed on a railroad flatcar and moved two miles west. This new location became Barrington Station. In 1856, a post office was established with John M. Porter appointed postmaster. Porter's office was reportedly in a building on East Station Street. Barrington was on its way to becoming a vibrant and thriving community. The area around Barrington Station continued to grow, with relocated buildings and newly erected structures, and in 1863 residents approved the creation of a village organization. On February 16, 1865, the Illinois Legislature granted a charter making the incorporation a reality.

Barrington was an agricultural community into the 20th century. Following the post–World War I era, a number of Chicago business leaders started constructing their residences on large woodland tracts around the Barrington countryside. In 1929, a new office for the Jewel Tea Company was also constructed. Barrington celebrated its centennial in 1963 and continues to grow and change. New homes and subdivisions have been built and older architecturally and historically significant homes and downtown buildings still stand proudly along the tree-lined village streets. The community's residents recognize the importance of the roles of history, culture, and the arts in the development of their community and actively work through committees, the local historical society, and many cultural and civic groups to retain and maintain an environment dedicated to the ongoing growth of Barrington. The postcards in this book illustrate the true importance and value of maintaining a photographic history of the community.

Photography has been an important component of human life for well over 170 years, from the first daguerreotypes in the late 1830s and early 1840s through the development of the ambrotype and tintype. In later years, paper images—known as calotypes or talbotypes—began to appear, followed by salted paper prints, *cartes-de-visite* (or visiting cards), and cabinet card photographs, which were popular from 1863 to 1920.

The first known postal-type card in this country was a privately printed card from 1861. Between 1870 and 1898, postcards were popular in European countries. Many of them were printed as advertising cards or specially produced for a historic event, such as the Columbian Exposition in Chicago. From 1898 to 1901, the Private Mailing Card Era allowed American publishers to print and sell cards for the purpose of sending written messages to friends and families. This was followed by the Undivided Back Era (1901–1907), the Divided Back Era (1907–1915), the Early Modern Era (1916–1930), the Linen Card Era (1930–1945), and the Photochrome Era (1939 to the present).

The divided-back card, which became popular in 1907, offered the opportunity for an image on one side and message and address on the other. Postcard production became a booming business for photographers, printers, and artists. As a result, the Eastman Kodak Company built a market for photographic postcards by introducing a photograph stock product specifically for postcards and urging their dealers to encourage postcard production among professionals as well as amateur photographers.

The author's collection contains many examples of real-photo postcards, which have a photographic view printed on photosensitive paper with a postcard back, printed by local photographers. Some cards in this collection were originally created by George Froelich Jr. (1888–1972) of Barrington, who documented many community scenes and events through real-photo postcards. Froelich left a valuable gift to the community with these important photographic records. Other postcards selected for this book are either printed or lithographed, with some later postcards printed in color.

Postcards offer a true visual record of the history and growth of the cities and villages in America and provide strong evidence of the determination of our forefathers to document American life and history.

One

GREETINGS

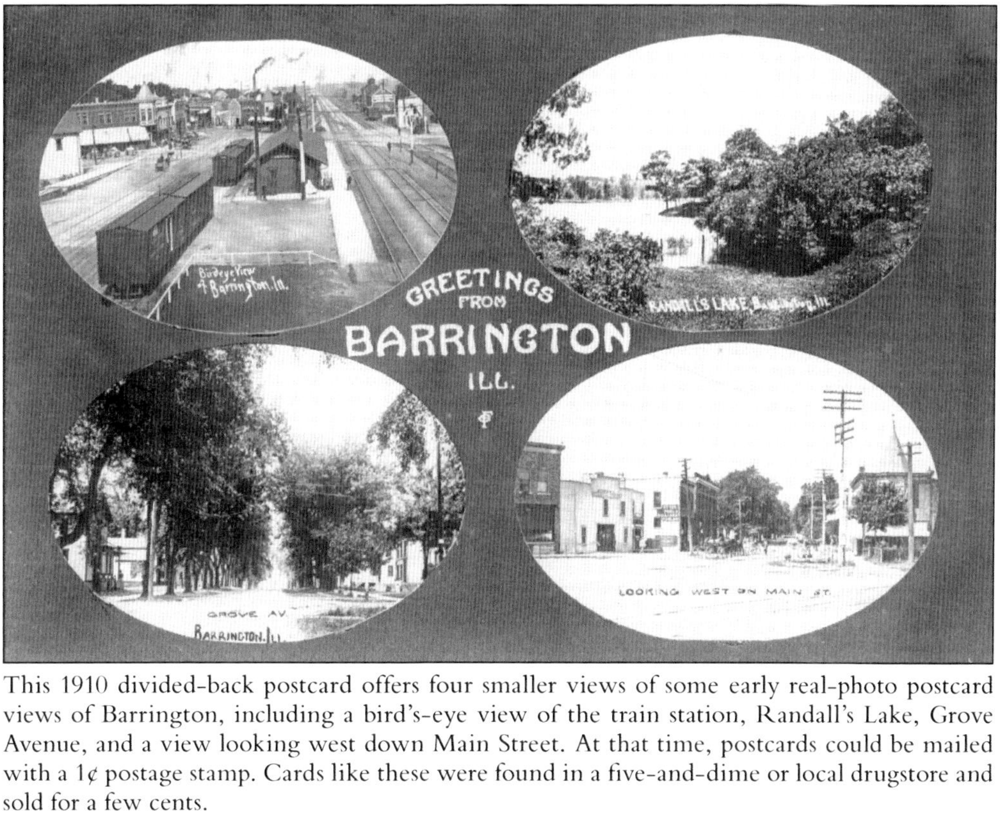

This 1910 divided-back postcard offers four smaller views of some early real-photo postcard views of Barrington, including a bird's-eye view of the train station, Randall's Lake, Grove Avenue, and a view looking west down Main Street. At that time, postcards could be mailed with a 1¢ postage stamp. Cards like these were found in a five-and-dime or local drugstore and sold for a few cents.

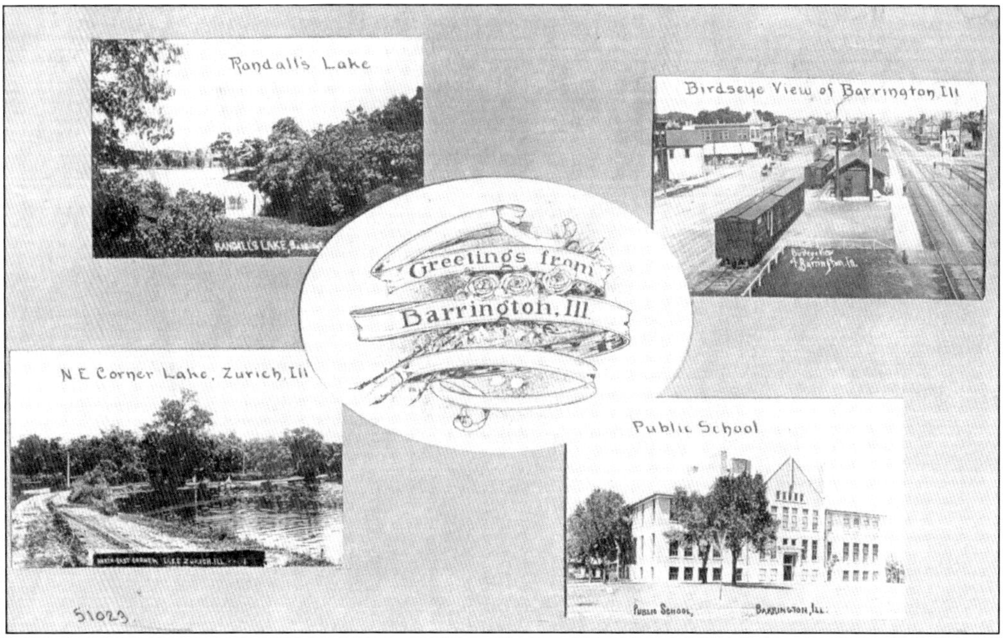

This greeting card consists of several smaller views of Barrington, including Randall's Lake, a bird's-eye view of Barrington, the northeast corner of Lake Zurich, and the public school in town. The photographs were taken by Charles R. Childs.

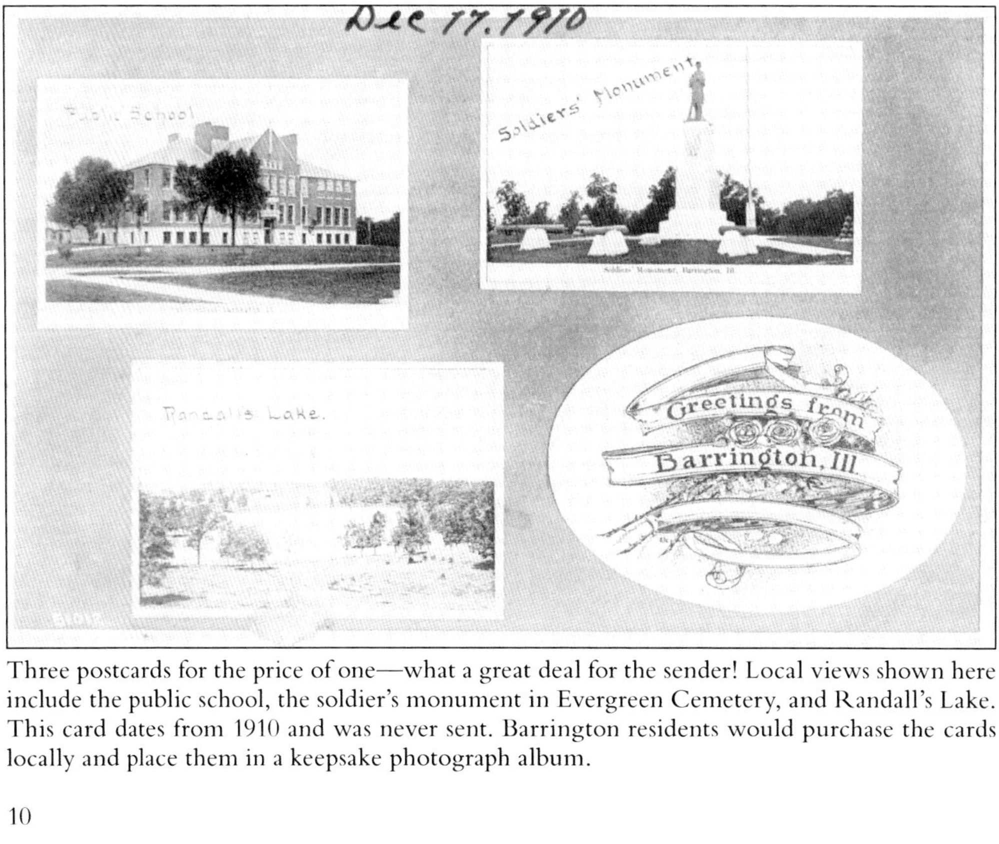

Three postcards for the price of one—what a great deal for the sender! Local views shown here include the public school, the soldier's monument in Evergreen Cemetery, and Randall's Lake. This card dates from 1910 and was never sent. Barrington residents would purchase the cards locally and place them in a keepsake photograph album.

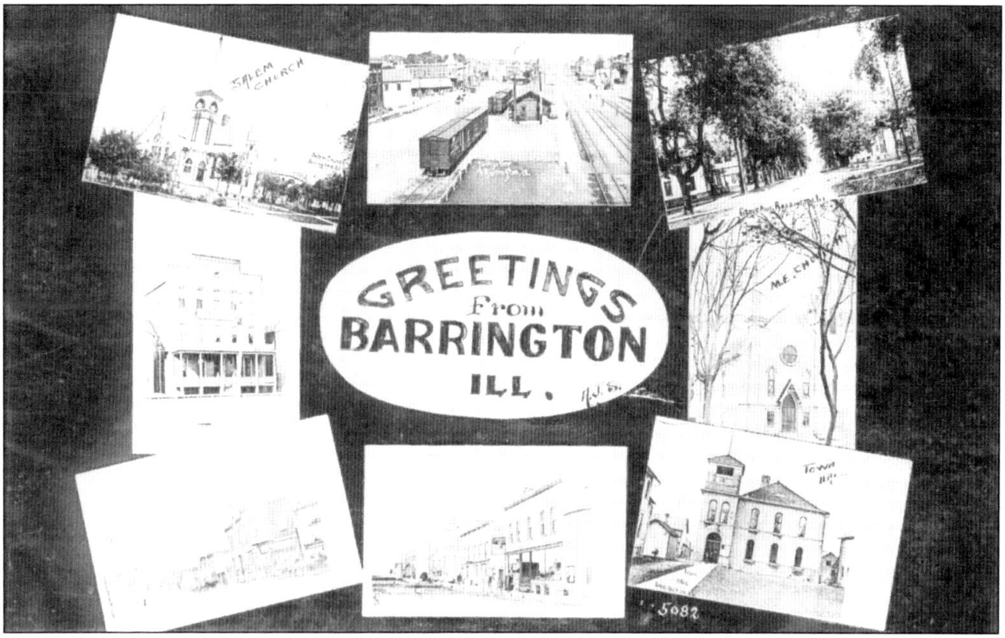

These eight views of Barrington are a bit smaller but in close-up are quite clear with amazing detail. Views include the Salem Church, a bird's-eye view of downtown Barrington, Grove Avenue, the Commercial Hotel, the M.E. Church, Cook Street, Railroad Avenue, and the Barrington Village Hall.

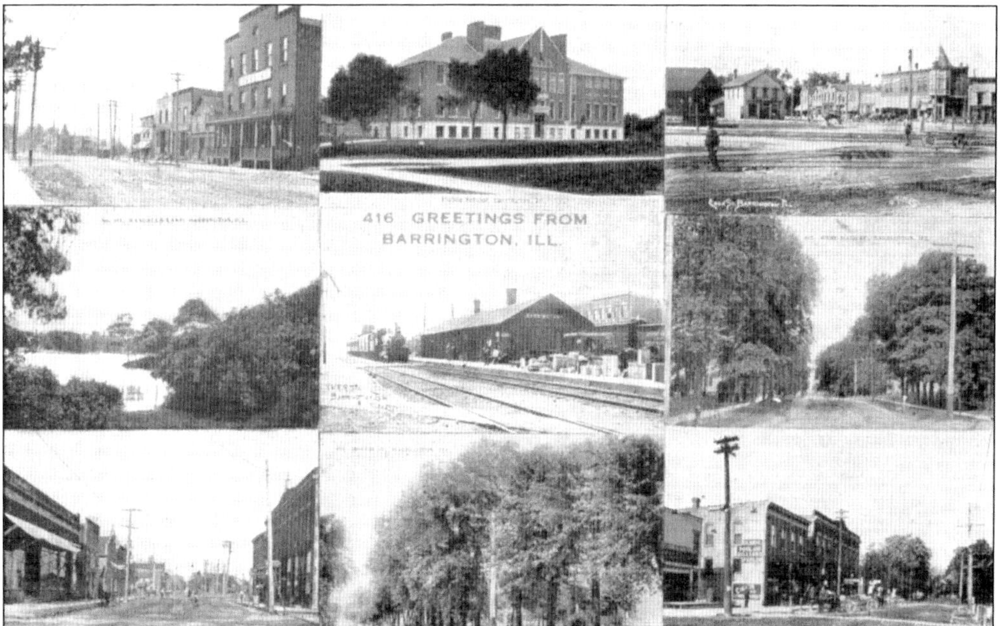

William D. Hoffman of Chicago, Illinois, printed and sold this multi-view postcard in 1915. The nine images include East Main Street, the public school on Hough Street, a view of Cook Street, Randall's Lake, the Barrington train station, a streetscape of West Main Street, East Main Street, tree-lined Hough Street, and downtown Main Street.

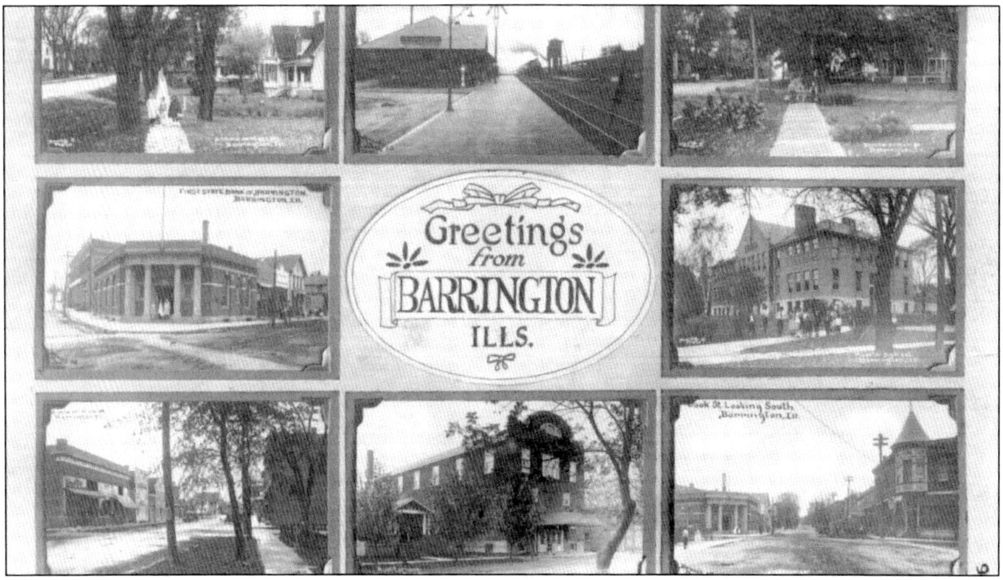

The eight views on this real-photo postcard by H.B. Brooks of Chicago, Illinois, include a scene on Main Street with small children, the Barrington Chicago & North Western (C&NW) train station, a view of West Main Street with small children, the First State Bank of Barrington, the Hough Street School with children posing in front of the school building, scenic Main Street with vintage automobiles, the auditorium where residents could view the latest movies, and a southward view of Cook Street.

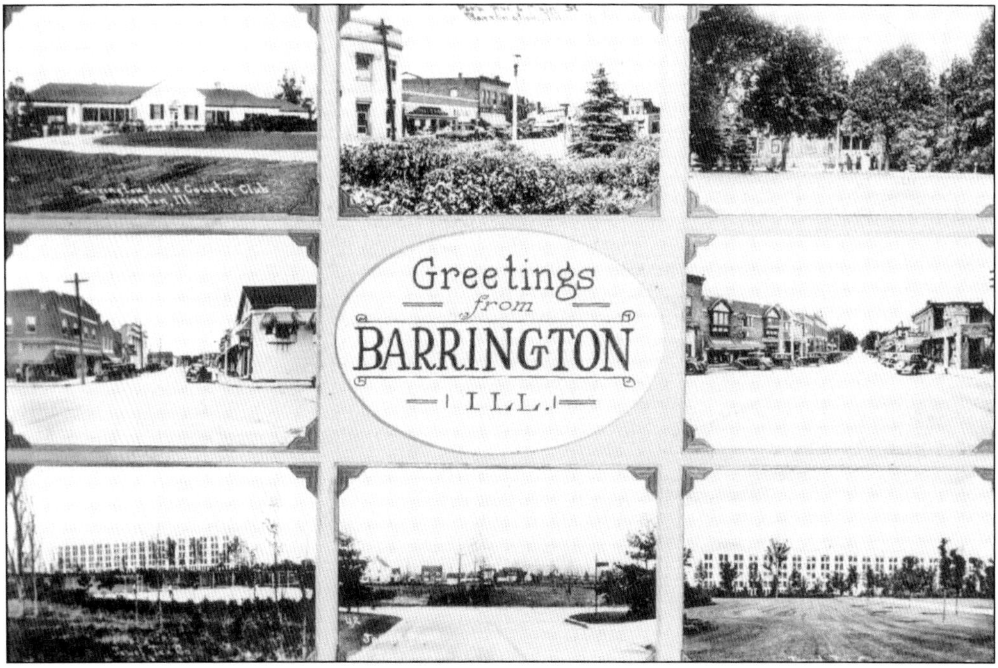

Another eight-view 1937 postcard from Barrington depicts the Barrington Hills Country Club, Park Avenue and Main Street, the Biltmore Country Club, Cook Street, West Main Street, the Jewel Tea Company offices, Jewel Park, and a closer view of the Jewel Tea building. Each of these images could also be found on separate postcards.

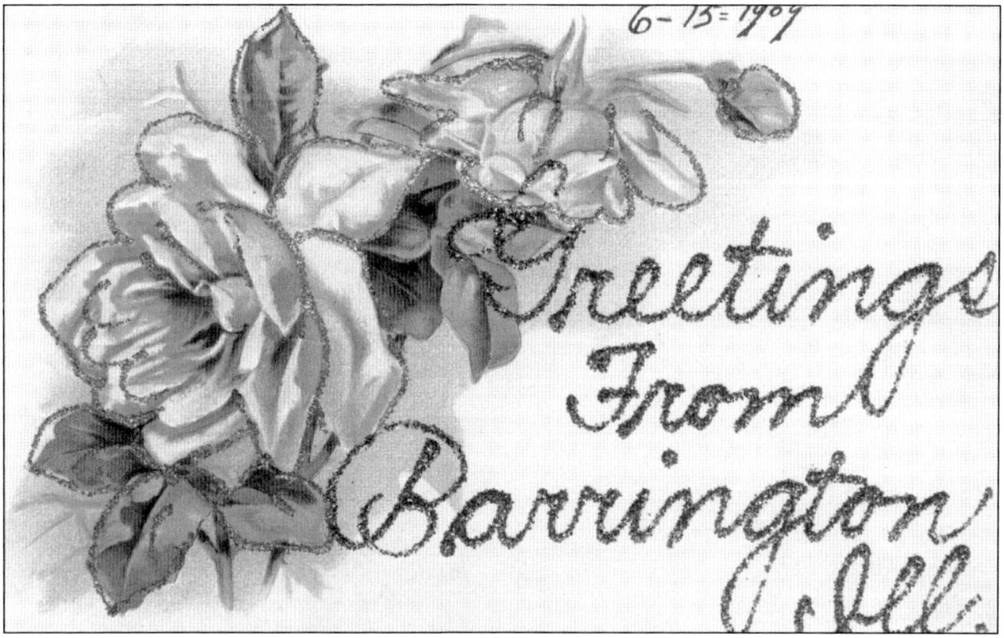

This colorful and elaborate 1909 greeting card, originally printed in Germany, was from a flower series offered by an unknown postcard retailer. The "Greetings From Barrington, Ill." was done in blue glitter with red, pink, and yellow flowers outlined in gold glitter and embossed on the front side of the card.

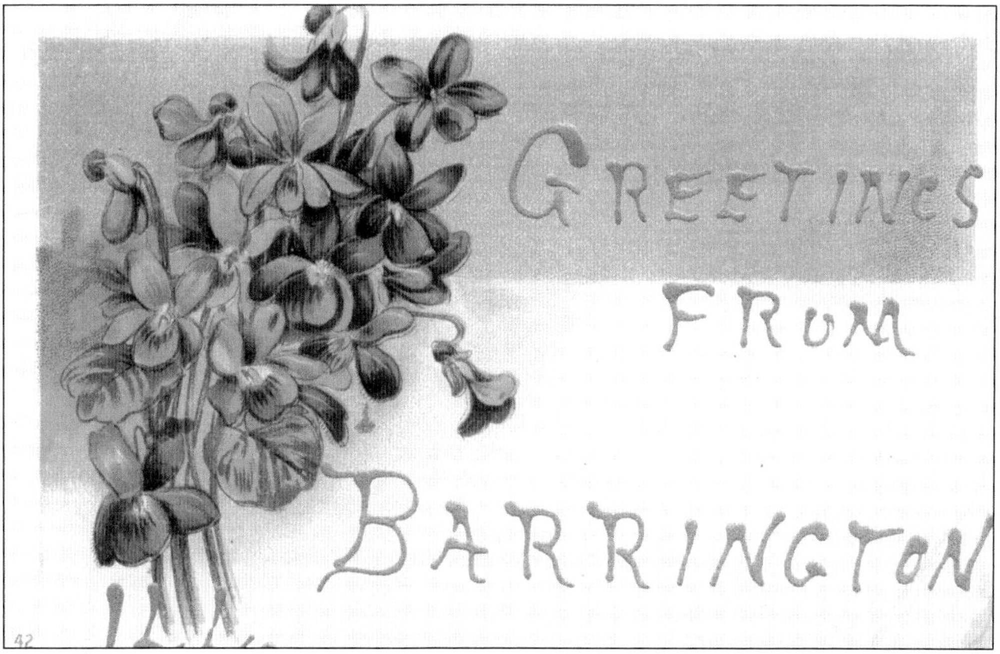

This card featuring purple violets was printed in Germany and has the word "postcard" printed in several languages on the reverse side. The violets are embossed on the surface of the card and the wording is done in raised gold lettering.

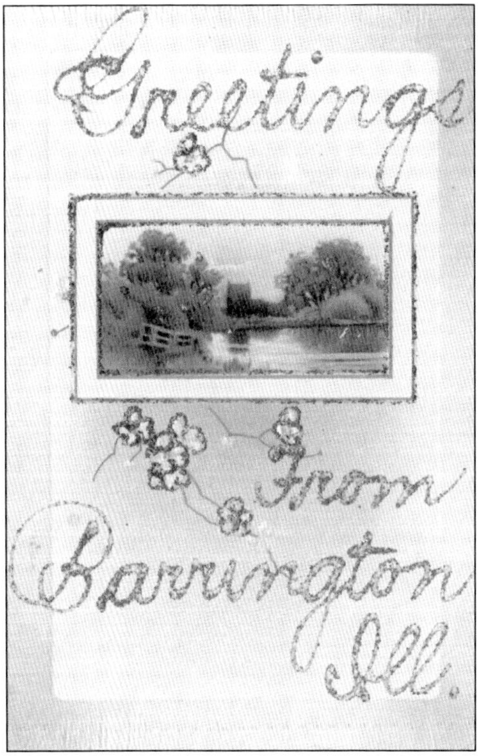

This German printed card from the early 20th century depicts a pond scene with "Greetings from Barrington, Ill." written on the card with purple glitter. Other colors on the card include yellow, green, and cream. Glitter was only used on postcards for a few years because mail carriers could get skin irritations from delivering them.

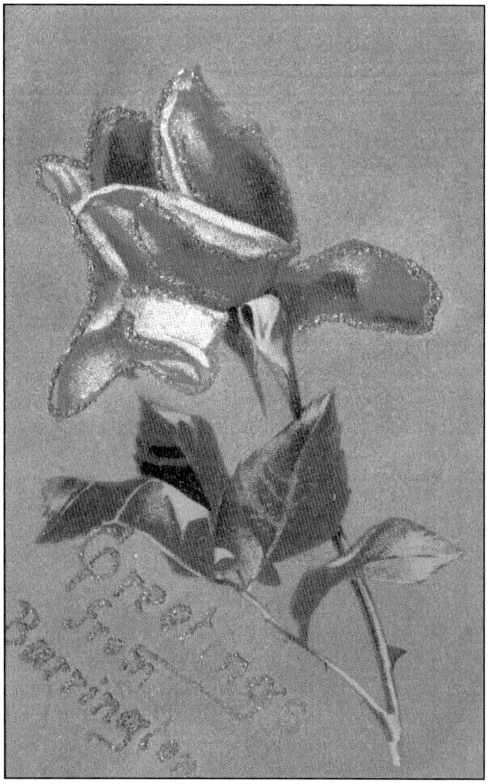

This card depicts a rose with "Greetings from Barrington" in silver glitter. The card has a dark olive background and a red rose highlighted with silver glitter with light and dark green petals. The card was printed by a manufacturer from Monroe, Wisconsin.

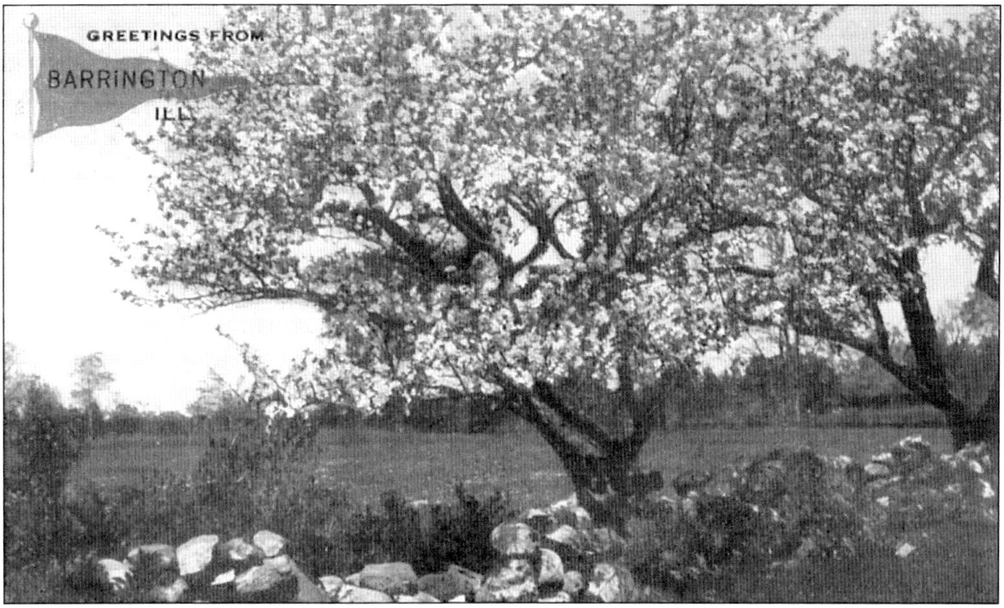

An early card from 1916, published by the E.C. Kropp Co. from Milwaukee, Wisconsin, depicts blooming crab apple trees. A red pennant appears in the upper left corner with "Greetings from Barrington Ill." This card was a generalized postcard, meaning that the manufacturer had a stock photograph and would overprint the "greetings" with the local community's name. The image quality on this card was not as clear as on a real-photo postcard.

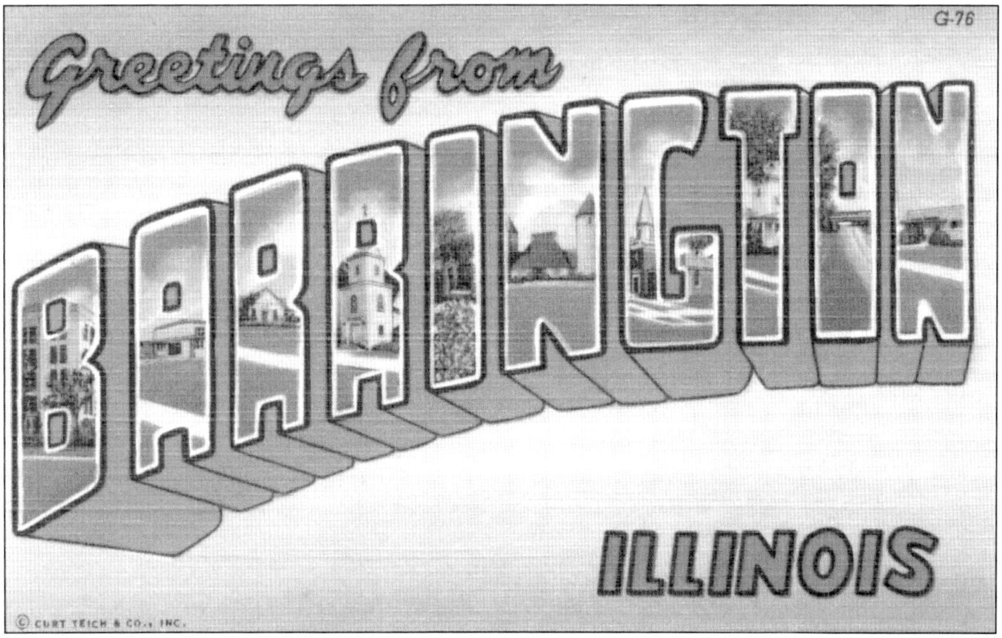

This bright yellow and orange postcard depicted various locations around Barrington inside each individual letter spelling out the name of the community. Images depicted on this card include the Jewel Tea Company, Barrington High School, a home, St. Paul Church, a flower garden, the building at Inverness, the Community Church of Barrington, the Methodist church, a road scene, and an unidentified building.

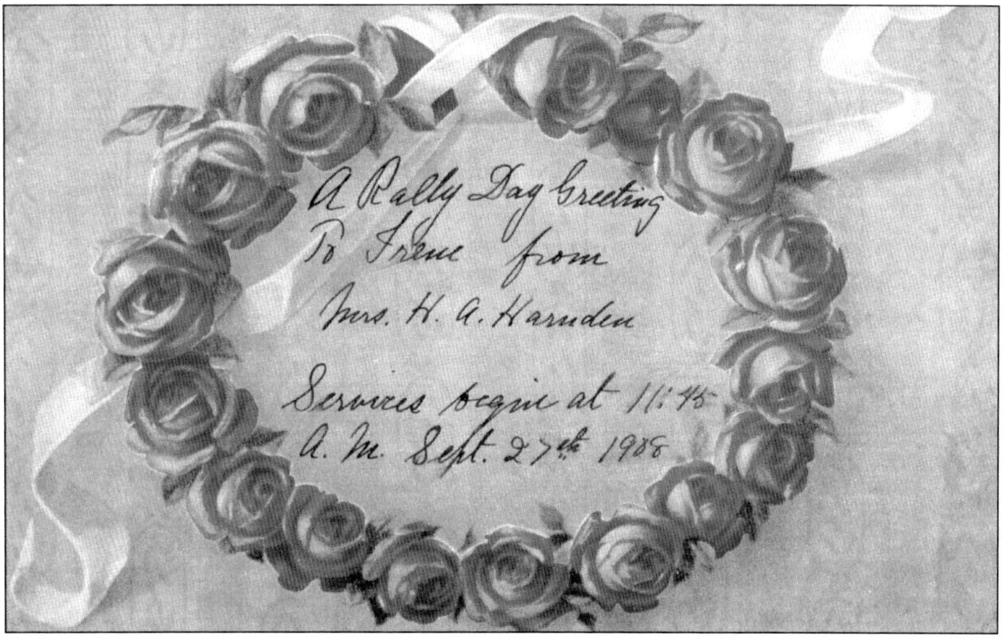

A Rally Day greeting card sent to Irene Holmes from Mrs. H.A. Harnden reminds her of services for Rally Day at one of the local churches. Services began at 11:45 a.m. on September 27, 1908, with a nice program at the regular time for Sunday school. Harnden stated that she would like to have a full class: "They were all there but two last Sunday." The card features a wreath of red roses with a white ribbon and a center space for short messages.

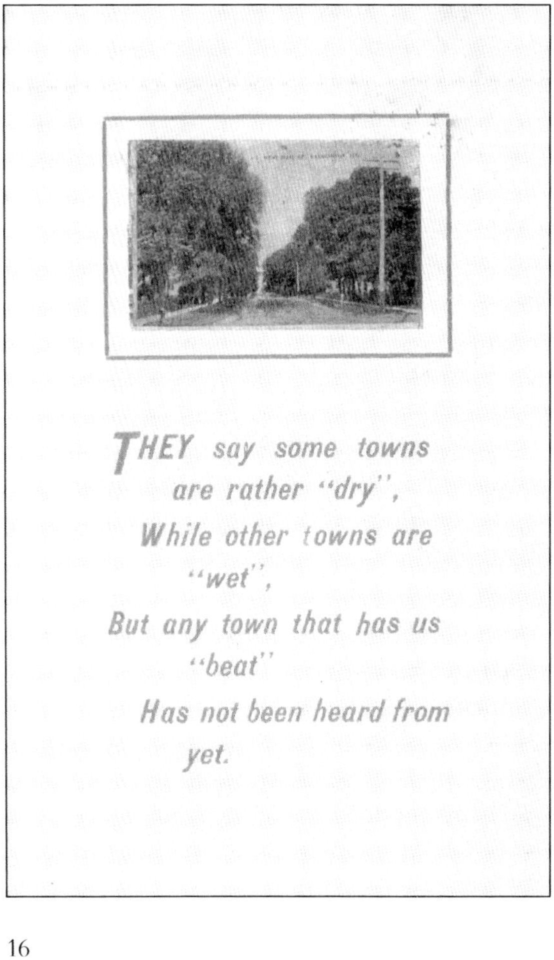

This card, published by William Hoffman Publishing, contains a miniature view of West Main Street and references the lack of taverns within the community. At one time, Barrington had as many as five taverns. In 1908, four saloons went out of business or stopped selling hard liquor in response to campaigning by local "dry" advocates. The town's "dry" spell ended in 1933 with the approval of the 21st amendment to the US Constitution, which repealed Prohibition.

Two

Downtown and the Railroad

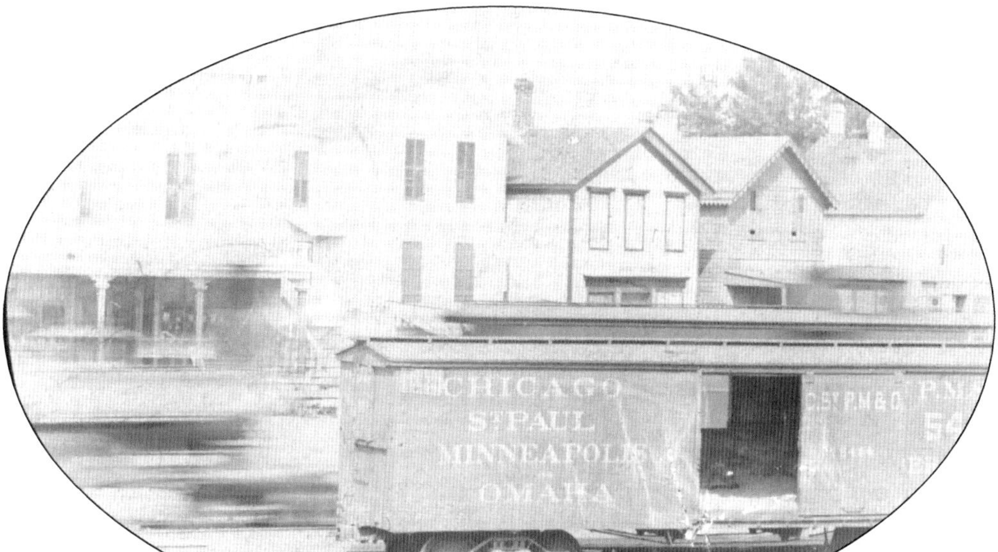

This view depicts the north side of East Main Street in 1870 or 1871, before the big fire. The buildings shown in the background housed a hotel, coppersmith shop, a tin shop, and a harness shop. This is one of the earliest photographs of downtown Barrington. The Chicago & Northwestern (C&NW) was the main line. Apparently, the freight shipment came along the Chicago, St. Paul, Minneapolis & Omaha line, and the railroad car was moved to the C&NW line for the delivery of goods to local merchants.

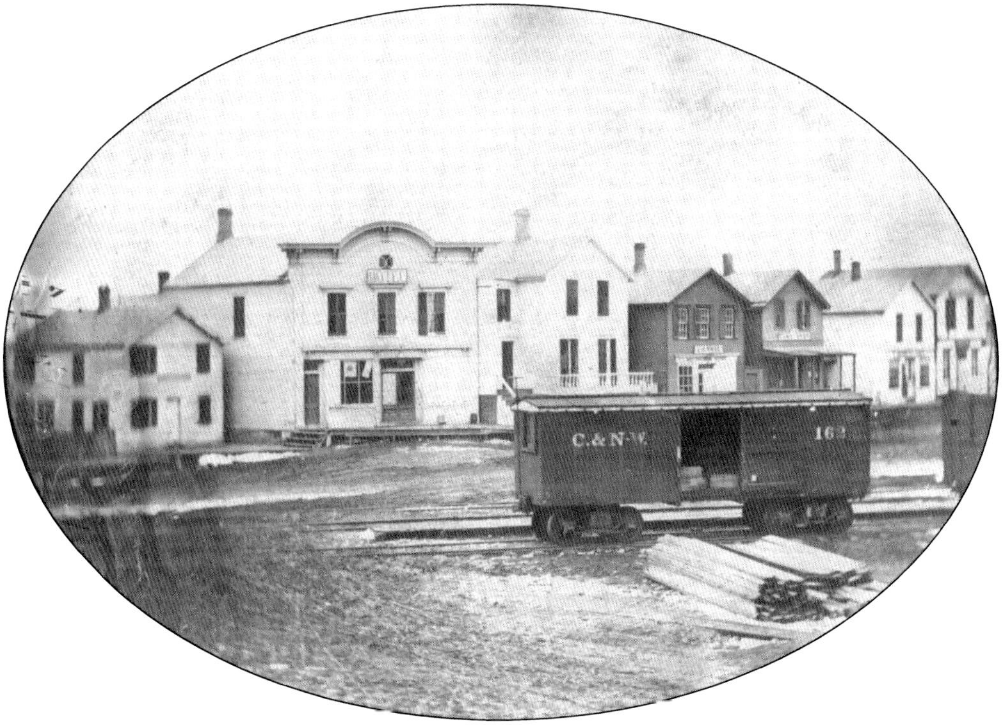

This view of East Main Street was taken from a greater distance, showing some additional businesses and clearer detail of the buildings and railroad. Additional businesses pictured include a market shop and the Colburn House.

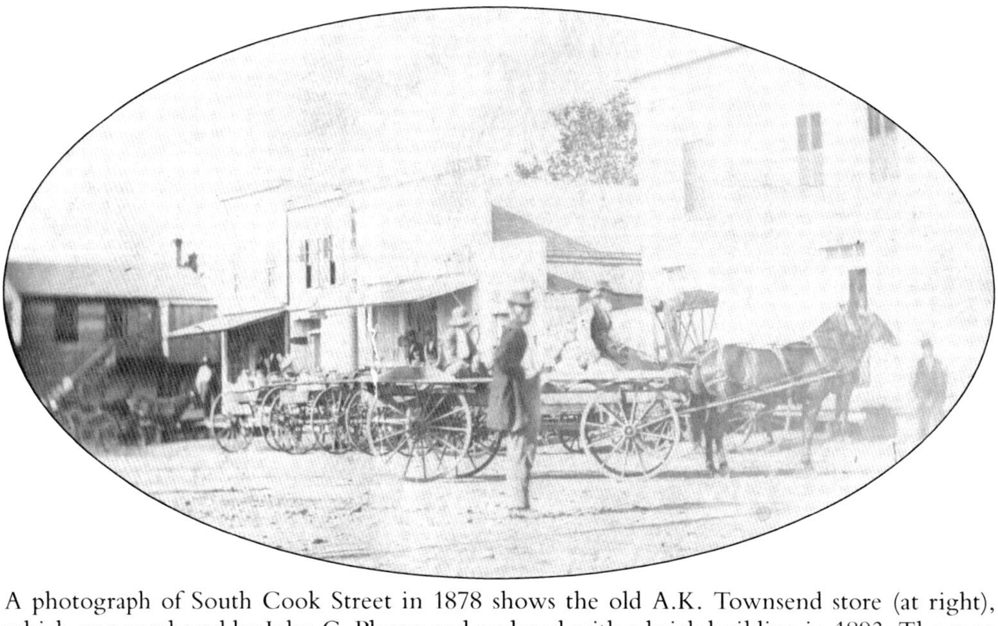

A photograph of South Cook Street in 1878 shows the old A.K. Townsend store (at right), which was purchased by John C. Plagge and replaced with a brick building in 1893. The man on the hayrack is Linus Lines Sr., the grandfather of Max, Arnett, and Jennie Lines. McIntosh Lumber is the third building from the left.

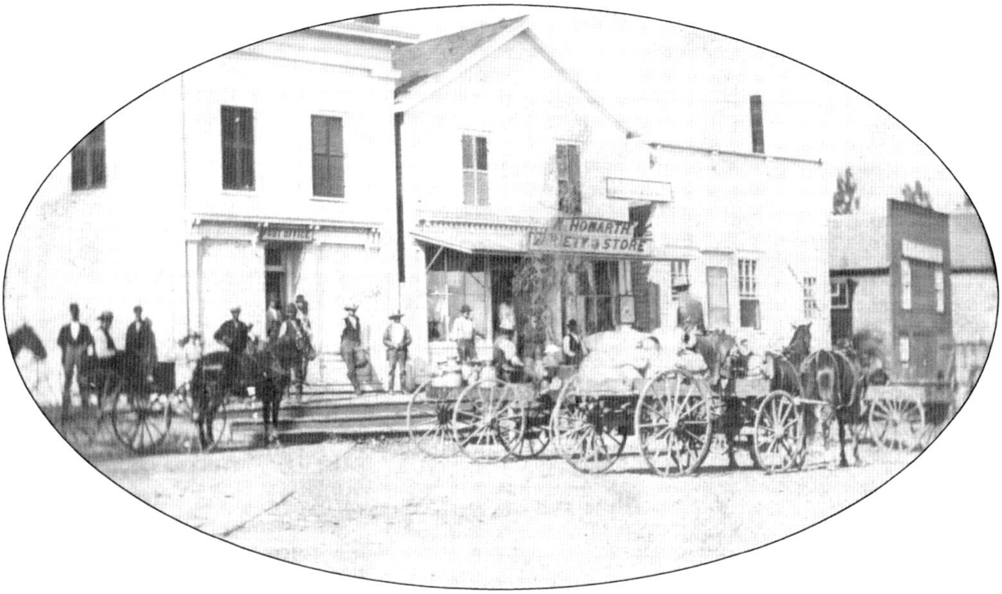

This is an 1870s downtown view of South Railroad Street (later renamed Park Avenue) from Cook Street, looking west. Businesses depicted in the photograph include the Townsend Store that housed the post office (Townsend was the postmaster), the William Howarth Variety Store, and the Wallace Benedict Photograph Studio.

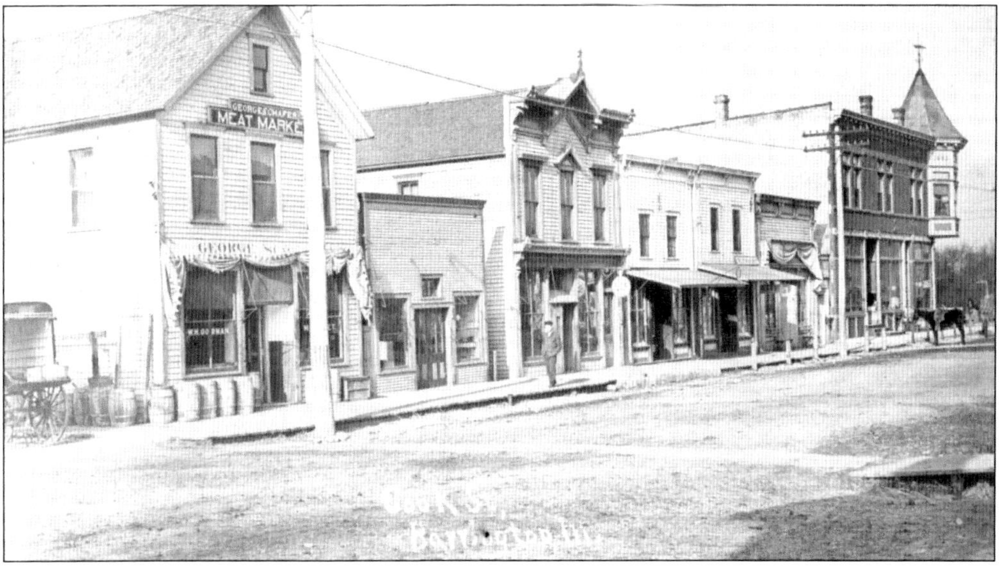

An early postcard view of Cook Street depicts local businesses, including the George Schafer Meat Market (in the corner building on the left). Note the barrels on the wooden sidewalk in front of the store and a restaurant/café (third building from the right). At the far right, a horse tied to the hitching post near the restaurant waits for his owner to return. In the very early years, sidewalks often consisted of wooden planks laid end to end that led to a path of ashes or gravel. An ordinance was passed in June 1887 requiring that all sidewalks be made of pine boards that were one inch thick, four feet long, and laid on well-supported stringers, with the boards set one quarter-inch apart. The spacing was required to allow air between the boards, which kept them from rotting.

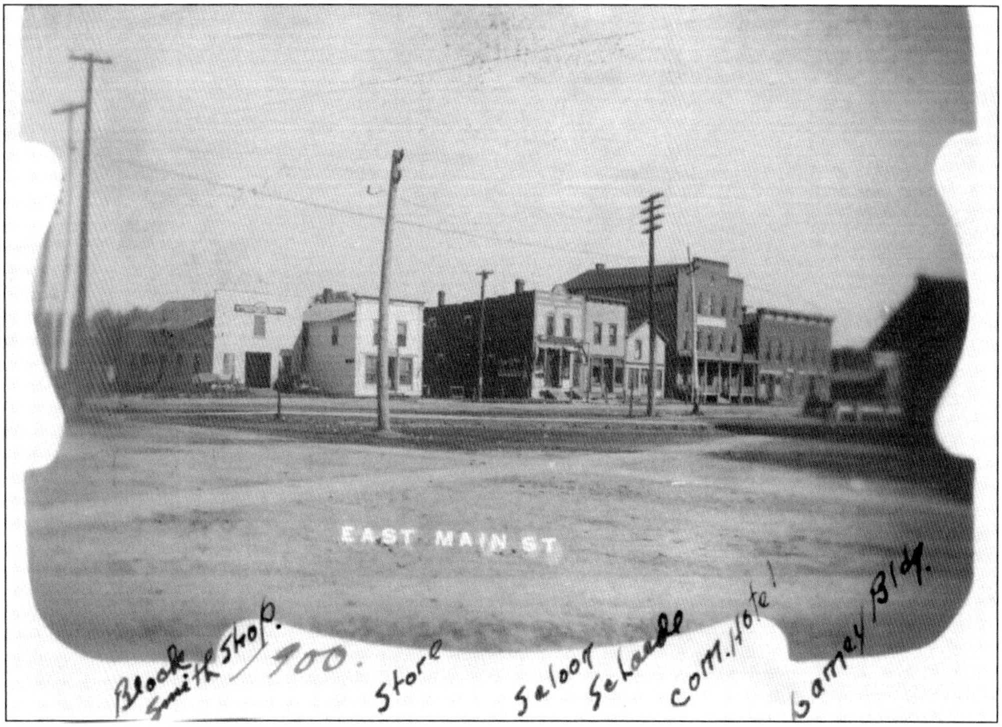

This 1900 view of East Main Street shows a blacksmith shop, an unidentified store, a saloon, a hotel, and the Lamey building. The photograph was probably taken very early in the morning, when no residents were visible along the walkways.

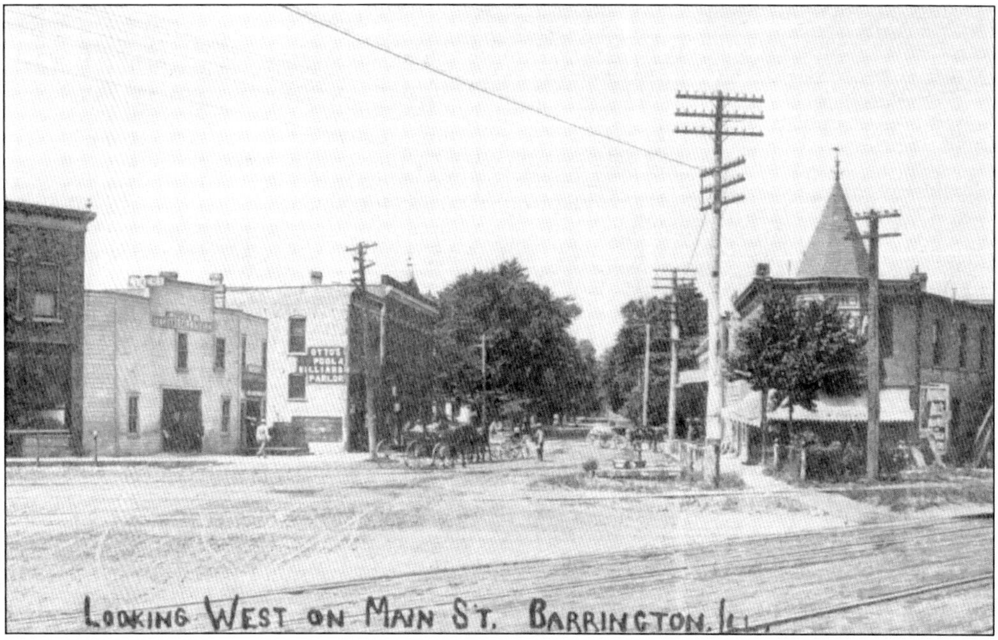

This 1911 card was published by John C. Dodge and looks west on Main Street in downtown Barrington. The sign on the side of the central building promotes Otto's Pool & Billiard Parlor, while the large building to the left of the sign houses a livery and feed store.

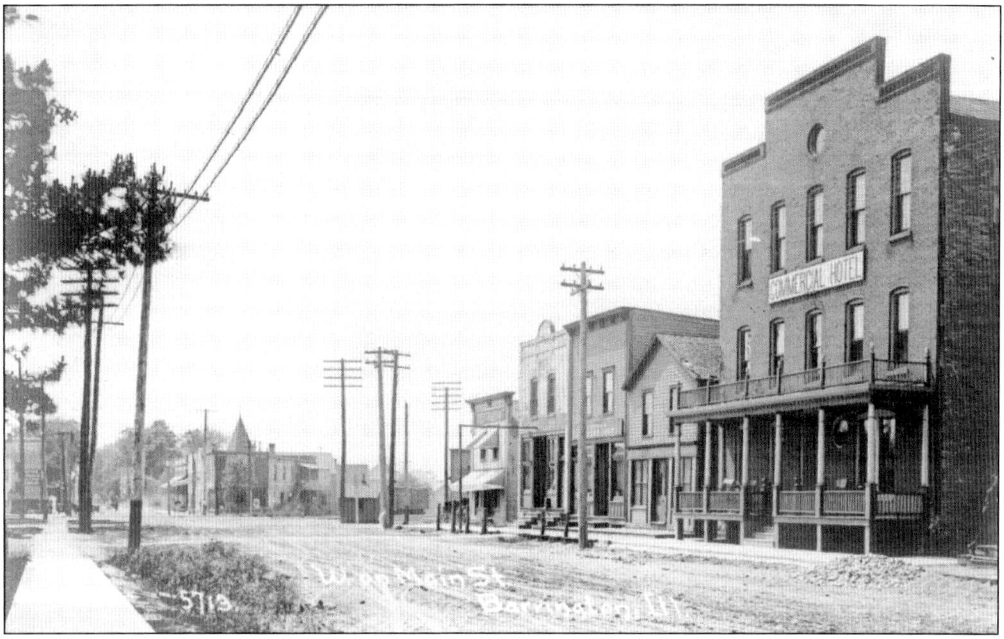

Charles R. Childs captured this 1911 view looking west on Main Street across the railroad tracks toward Hough Street. Childs probably took this photograph early in the morning, before local residents arrived downtown. In the distance, a lone horse and wagon team can be seen heading east on Main Street.

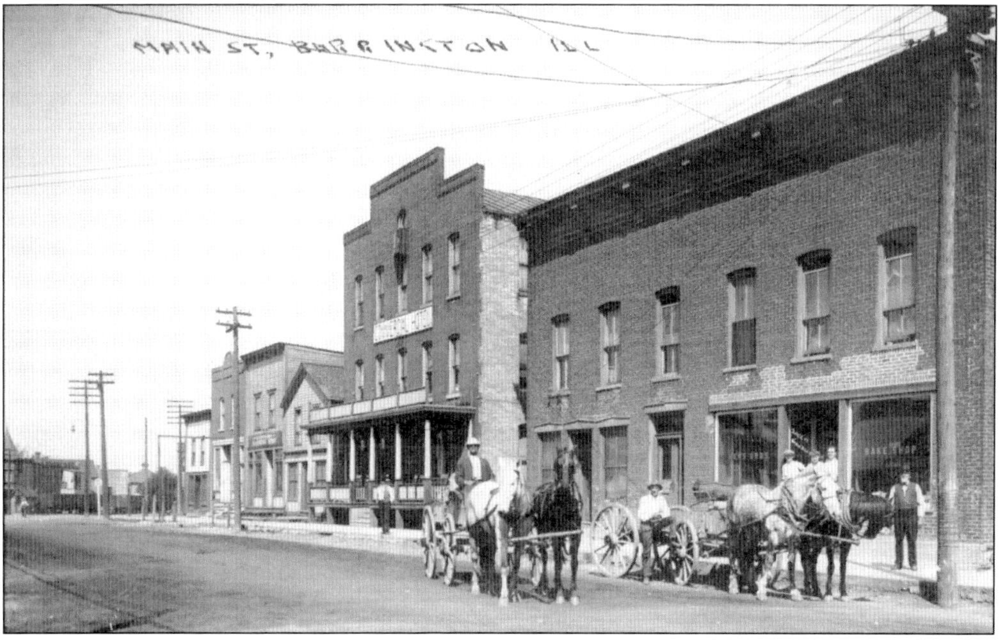

P.L. Huckins of Chicago, Illinois, photographed this 1912 scene on Main Street, with horses and wagons outside of the local bake shop. Visitors to Barrington could stay at the Commercial Hotel and walk a few steps for freshly baked goods. The third floor of the hotel housed the meeting rooms for the Freemasons. The hotel also faced the Barrington train station, offering a brief walk to catch a train.

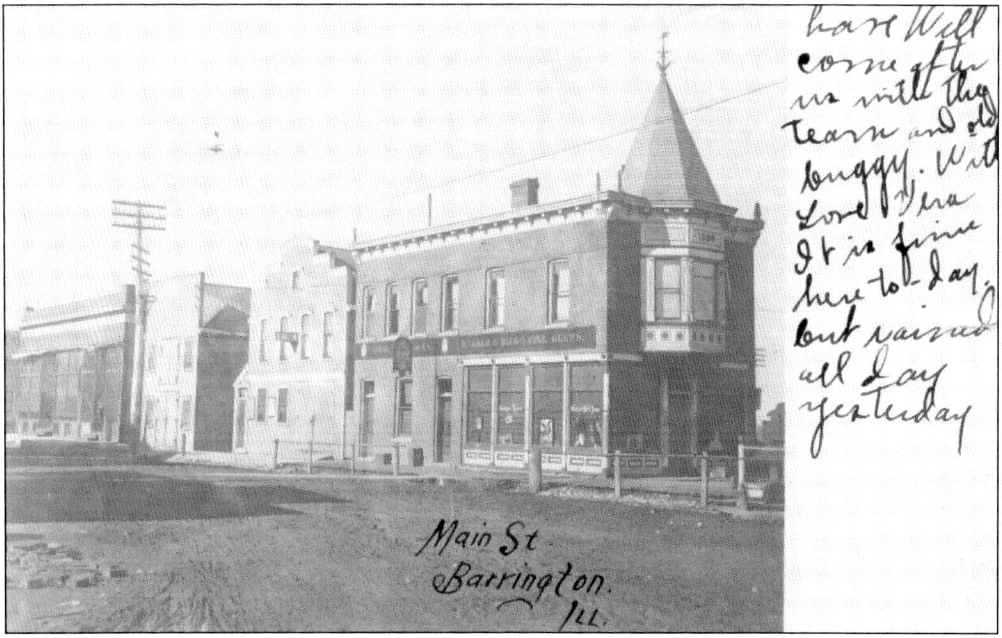

This well-detailed and rare real-photo postcard shows the Wacker and Birk Fine Beers store, offering a beer sampling room, with Barrington's YMCA next door. The beer business was adjacent to the railroad tracks, allowing for easy delivery of beer shipments from Chicago. The Victorian building, complete with turret, was constructed in 1898.

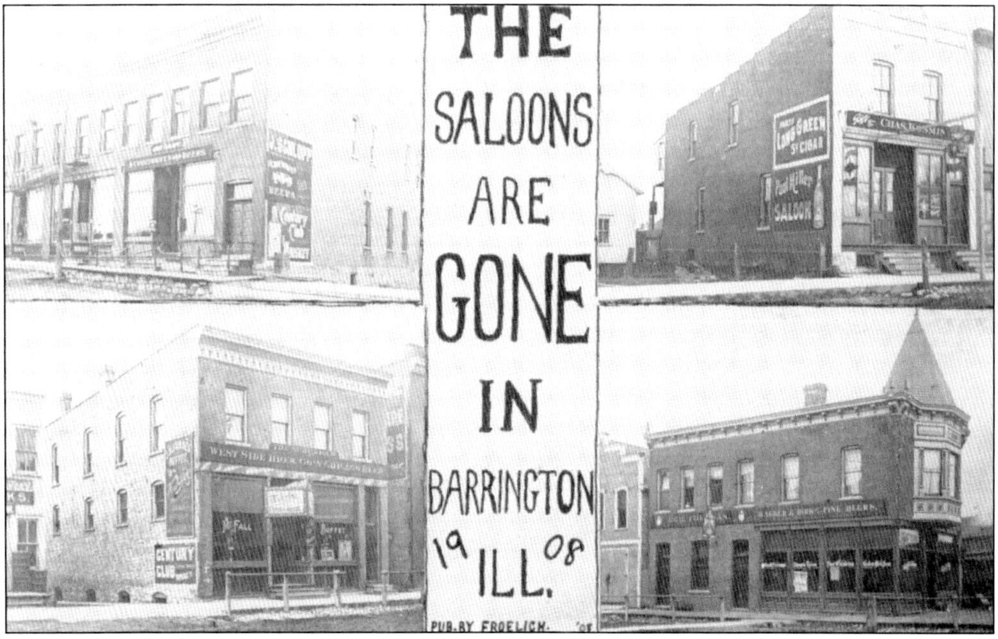

This postcard's statement—"The saloons are gone in Barrington, Ill."—provides a commentary on Barrington's status as a "dry" town. These images, taken by George Froelich Jr. in 1908, depict the Schoenhofen Beers, Charles Kosmin, Suburban West Side Brew Company's Chicago Beer, and Wacker and Birk Fine Beers establishments, which disappeared from the downtown business streetscape during Prohibition.

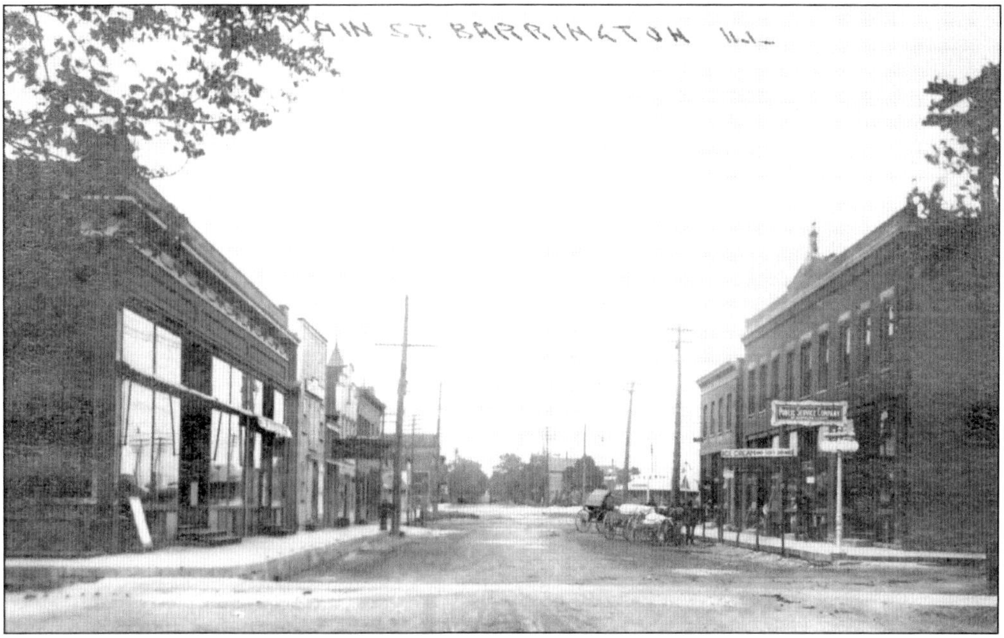

P.L. Huckins captured this view of Main Street looking east from Hough Street and showing the Public Service Company office, the local ice cream store, and the Barrington train station. The A.W. Meyer store is visible on the left. Note the horses tethered to hitching posts.

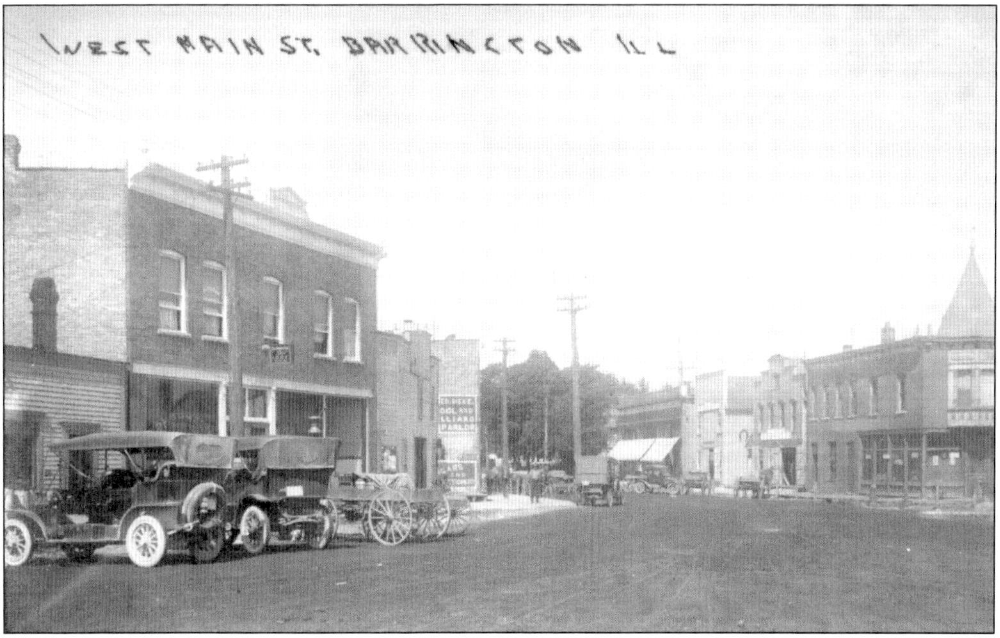

This early 1900s view of Main Street, looking west, was photographed by P.L. Huckins and shows both horse-pulled wagons and automobiles. The wagon to the right of the two cars has a number of milk cans under a covering in the wagon. The cars and wagon are parked in front of the pharmacy, as evidenced by the large mortar and pestle in front of the building. The second floor of the pharmacy building housed the Barrington IOOF.

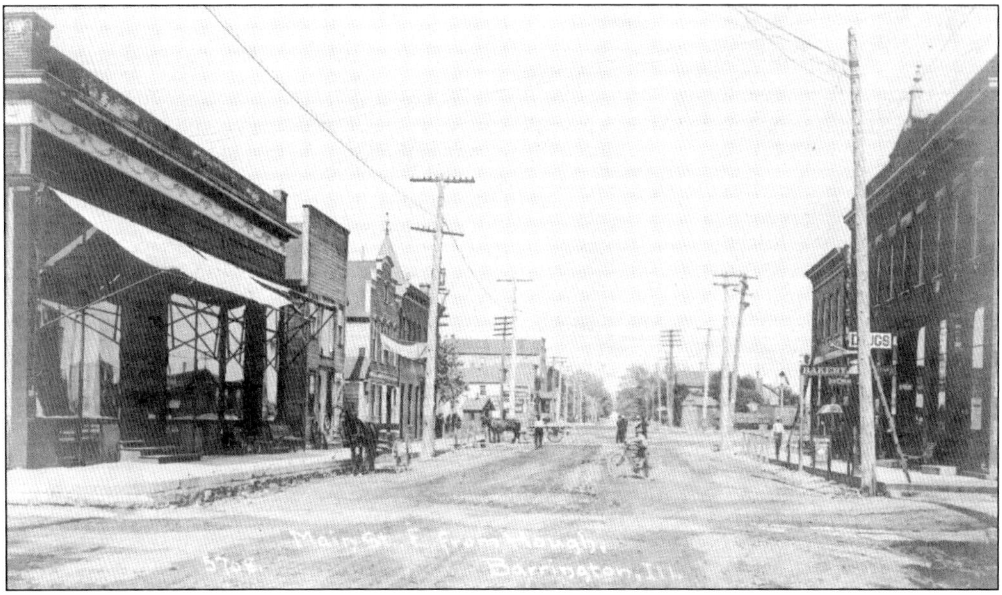

This real-photo postcard contains a picture taken by Charles R. Childs that depicts the local business district as seen from Hough Street, looking east on Main Street. Childs captured a child walking his bicycle across Main Street, possibly after the boy's visit to the local bakery or ice cream shop.

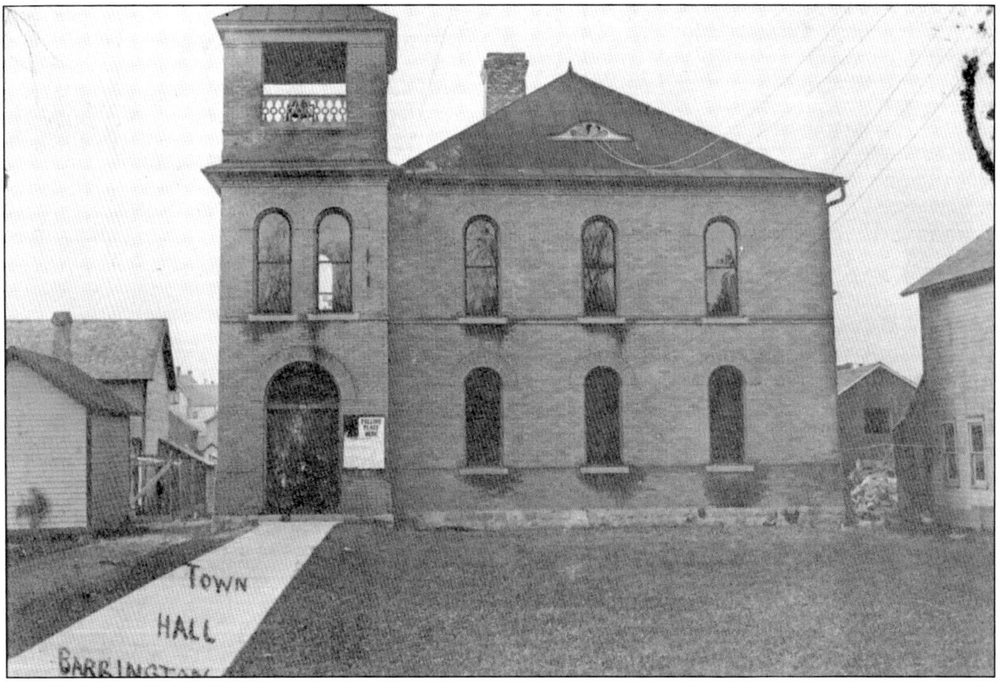

A very early real-photo postcard of the original Barrington Village Hall, located on Hough Street, dates from 1907 (as evidenced in the upper right corner of the card). On the reverse side of the card, the sender wishes her cousin a very merry Christmas and a happy new year. The sign on the building indicates that on the day the photograph was taken, the Village Hall was a polling place. The croquet court was not yet installed in front of the building. In the early 1900s, motion pictures were shown on the second floor.

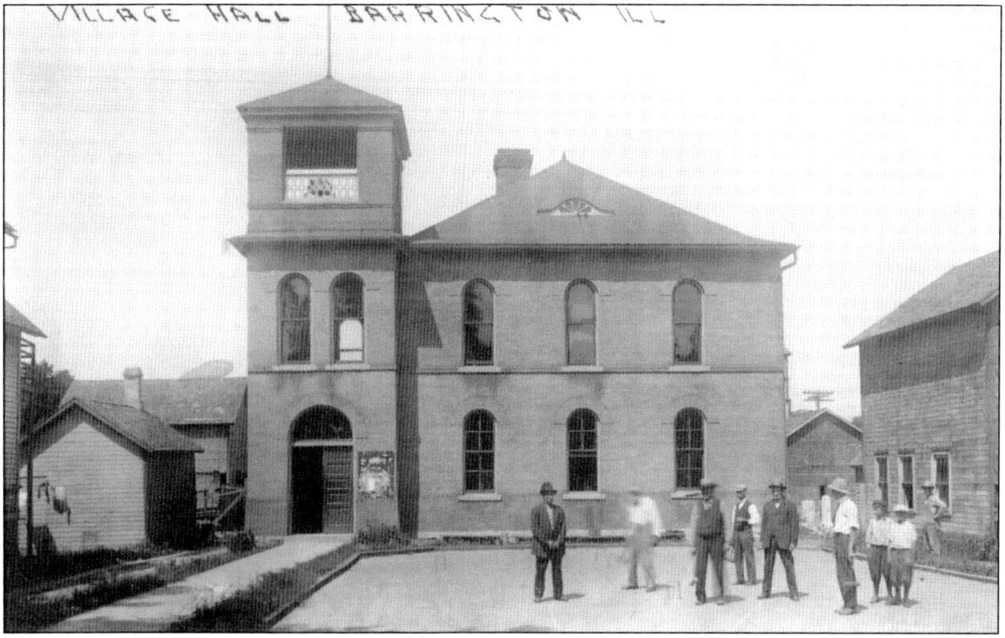

A croquet court was constructed in front of the Barrington Village Hall. This must have been a popular sport, as evidenced by the number of people on the court.

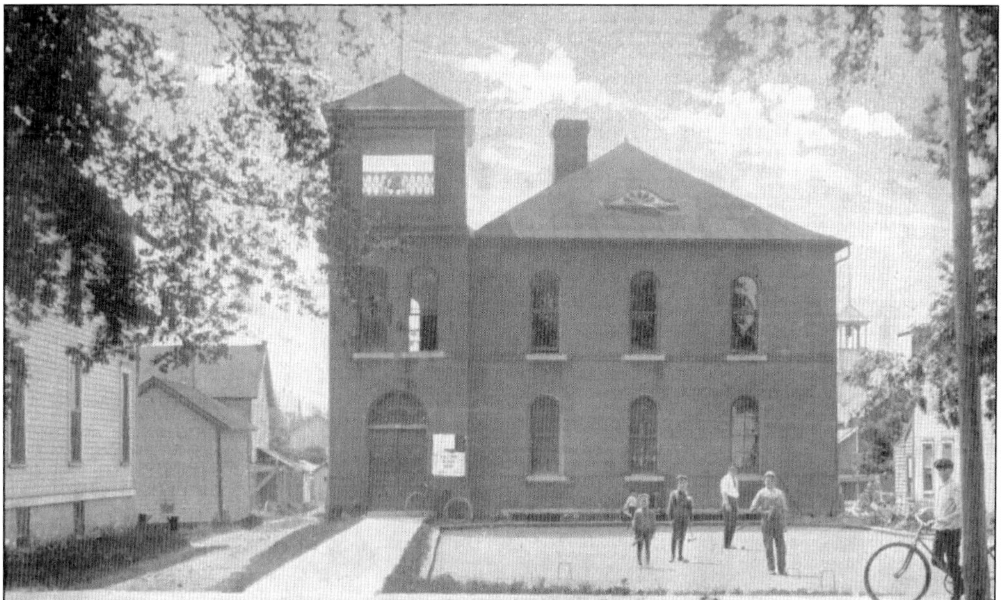

This colorized postcard of Barrington Village Hall shows the croquet court being used by both children and adults in 1909. This court was one of the most important social areas in the community and offered townspeople an opportunity to catch up on the latest news and happenings.

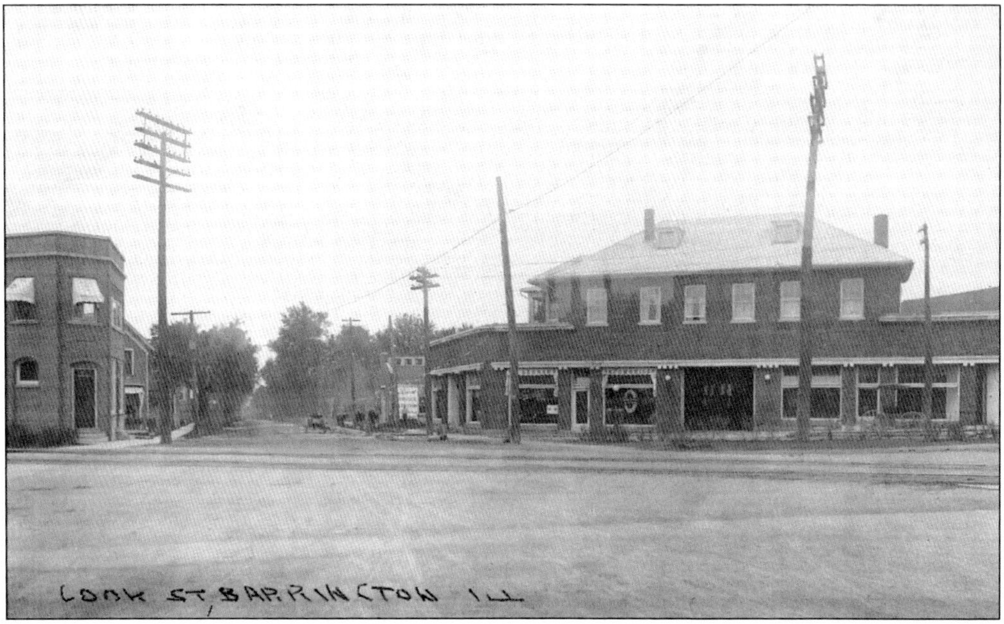

This 1917 postcard image captured by P.L. Huckins depicts business establishments at Cook Street and Main Street. The large building on the right was originally constructed as a garage building and housed the Percy Leonard Automobile business.

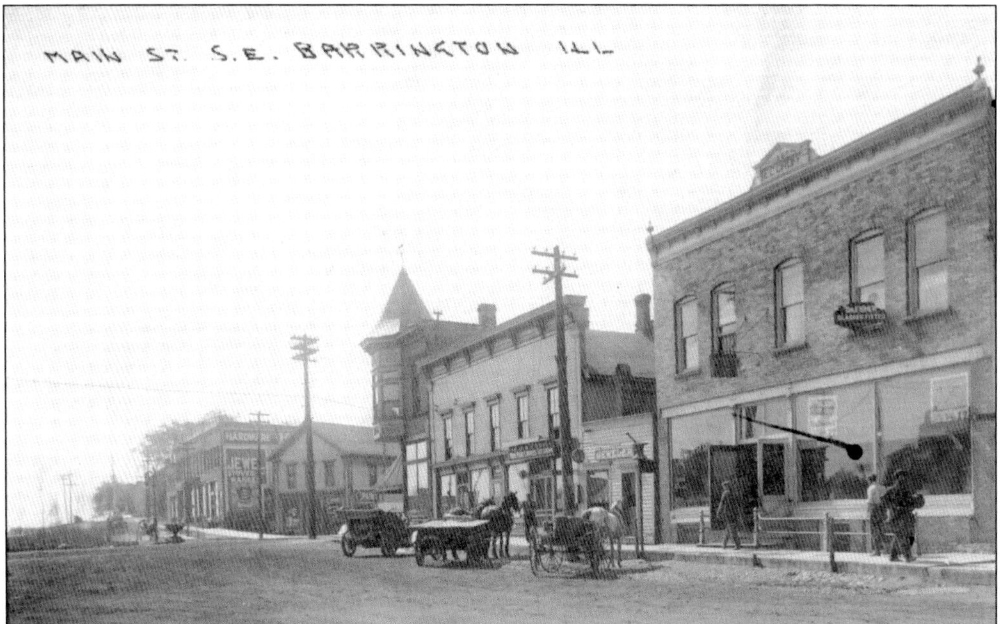

People came to town by horse and wagon or by car. P.L. Huckins captured both modes of transportation "parked" in front of Fostone's homemade candies and ice cream store. The stores to the right of Fostone's include a jeweler and a pharmacy. Doctor Fisher's optometry office was located on the second floor of the E.C. Groff building.

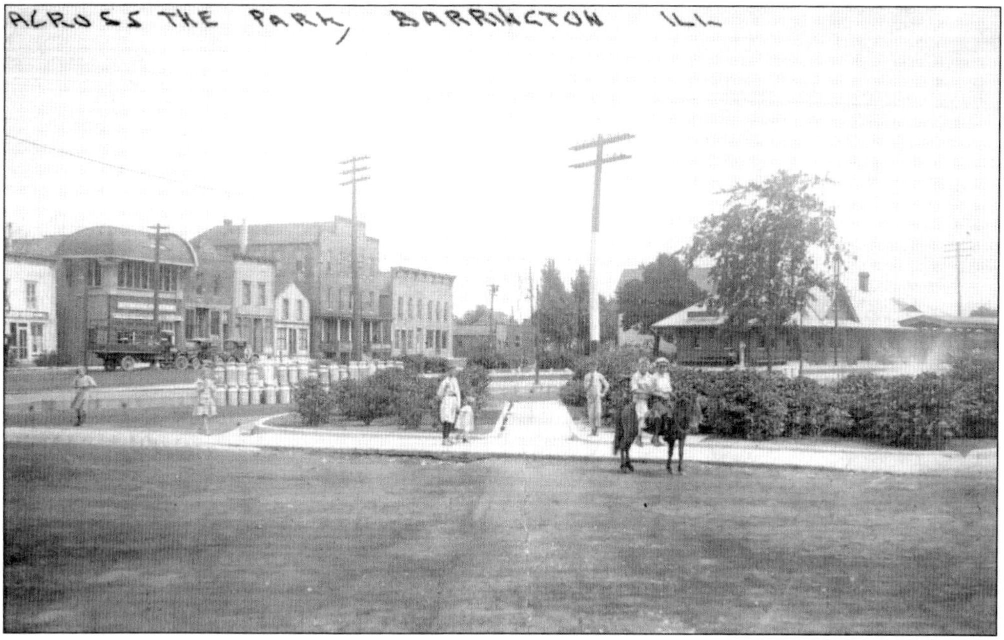

P.L. Huckins recorded this interesting scene, titled "Across the Park," near the Barrington train depot. Stacked milk cans await pickup by the dairy farmers and several children pose in the image. Note that there is only one horse visible, which the children are sitting on, with only automobiles and trucks parked in front of the buildings on the other side of the railroad tracks.

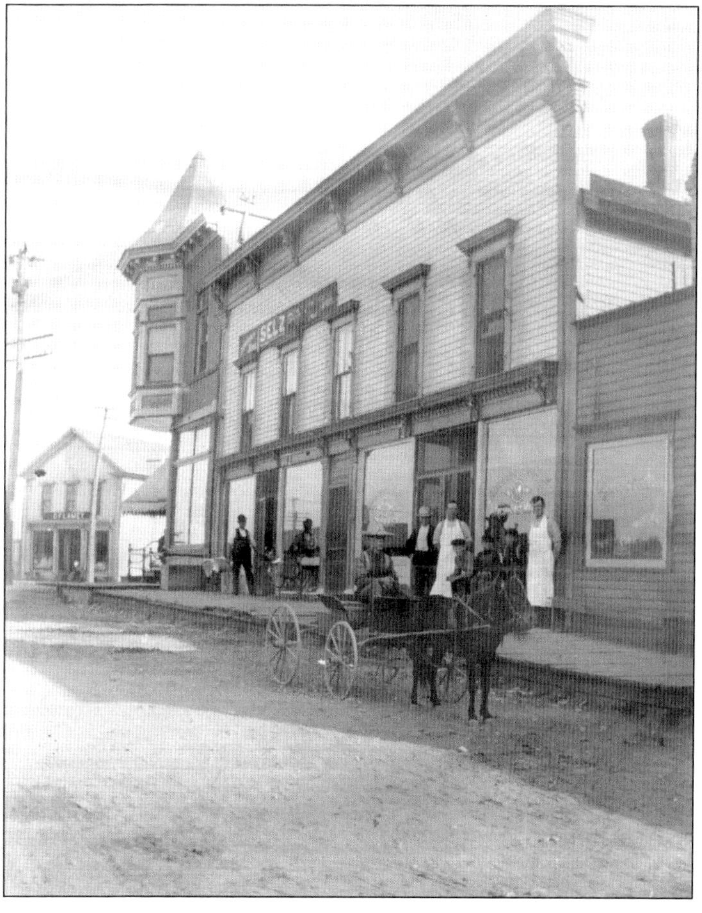

This well-defined image shows the D.F. Lamey Barrington Fair Store and the Alverson and Groff meat market in downtown Barrington. Note the wooden sidewalks in front of the businesses. A cigar and tobacco store is visible immediately to the right of the meat market.

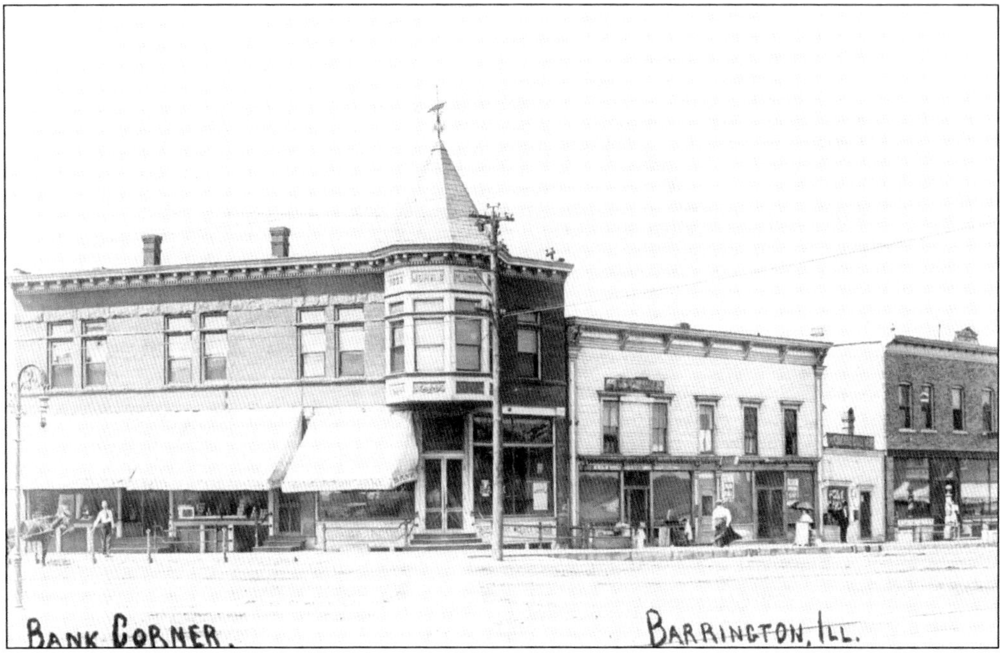

The John C. Plagge building housed the Barrington Bank and a notions, boots, shoes, and grocery store to the left of the bank. The lower level of the building contained the Ladies and Gents Lunch Restaurant, where one could get a quick lunch "with meals served at all hours."

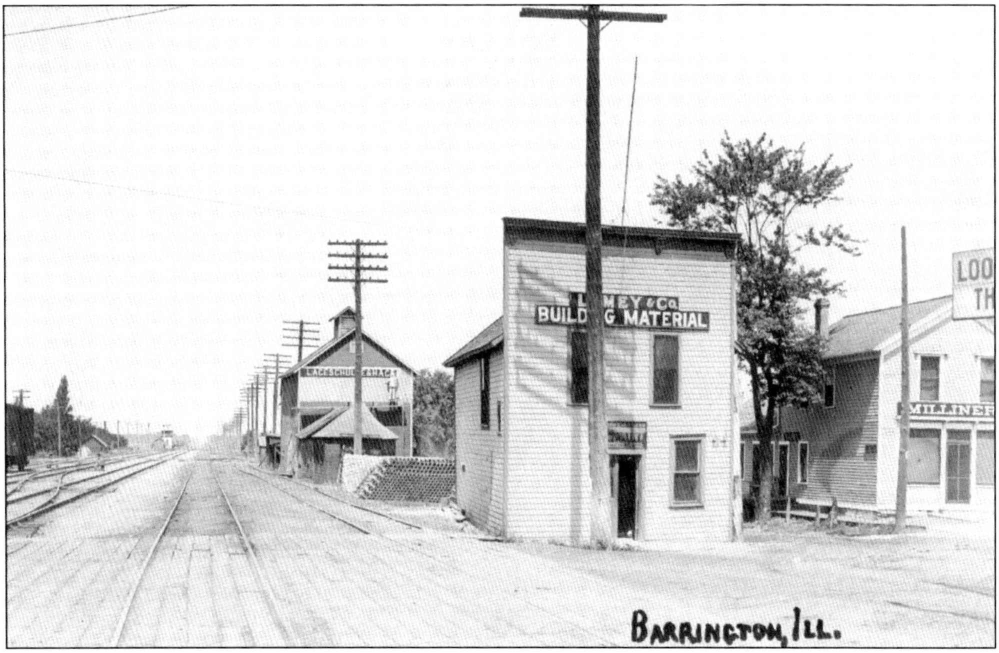

The Lamey and Company Building Material office and the Jukes Sisters millinery shop are shown in this early-1900s photograph taken near the C&NW tracks. In the background, a painter works on a new building sign for Lageschulte and Hager.

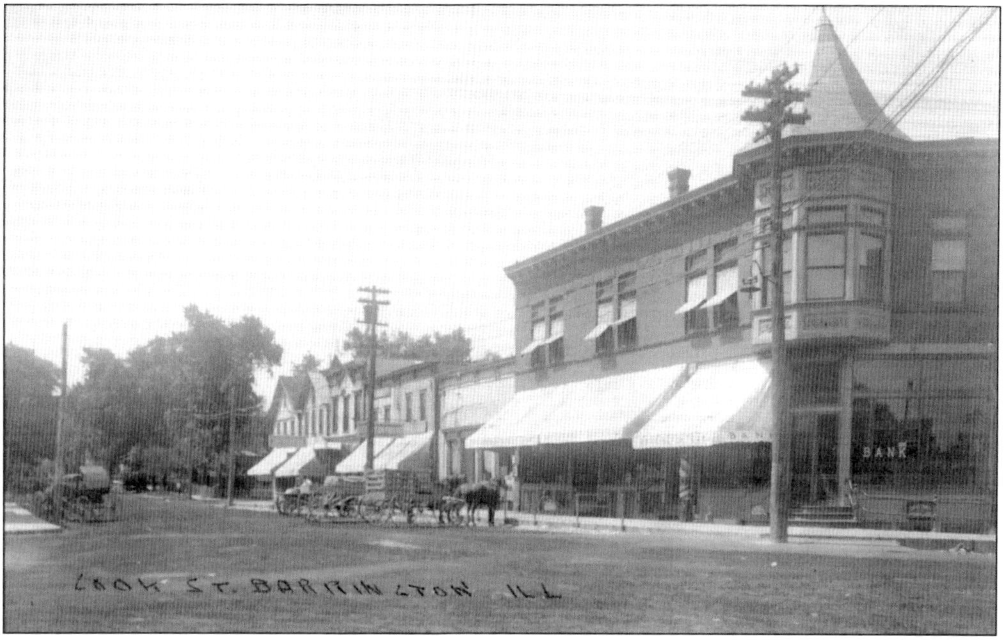

This view offers a broader perspective of Cook Street and the various businesses visible to the left of the Plagge building, including an ice cream parlor. The Charles Thies barbershop business sign can be seen near the basement entrance to the Plagge building.

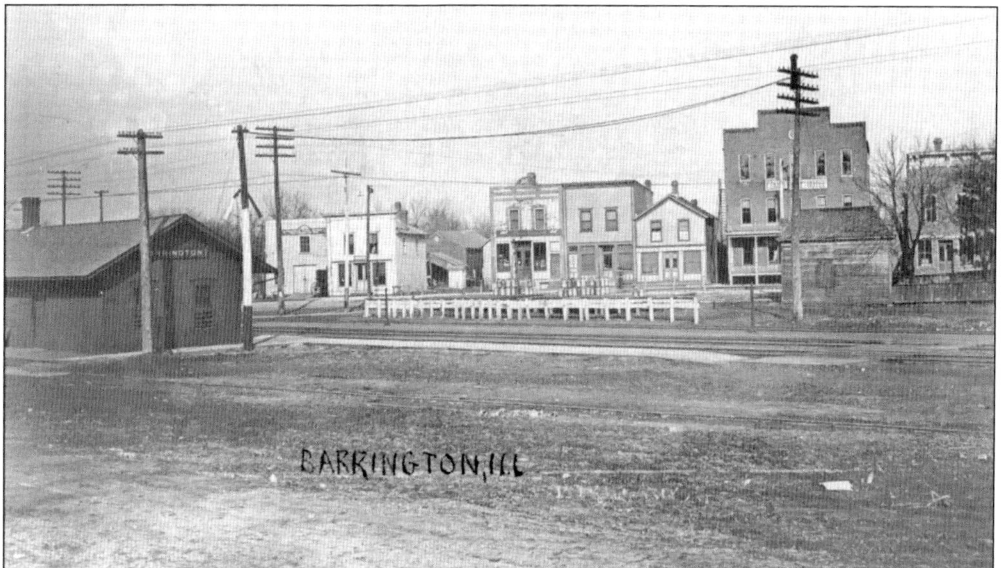

Photographer George Froelich Jr. captured this 1900 view of downtown Barrington, looking across the railroad depot area onto East Main Street. Milk cans are stacked on the train depot platform awaiting pickup by the next train.

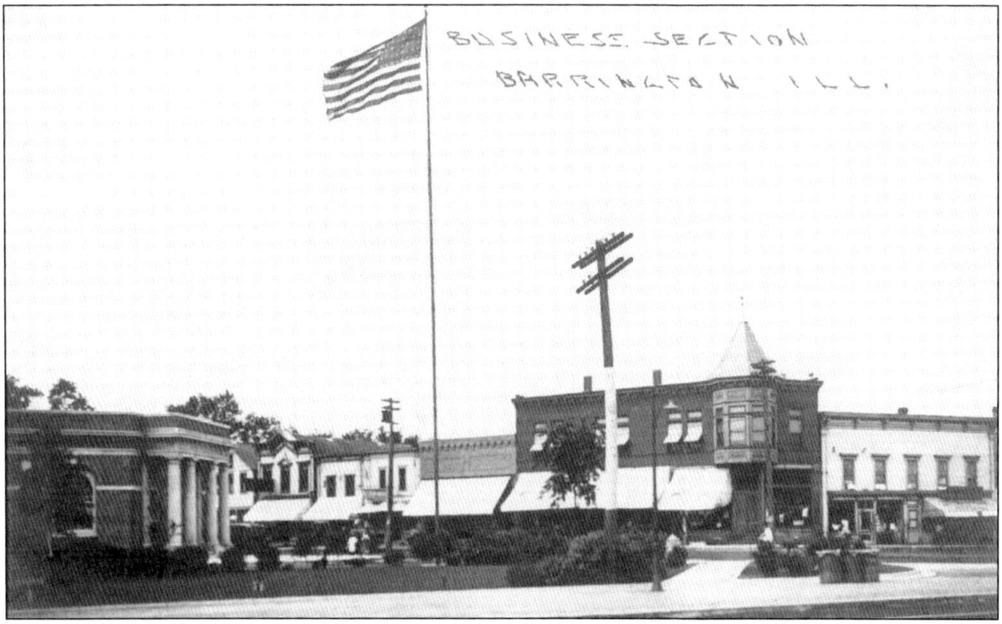

P.L. Huckins recorded this picture of the "business section" of Barrington. This view was taken from East Main Street looking across the railroad tracks to Cook Street. Note the huge American flag flying in the park area of downtown. The wind must have been very gusty that day, as the flag is flying straight out.

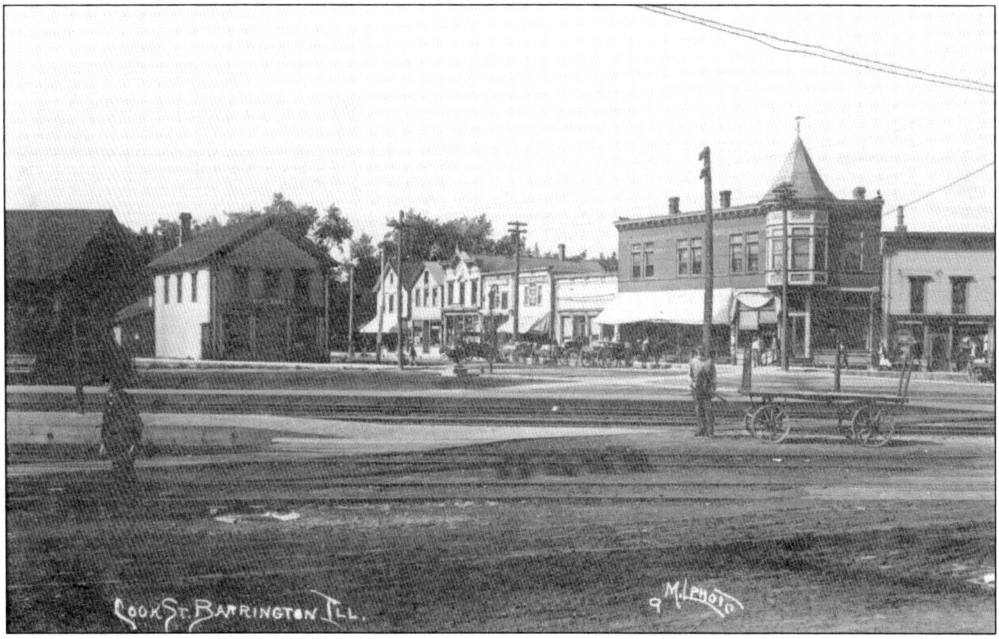

This 1911 photograph, taken from the railroad looking towards Cook Street, offers perhaps one of the busiest perspectives of downtown Barrington. At right, a railroad employee waits with a baggage cart for the next arriving train. At left, it appears that a trainman is waiting for a train to back onto a siding track.

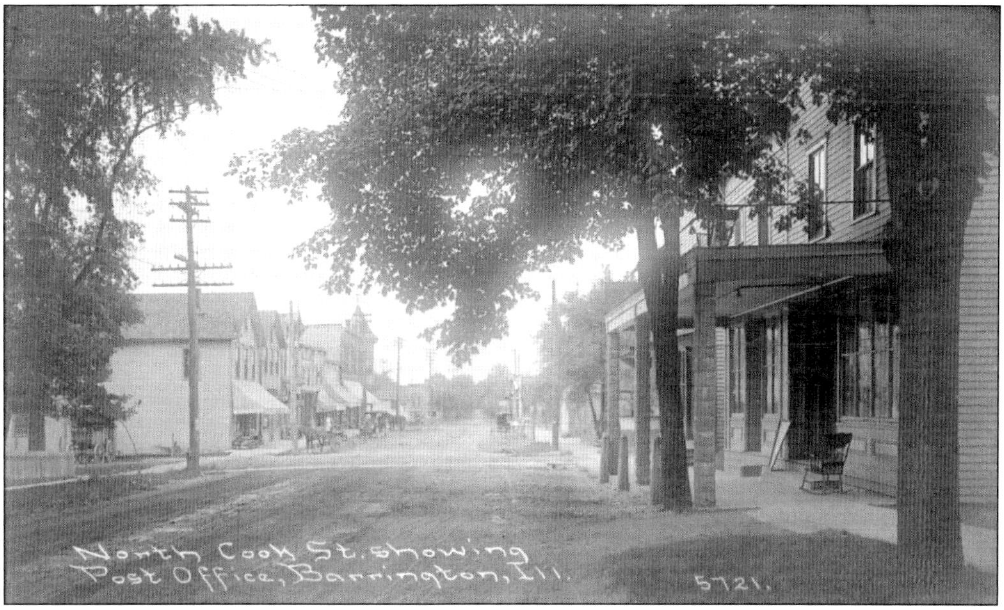

Charles R. Childs captured this photograph along Cook Street looking directly into the downtown business district in Barrington. It references "showing the post office," but it is difficult to identify its exact location in this photograph. Many times, the local postmaster had the post office located within his or her place of business. Note the watermelons stacked in front of the store at left.

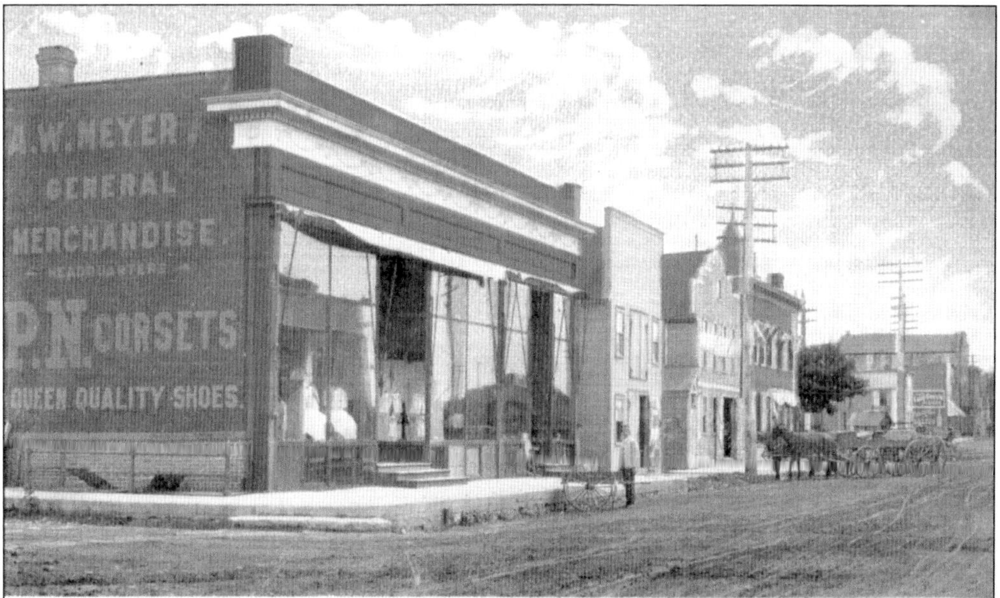

West Main Street, Barrington, Ill.

This colorized postcard view of West Main Street shows the A.W. Meyer Store, which sold general merchandise (including quality corsets). This card was published by William G. Hoffman of Chicago.

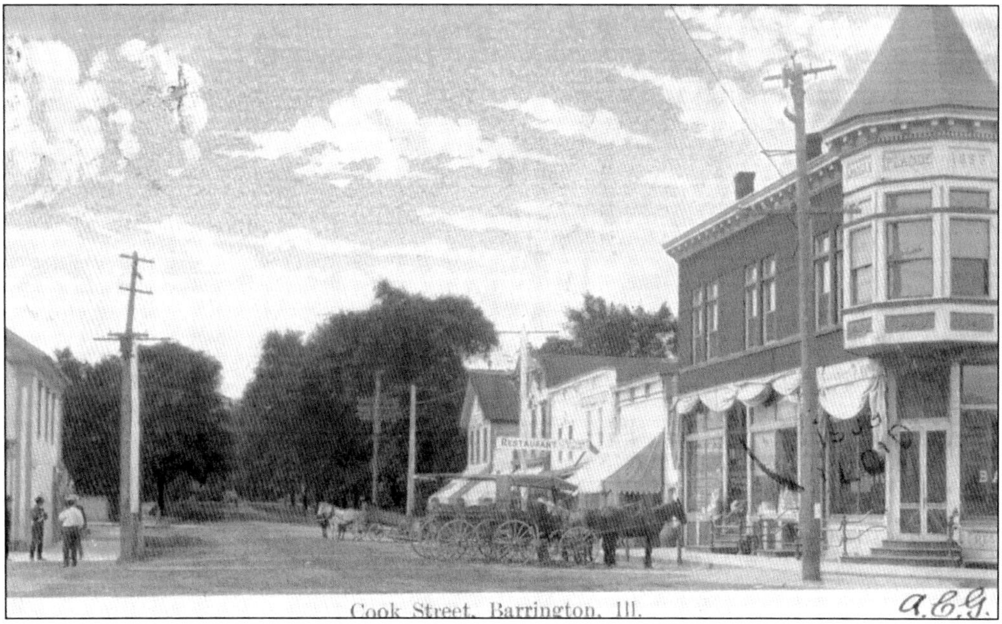

Another colorized postcard published by William G. Hoffman shows Cook Street and its local businesses in 1909. The sender notes that the street pictured on the card is the street her sister lives on and asks her cousin to please write soon.

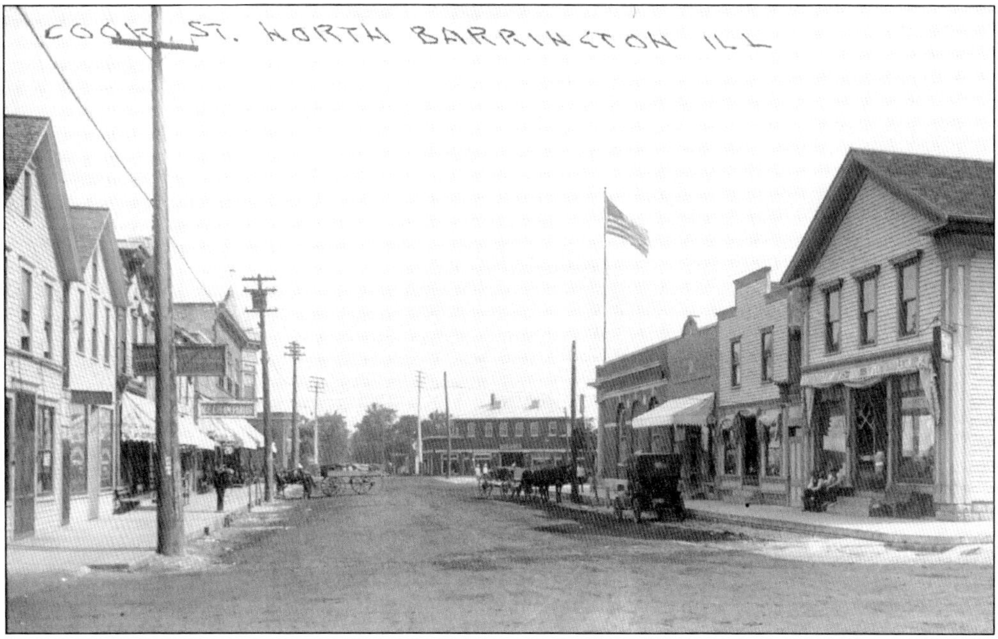

This very sharp postcard image of Cook Street looks northward into the downtown business district. The banner over the doorway of the store on the right indicates that starting on July 15, the Chautauqua would be coming to Barrington for six days. This card is postmarked 1918.

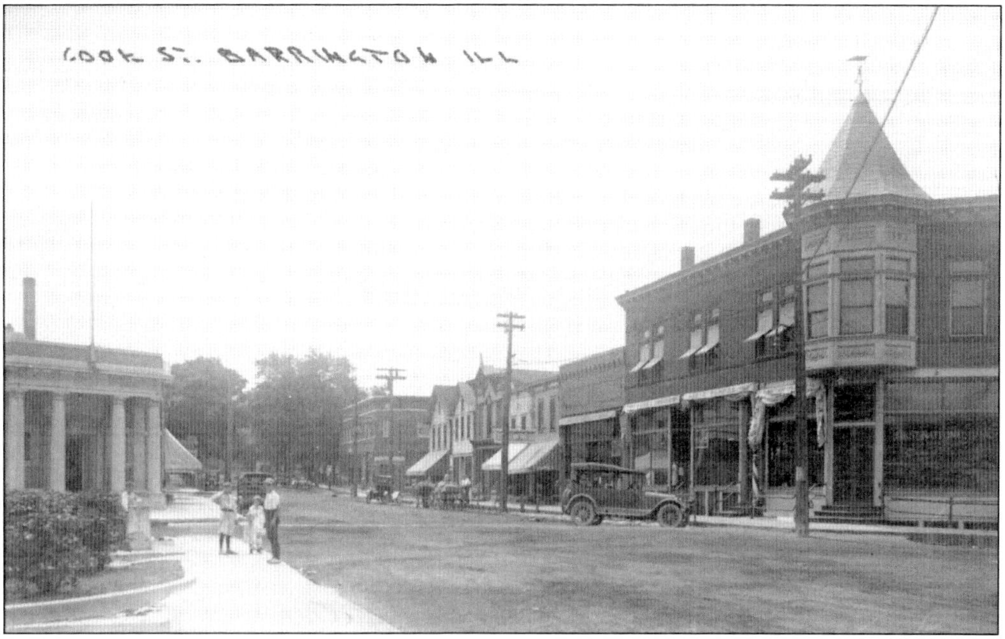

This photograph of Cook Street shows an increase in motor vehicles in the downtown business district. There is only one horse and wagon, parked near the ice cream parlor in the center of the picture. Horses and wagons were beginning to disappear as a method of transportation as more families acquired automobiles.

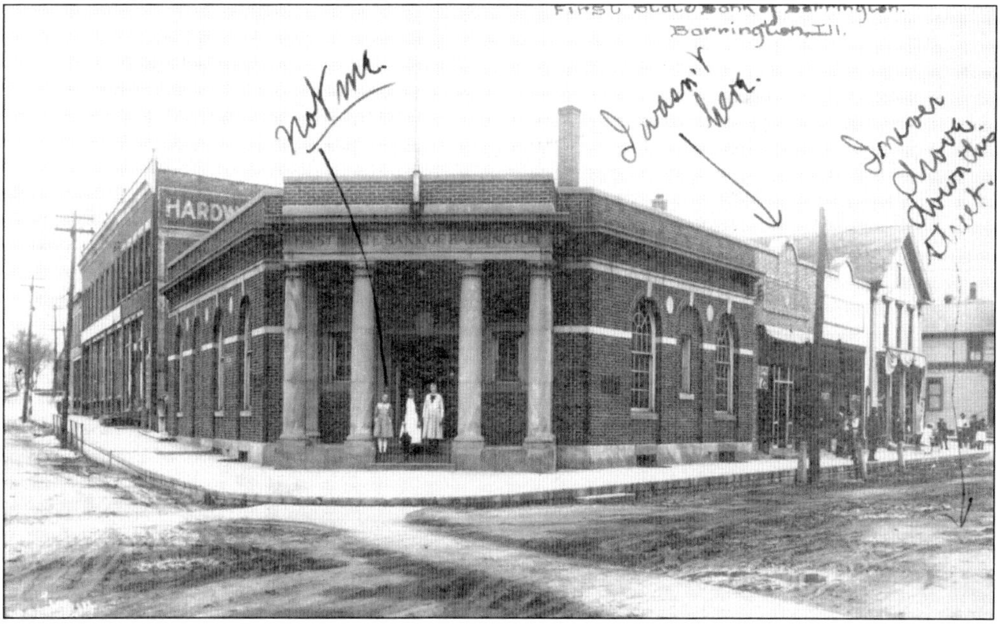

H.R. Brooks of Chicago captured this picture of the First State Bank of Barrington in the 1920s. Barrington had two downtown banks, including the First National (on the west side of Cook Street) and the First State Bank (on the east side of Cook Street).

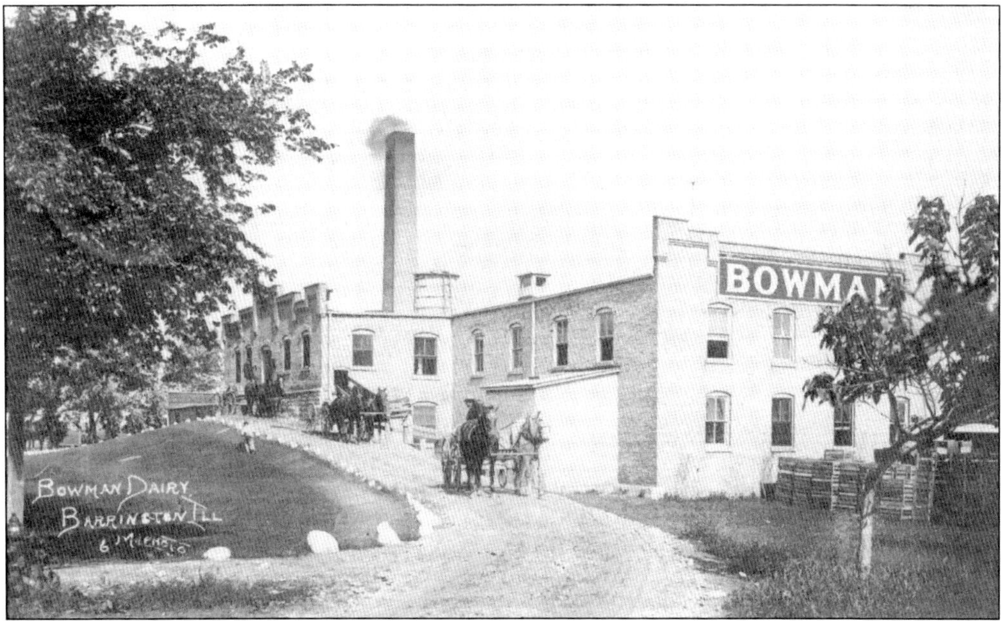

This M.L. Photo Company postcard shows the Bowman Dairy Company, which was built in 1904. It was located along the railroad tracks near Harrison Street, and its whistle was sounded to alert volunteer firefighters about a fire in town.

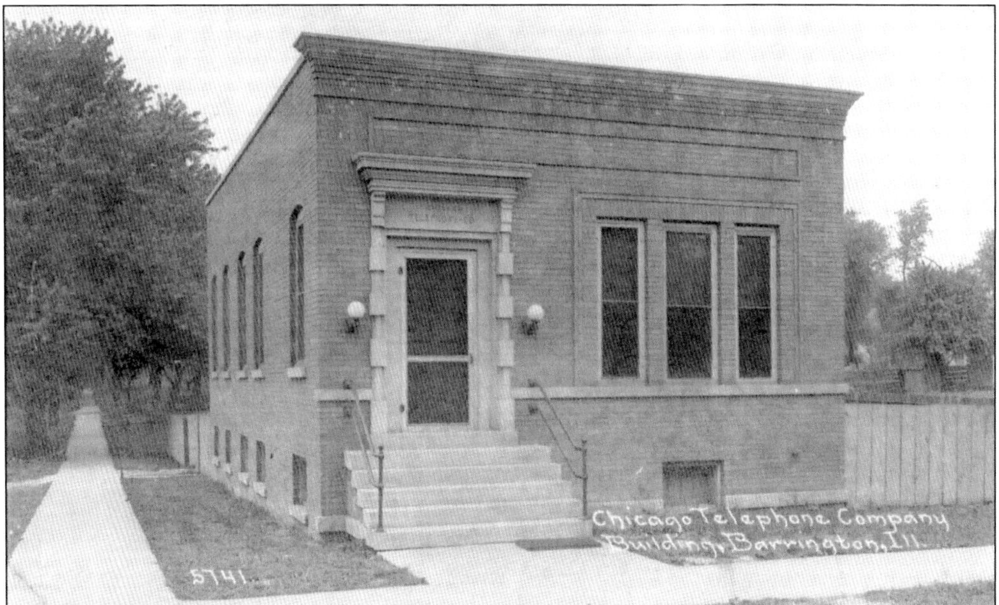

The telephone came to Barrington in 1898 on a village franchise. When the Chicago Telephone Company started its service, there were initially eight subscribers. The first switchboard was in the *Barrington Review* newspaper office and was later moved to the Commercial Hotel. As demand grew for telephone service, the switchboard was moved to its own building on Main Street.

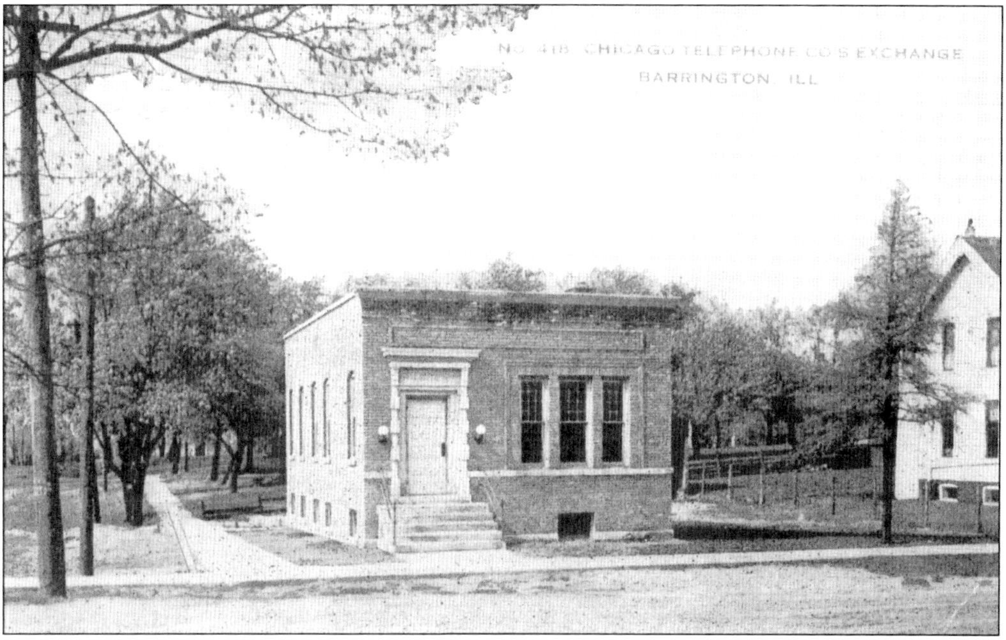

The Chicago Telephone Company became the Illinois Bell Telephone Company in 1923. By 1940, the Barrington switchboard had 1,550 phones, and by 1953, the town had 3,712 phones. The Chicago Telephone Company's exchange building housed switchboard positions for 38 operators.

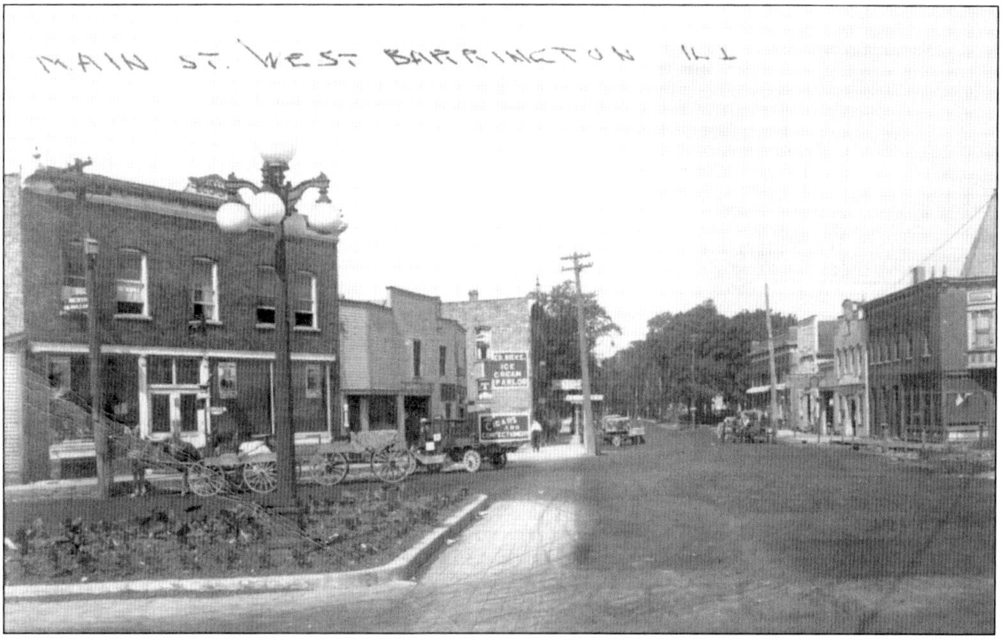

This 1923 photograph of Main Street looking west, taken by P.L. Huckins, offers a glimpse of the triangle area around Park Avenue. This image illustrates the downtown area's transition from horse-and-buggies to motorized vehicles.

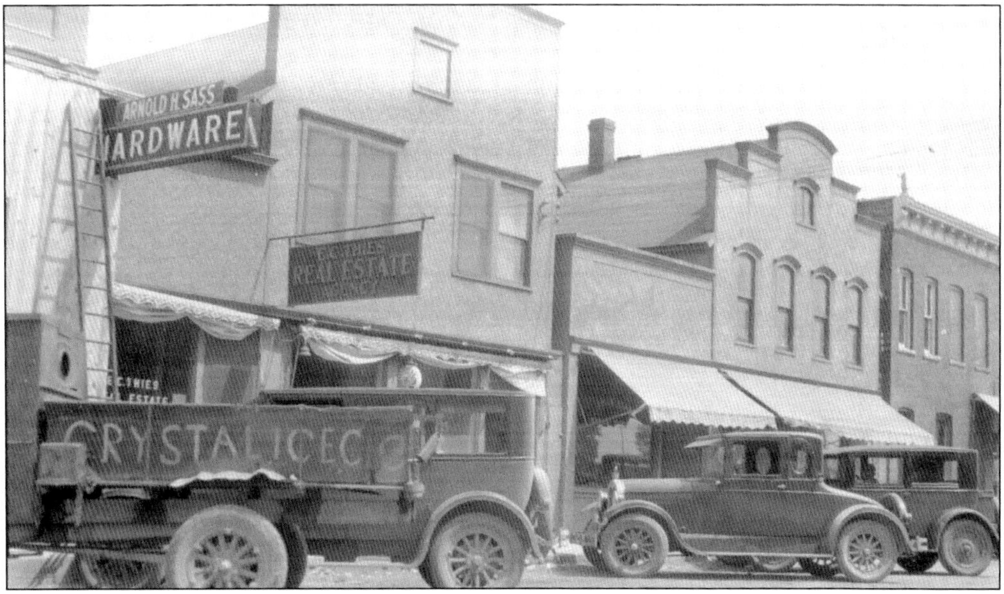

The north side of Main Street included the Arnold H. Sass Hardware Store, the Ed C. Thies Real Estate Agency and the Charley Thies barbershop. Note the Crystal Ice Company truck in the foreground.

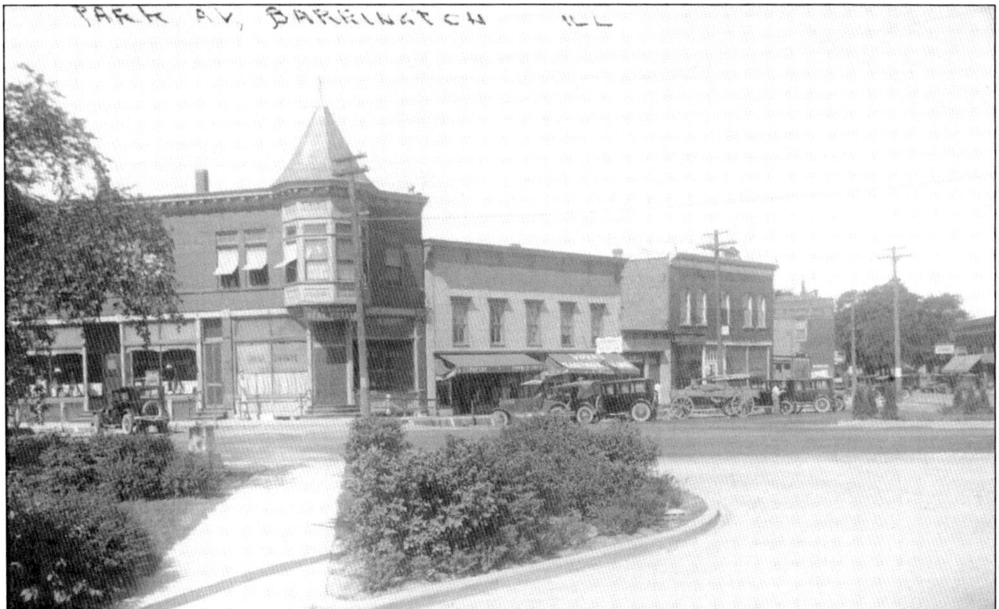

Park Avenue businesses included the Martin Real Estate Office, Lipofsky's Furnishings Store, McLeister's, Peerless Film Store, and the Peerless Market.

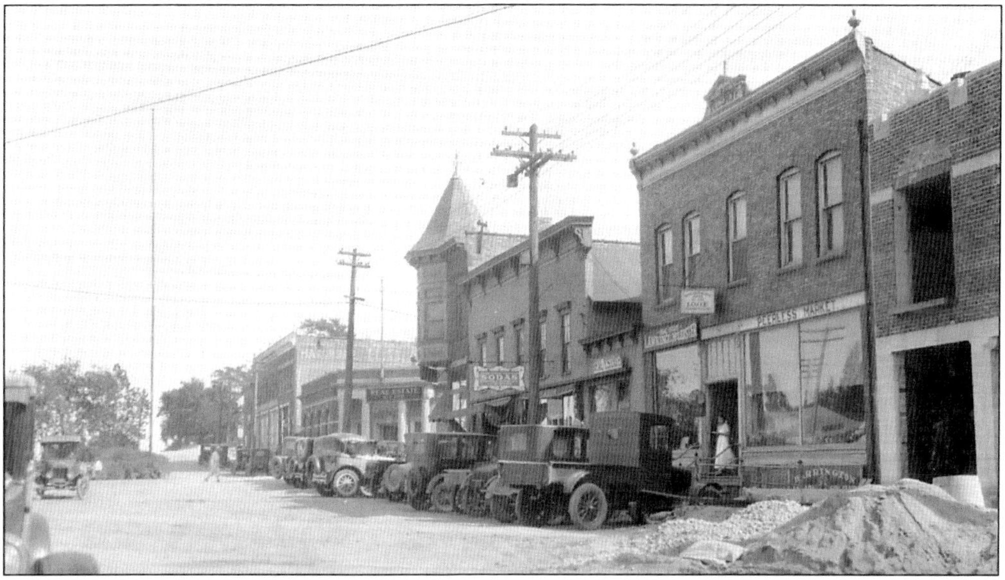

As evidenced by this view looking east down South Railroad Street (now Park Avenue) toward Cook Street, the downtown Barrington shopper had many choices. A new brick building is being constructed (on the far right) by owners Clarence Landwer and Paul Pohlman. This image also offers a more detailed view of the Peerless Market. The Lawrence & McLeister Real Estate Office is to the left of the market.

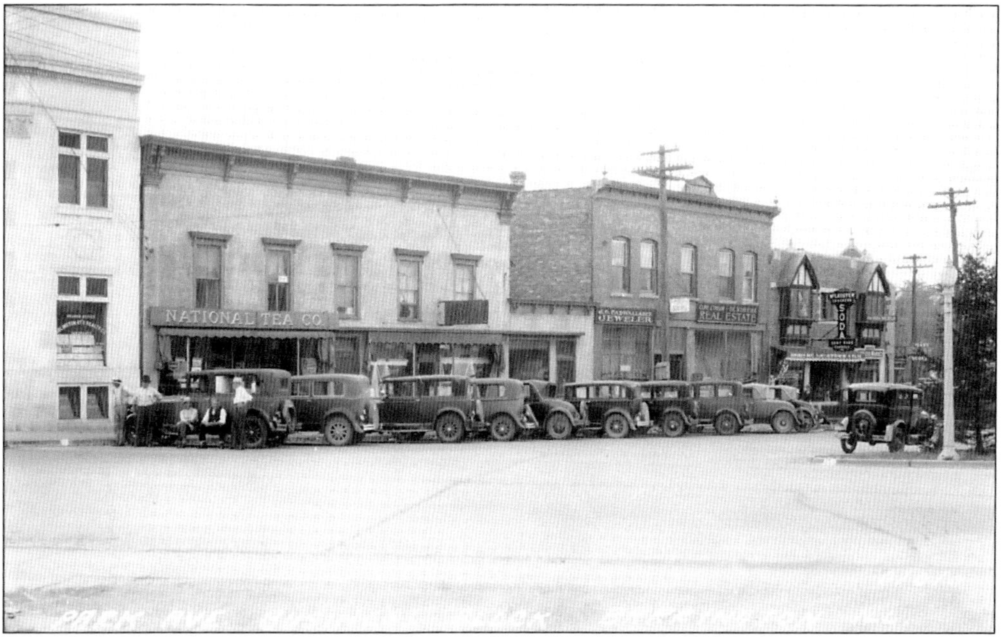

The downtown Barrington business block, on the south side of Park Avenue west of Cook Street, offered an opportunity to shop for groceries at the National Tea Company, jewelry at J.C. Cadwallader, and real estate at the Clive J. Taylor and D.C. Schroeder Real Estate office. Next to the real estate office, the famous McLeister's offered sodas and homemade candies.

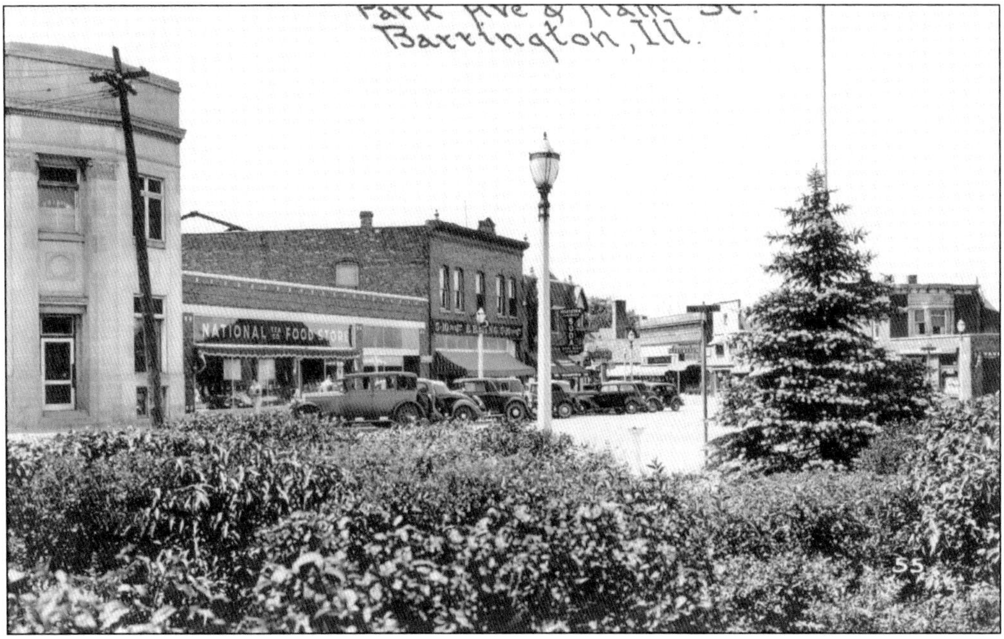

This more modern view of the Barrington business block on Park Avenue shows the modernized National Tea Company Food Store, the E.B. King five-and-dime store, and McLeister's.

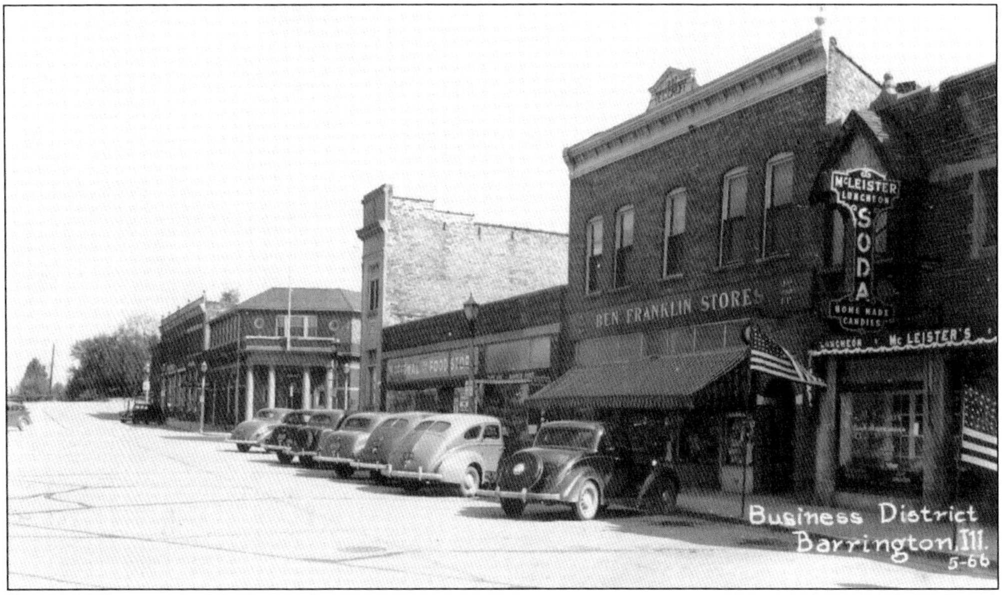

The face of Park Avenue changed again when the E.B. King five-and-dime store became a Ben Franklin Store. Visiting dime stores was a great American pastime for both children and adults. One could find almost anything, from thread and needles to stationery and cards, any kind of candy, souvenir and memento items, and—of course—a fine selection of local postcards!

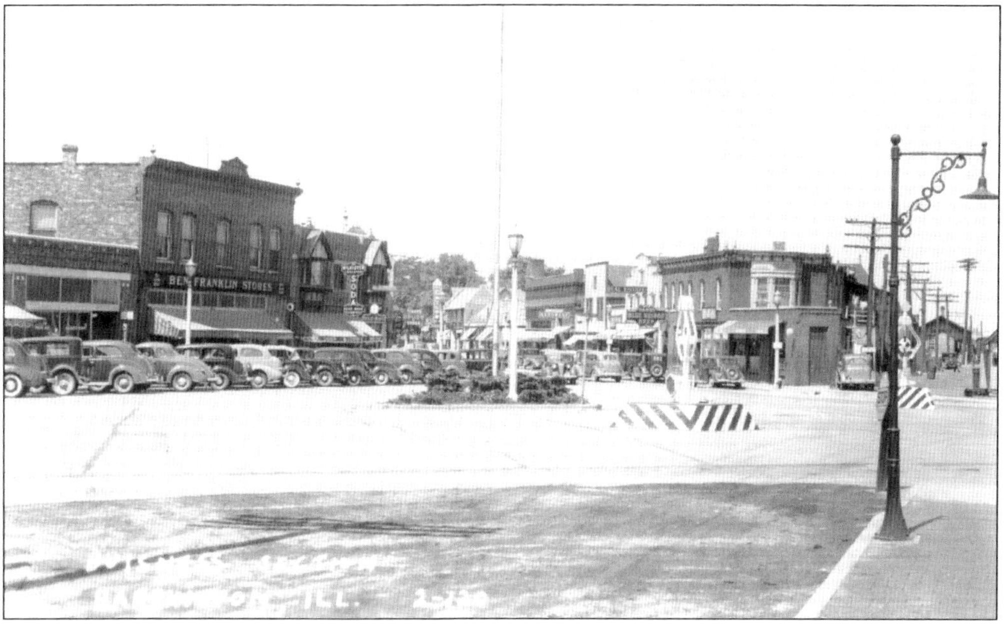

This 1937 image offers a broader perspective of Park Avenue and West Main Street, showing local businesses, the downtown triangle area, and the C&NW railroad crossing. The Catlow Theater building is visible in the distance, with its large sign listing the latest movie.

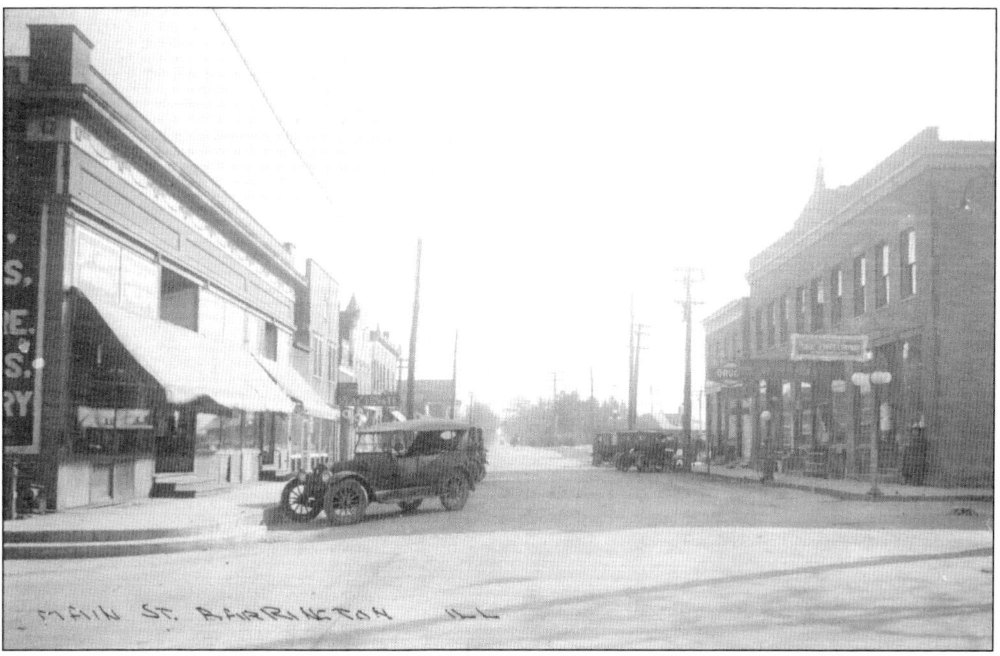

In this view looking east down Main Street, the A.W. Meyer store is at the immediate left and the E.C. Thies Real Estate office and the Barrington train station are in the far distance at the right. At the near right, an early gasoline pump stands in front of the Public Service Office of Northern Illinois.

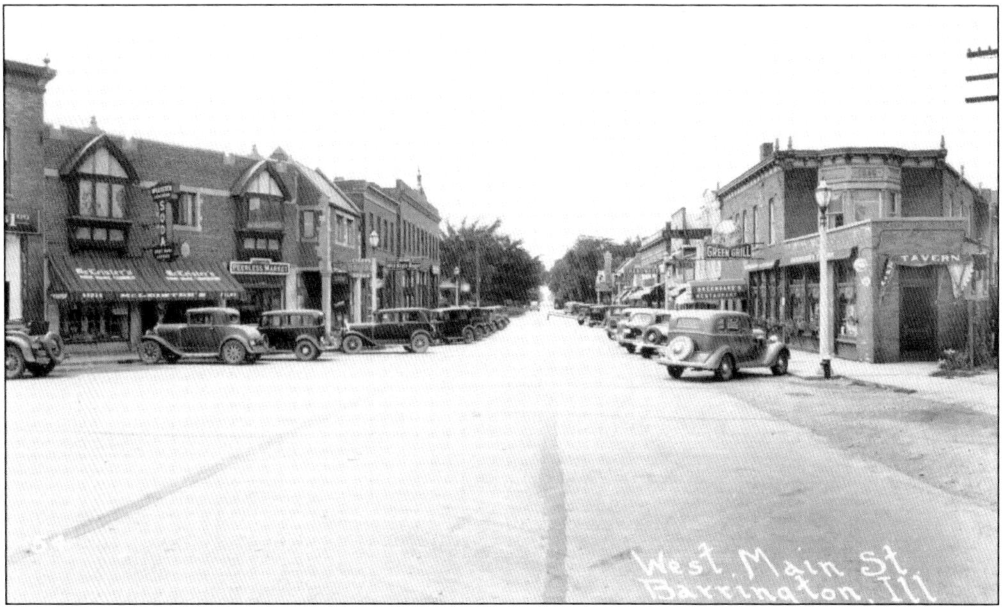

This 1935 image was taken from the middle of Main Street at the C&NW railroad crossing. It is amazing that the photograph was captured without any moving vehicles present on Main Street. Perhaps it was lunchtime, and everyone was enjoying lunch at McLeister's or at Greengard's across the street.

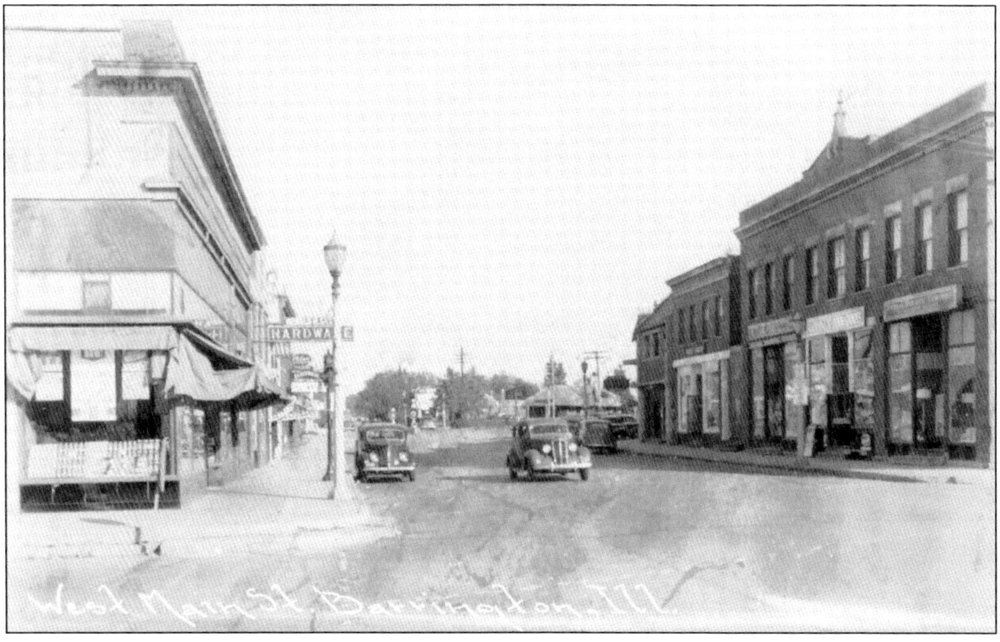

Local merchants continued to change in downtown Barrington as many retired and sold their businesses. Another change included the removal of the gasoline pump in front of the public service company; more and more service stations were built to meet a growing need for gasoline and oil. The A.W. Meyer store disappeared from the streetscape and was replaced by a local grocery store that offered two jars of grape jelly for 25¢ and out-of-date doughnuts for 10¢.

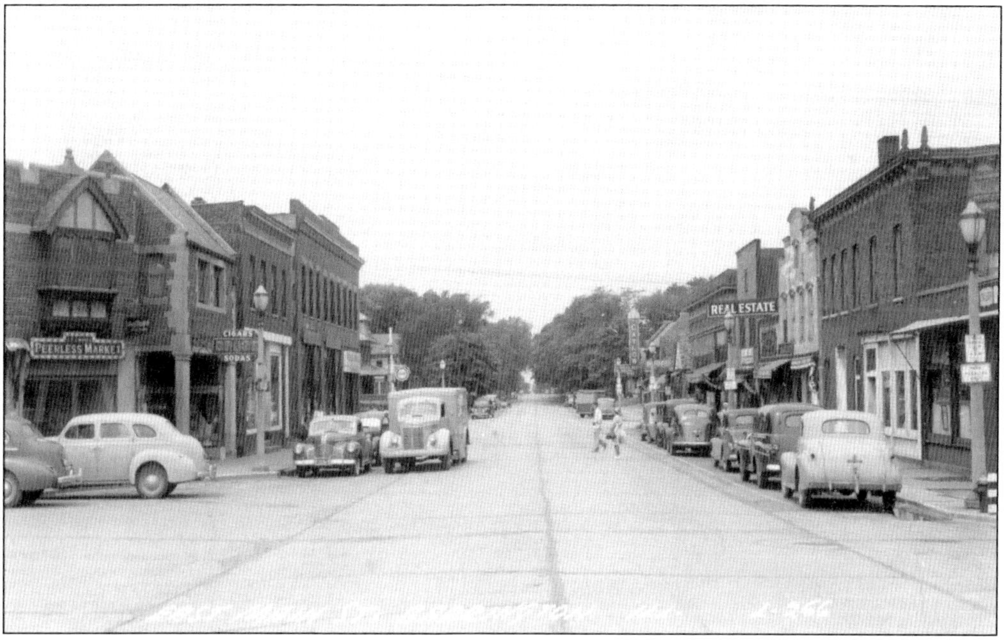

This 1940s image of West Main Street shows a new location for the Peerless Market, the new Pohlman's Pharmacy, and visible evidence of new service stations, such as the Pure Oil station located at Hough and Main Streets. Greengard's became a tailor shop, and *Abilene Town*, starring Randolph Scott, was opening at the Catlow Theater.

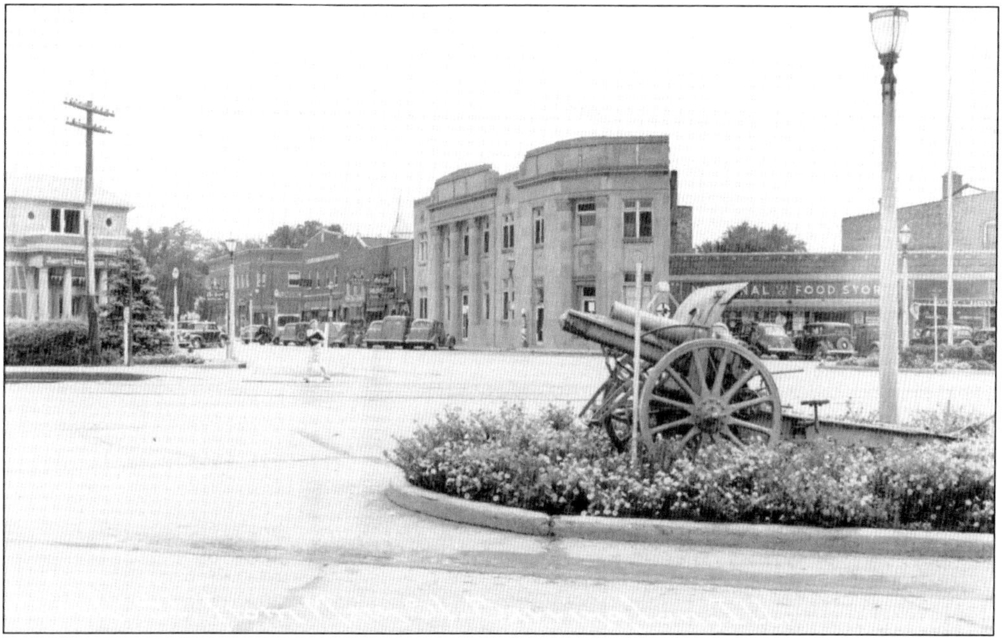

This image of Cook Street, taken from Main Street, offers prominent views of the National Tea Company Food Store and the new First National Bank Building. Adjacent to the bank building was a fountain service and liquor store, a Florsheim Shoe Store, a Royal Blue grocery store, Lipofsky's Store, and, across Station Street, the Ten Pin Bowling Alley.

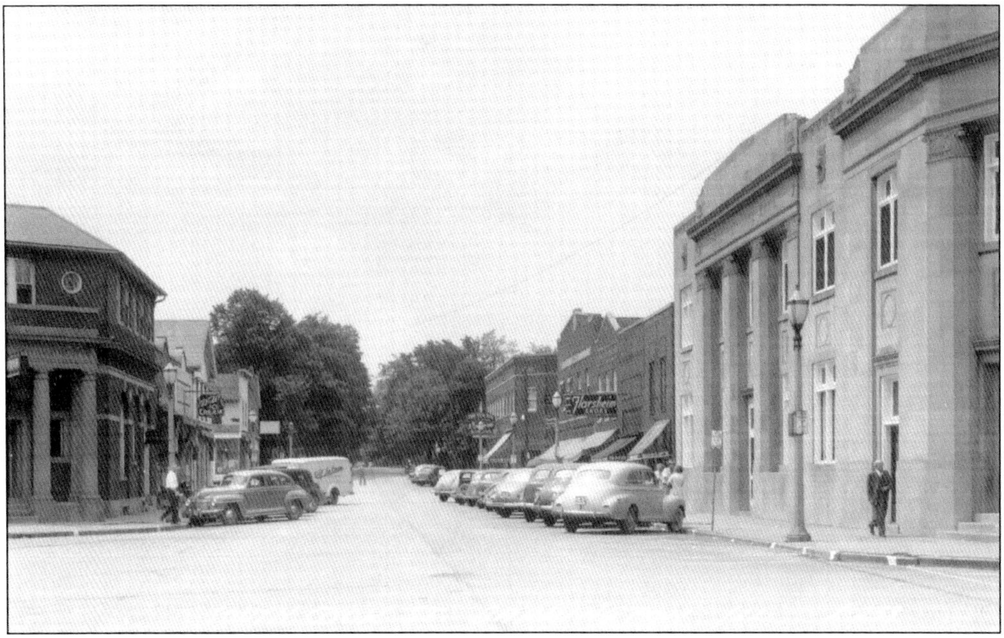

In this 1947 photograph of South Cook Street, one can see the Bank Tavern and the D&W Ice Cream Store at the left. Note the D&W ice cream truck parked in front of the store. The Florsheim Shoes has a new sign and a hardware store is next to the Ten Pin Bowling Alley.

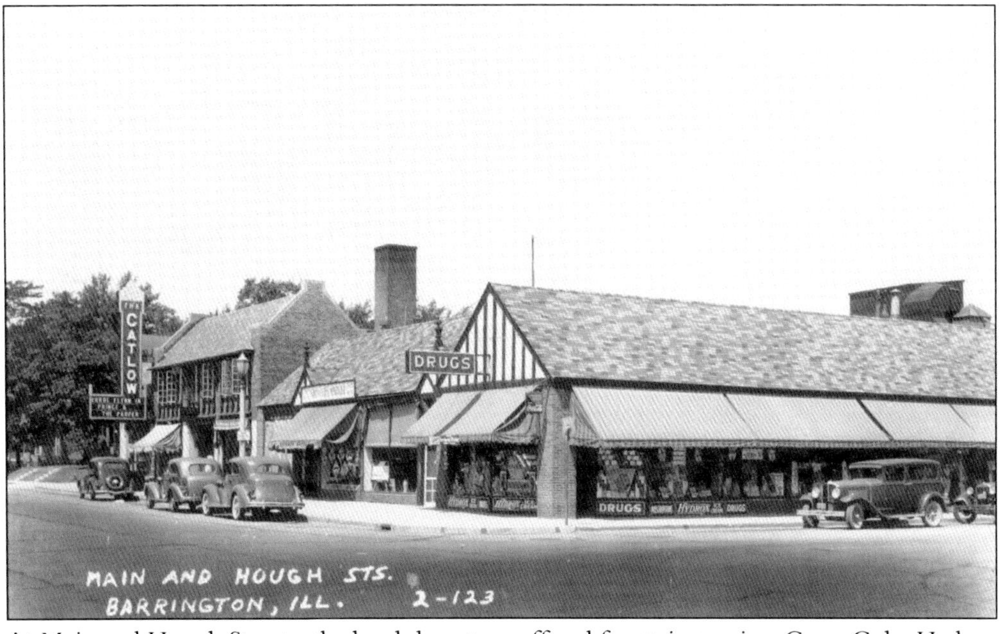

At Main and Hough Streets, the local drugstore offered fountain service, Coca-Cola, Hydrox ice cream, film developing, and photograph printing. Shinner's meat market is next door, and a few doors down, the Catlow Theater is showing Errol Flynn in *The Prince and the Pauper.* Wright Catlow started construction of the theater, designed by Betts & Holcomb of Chicago, in 1926. The theater's grand opening was held on May 28, 1927—Catlow's birthday. The Catlow Theater was listed in the National Register of Historic Places in 1989.

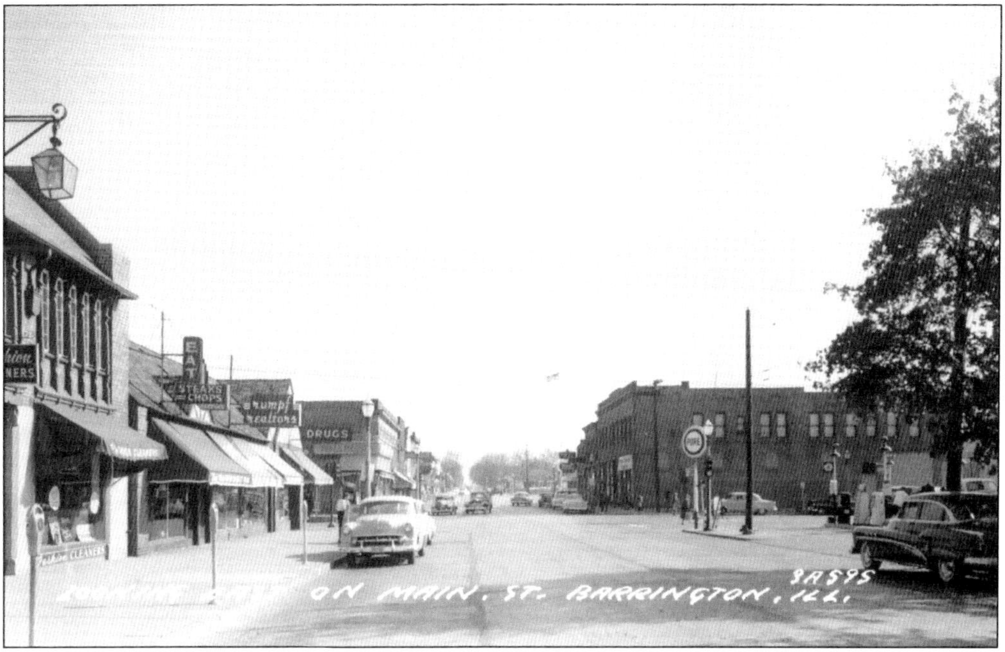

In this eastward view of Main Street, Fashion Cleaners is visible at the left, along with a restaurant offering steaks and chops. The local drugstore and the Pure Oil service station still occupy the prominent corners of Hough and Main Streets.

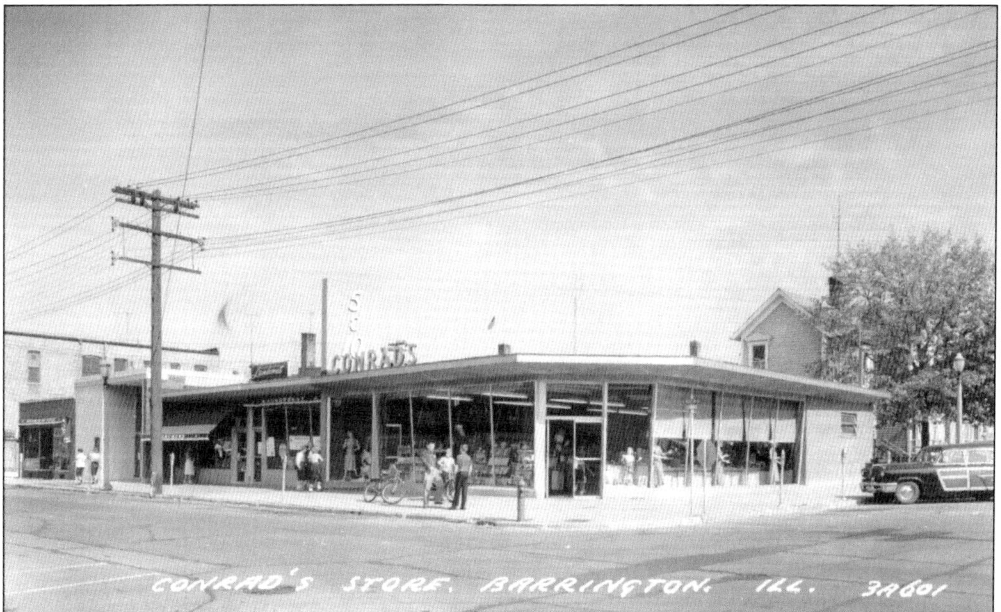

Conrad's five-and-dime, located at the corner of Hough and Station Streets, offered just about everything a shopper could need, including office supplies, children's toys, sewing notions, makeup, a fine selection of candies, and household cooking and baking items. The store also carried women's and children's clothing.

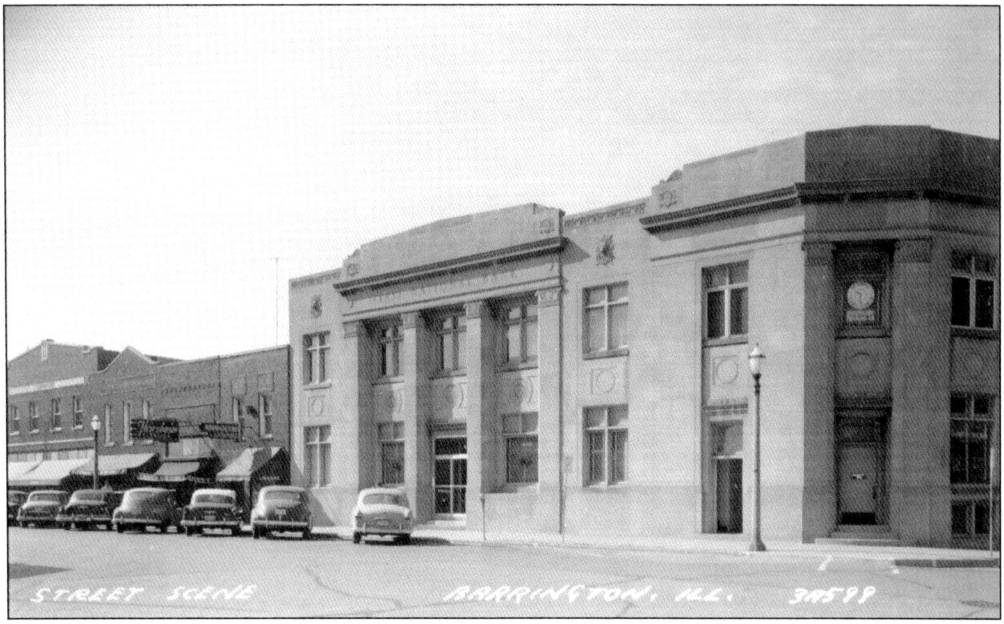

Although new businesses appeared on Cook Street, including a record and gift shop and Barrington liquors, Lipofsky's and the First National Bank continued to anchor this block. Note the clock on the bank building that promotes the Barrington Trucking Company and includes the slogan, "Our business is always picking up."

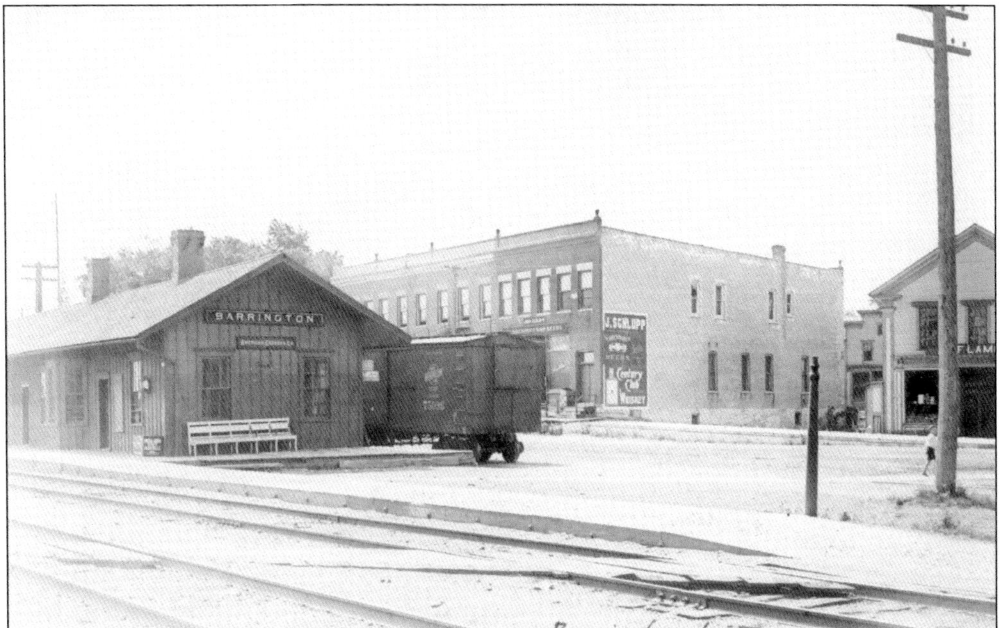

This American Express Company office in the early 1900s along the C&NW tracks also had a sidetrack for freight cars so that merchandise could be unloaded close to local businesses. The building in the background is the J. Schlupp business, offering Schoenhofen Beer.

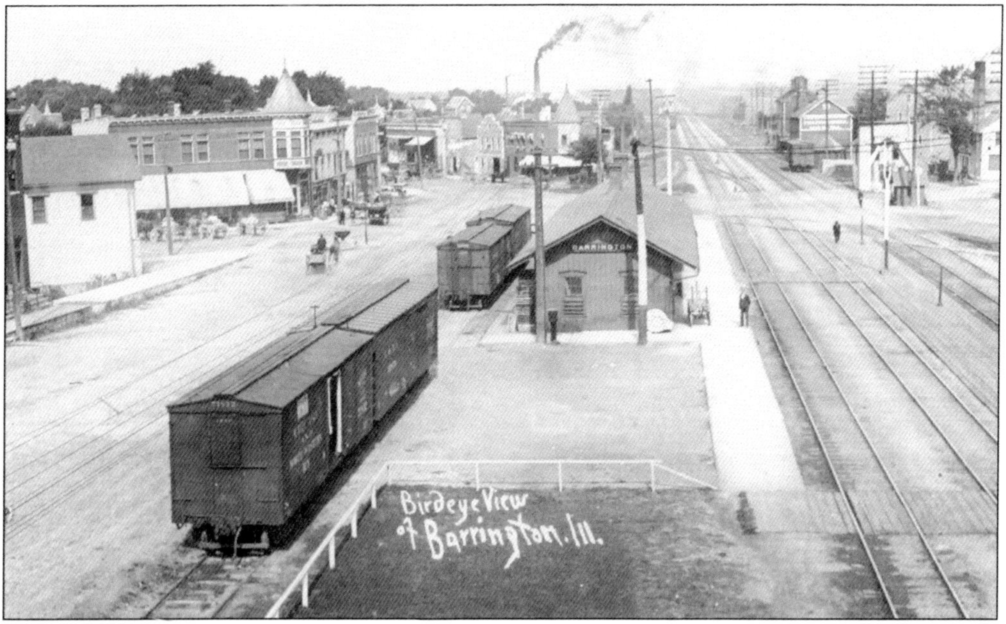

This 1908 bird's-eye view of downtown Barrington shows a progressive and vibrant town. The trainman waits on the platform for the next train to arrive and local residents go about their daily business. This photograph was taken from the railroad water tower and shows Park Avenue, Cook Street, and Main Street.

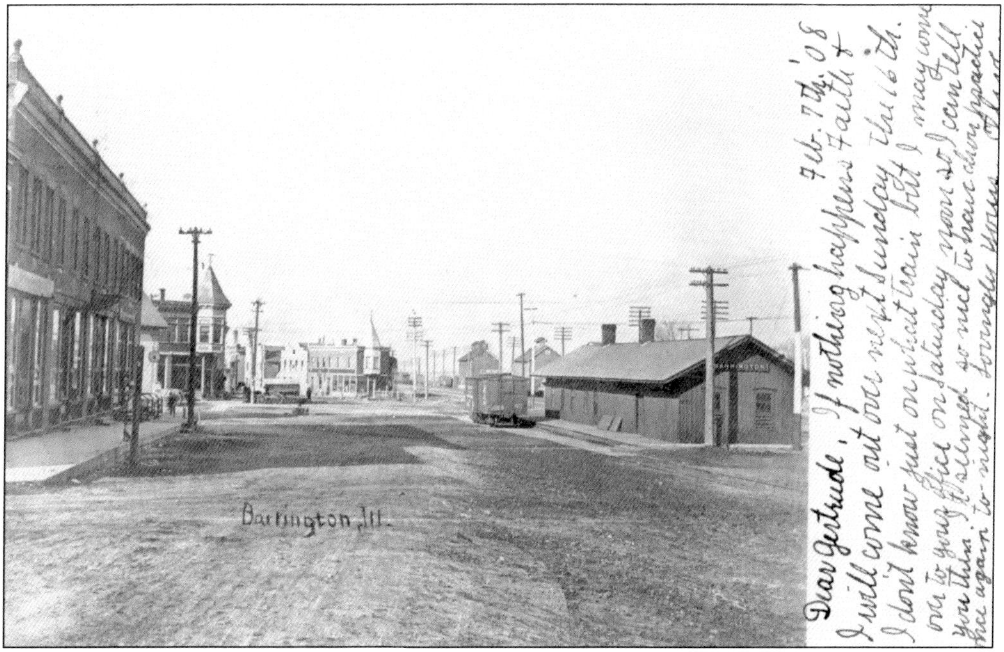

Downtown Barrington had wide dirt streets to provide room for turning wagons. This image of Market Street (later known as South Railroad Street and now called Park Avenue) offers a glimpse of the open and available space in the developing community.

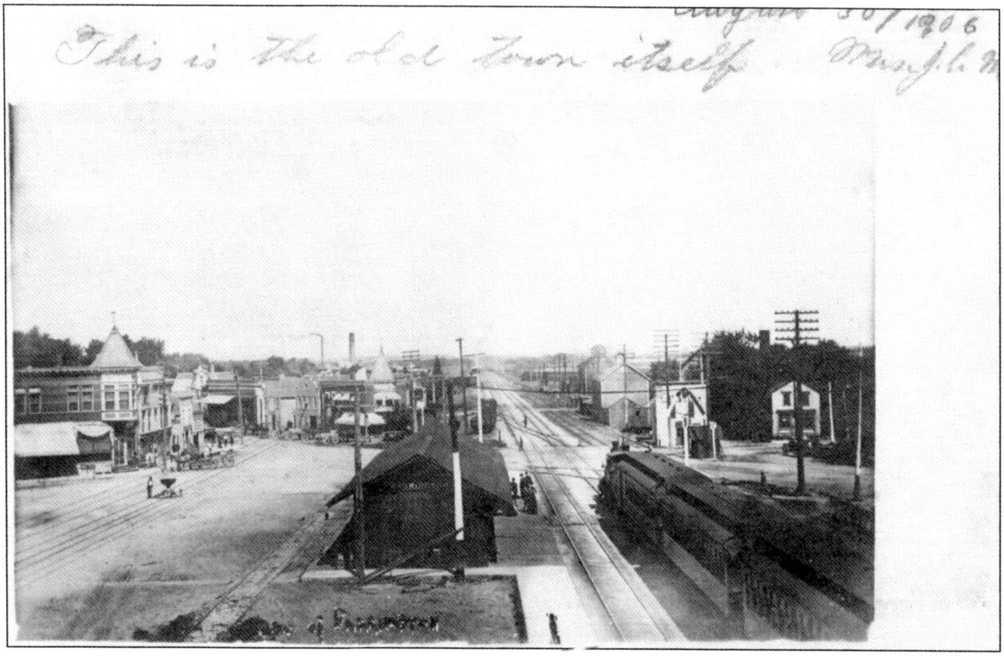

In this 1906 image, the C&NW train arrives at the depot, where people wait to board a train headed for Fox River Grove, Illinois. The town water fountain, where residents could water their horses, is visible at the left in the center of the street.

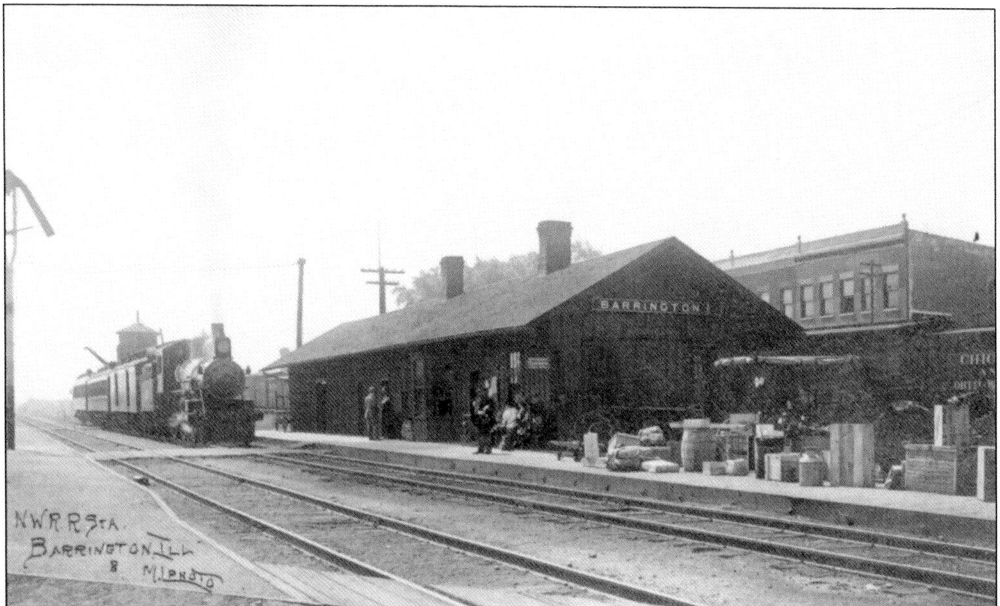

This 1913 image offers a different perspective of the C&NW train pulling into the depot. Most local merchants shipped products by rail; note the freight waiting for shipment at the right.

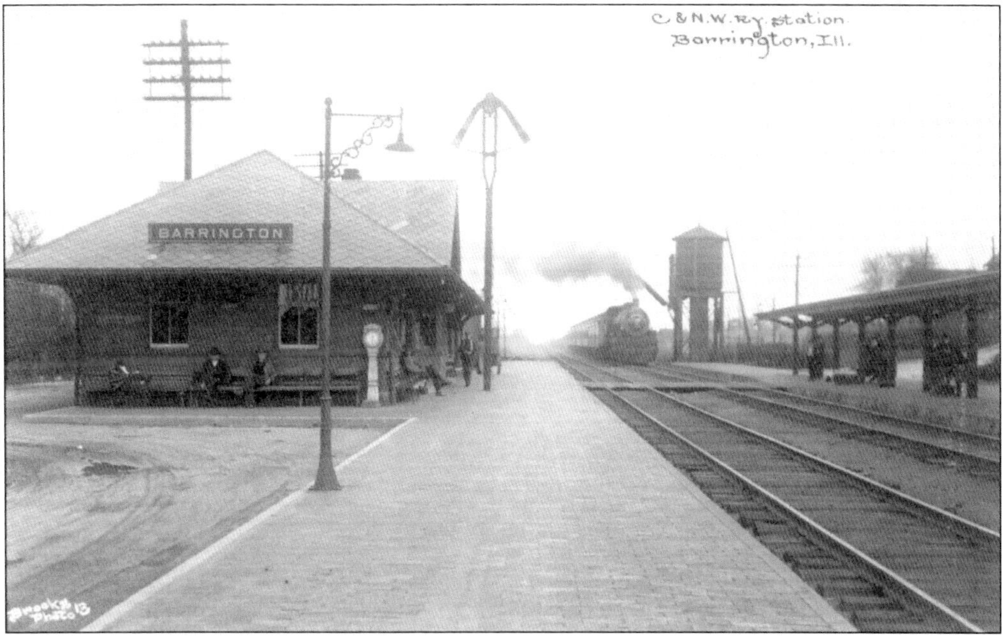

This 1926 photograph of the C&NW station shows a steam locomotive pulling into town to discharge its passengers. The water tower to the right of the locomotive was used to provide water to the engines so steam could be generated to propel the trains. A scale in front of the station offers to weigh a traveler for a penny.

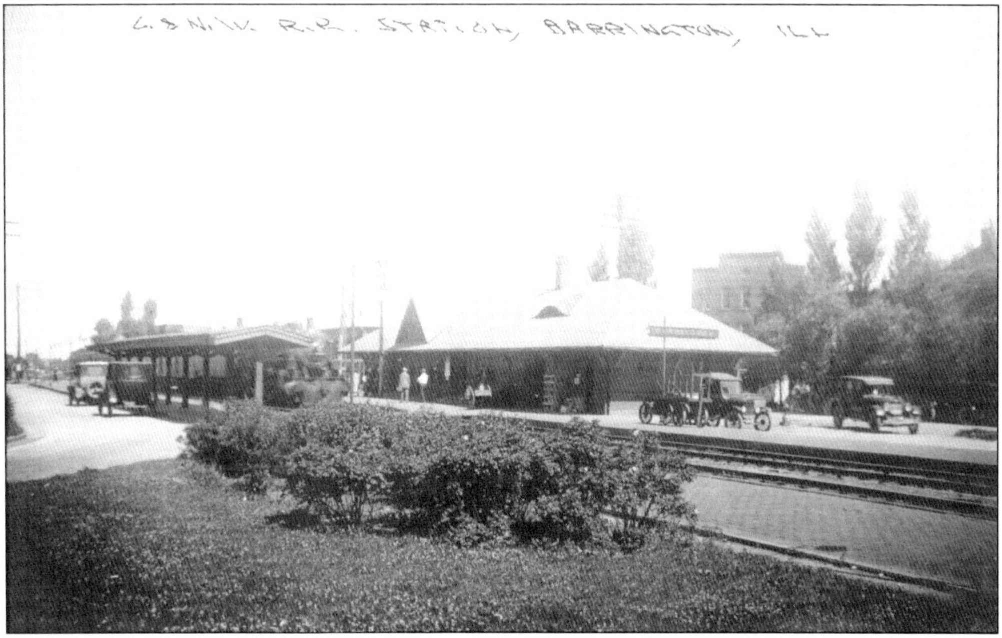

The convenient downtown location of the C&NW station offered travelers easy access to the hotel across the street or the opportunity to get a meal at one of the restaurants and eateries located within a few hundred feet of the station. A close look at this image reveals a Chicago-bound train in the station.

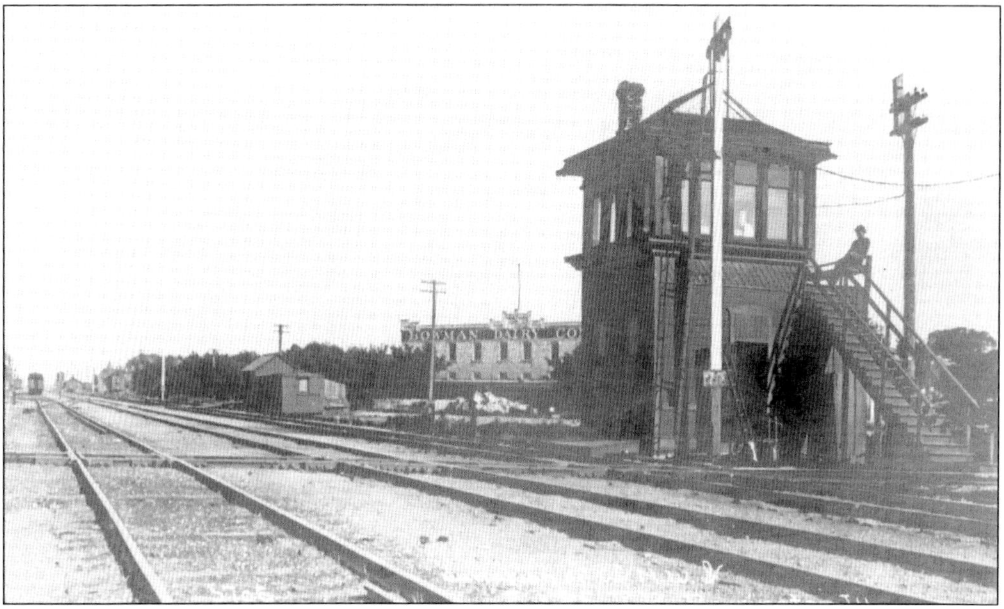

Charles R. Childs took this photograph of the train tower at the junction of the C&NW and the Elgin, Joliet & Eastern (EJ&E) railroad tracks. Standing 27 feet high and rumored to have been constructed at a cost of $10,000, this tower housed many hand levers operating train signals by wire cables at distances of as much as 300 yards.

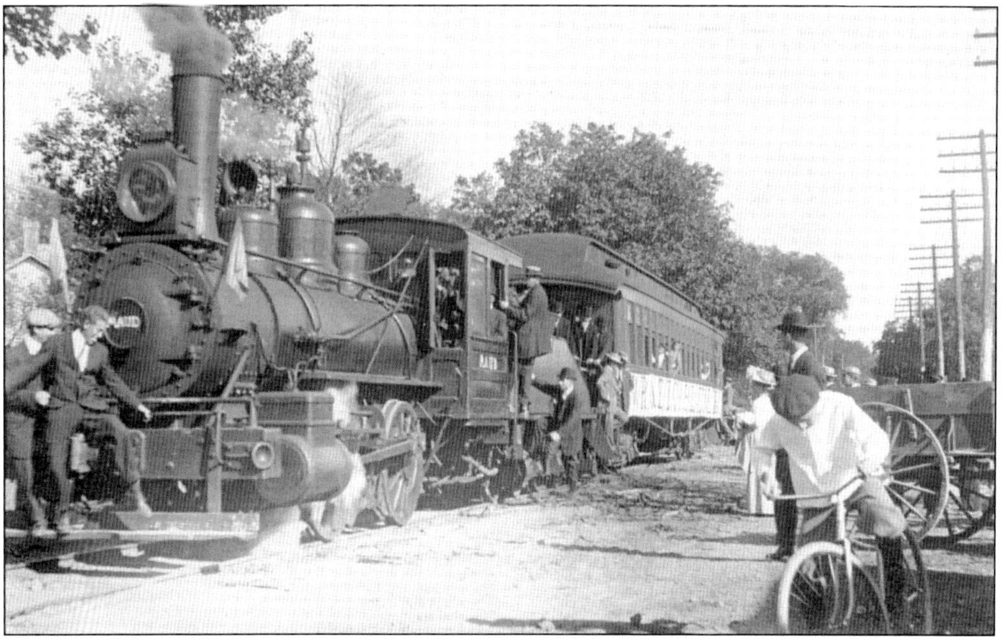

The Palatine, Lake Zurich and Wauconda (PLZ&W) Railroad was an 11-mile, short-line railroad built to connect the towns of Palatine, Lake Zurich, and Wauconda, Illinois. The route delivered commuters and freight to these communities, as well as to the Deer Grove picnic grounds. "Old Maud," the locomotive in this photograph, was originally purchased from the C&NW. Many Barrington residents rode the train to the resorts in Lake Zurich and Bangs Lake in Wauconda.

Three

Schools and Churches

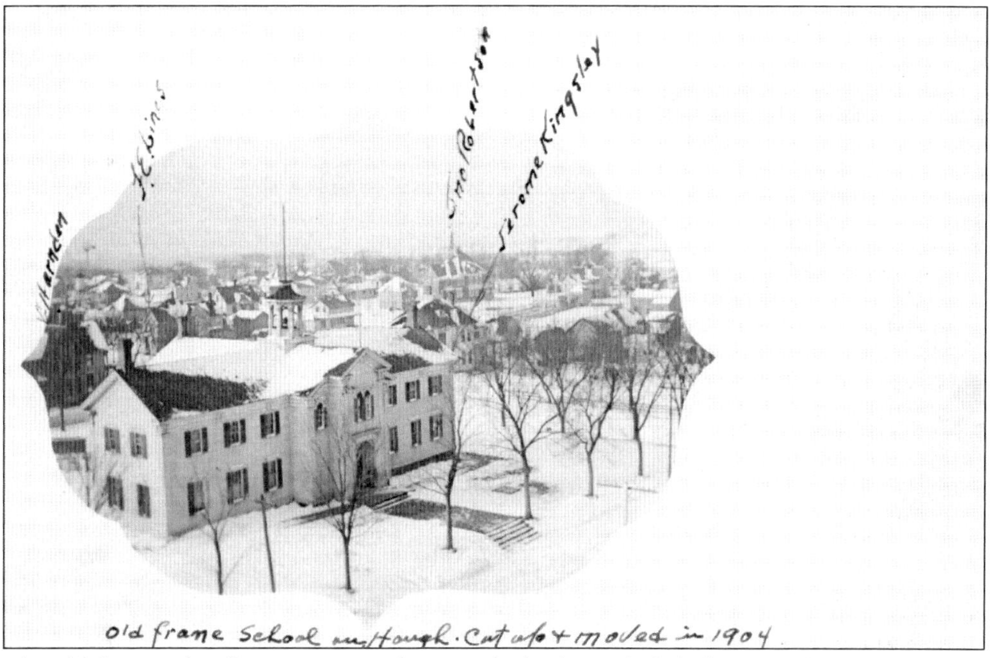

The old frame schoolhouse on Hough Street had a large dark hallway in the center section and winding stairways with wide, smooth banisters that offered students a quick exit when the school day ended. The original wood stoves were later replaced with hard coal base burners. The pupils in the back of the room shivered in the cold while those in the front suffered excessive heat; the problem was resolved by putting jackets around the stoves. The writing on this image identifies the owners of some local homes in 1904.

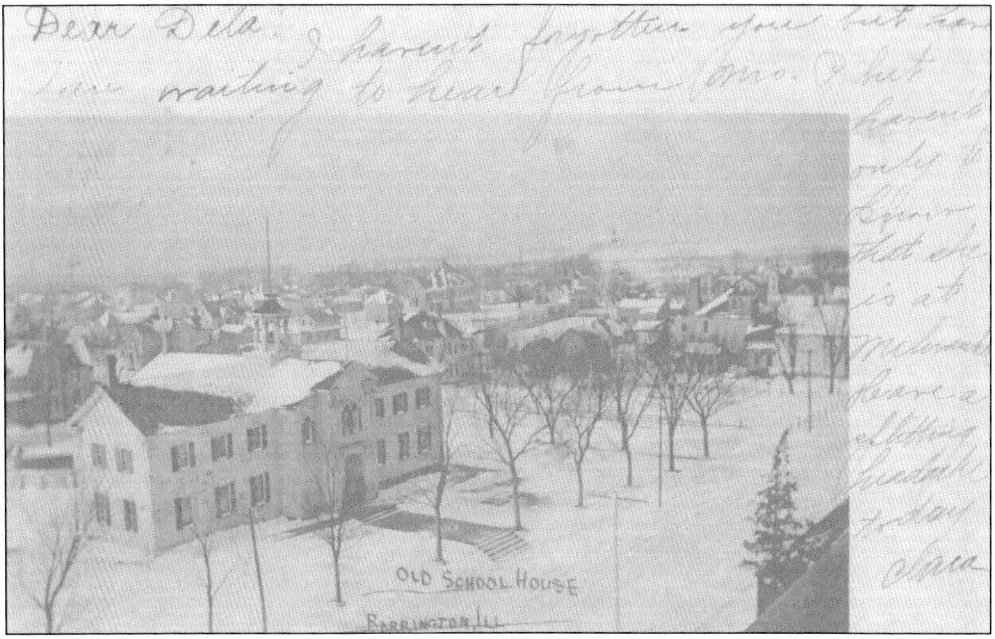

This 1906 photograph, attributed to photographer George Froelich Jr., offers a broadened perspective of the school in relationship to the neighborhood. There were two playgrounds at the school—one on the south side for girls and one on the northwest side for boys. Students had to buy their own slates, pencils, writing tablets, and books.

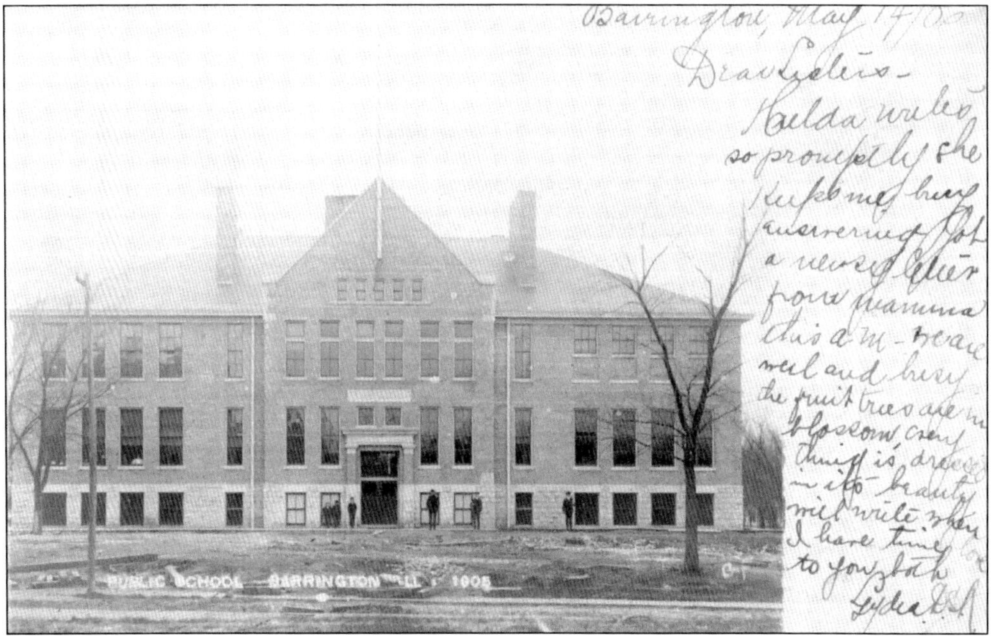

Eventually, the old schoolhouse on Hough Street became overcrowded and classes began meeting in the Zion church across the street. In 1905, a new brick building was constructed on Hough Street and the old frame school was divided into four sections that were sold as residences. This photograph shows the newly built school.

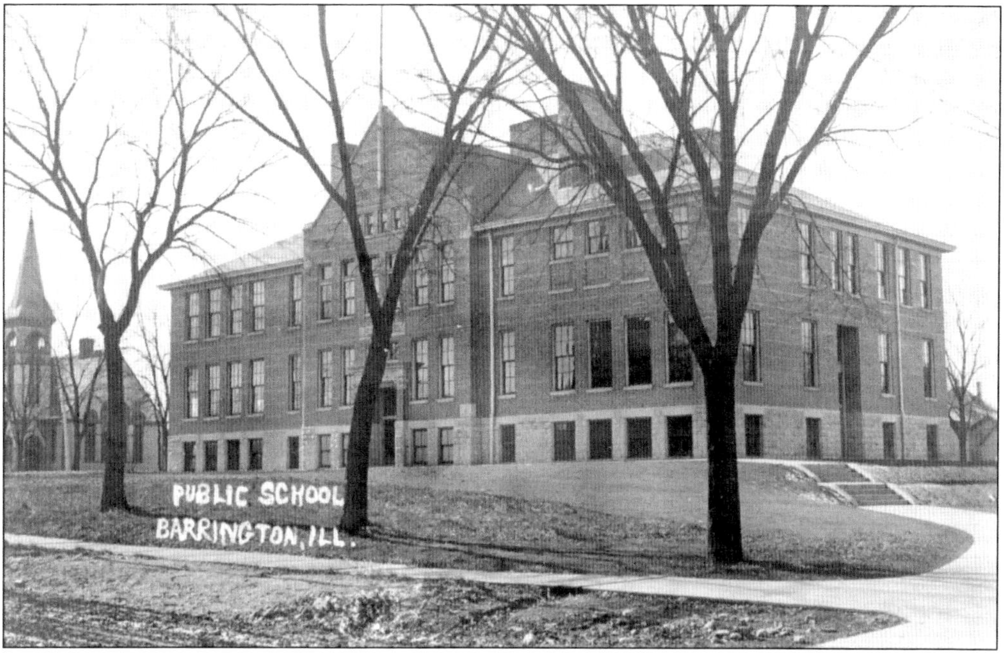

The new school, constructed for $35,000, stands on a hill overlooking the southwest area of Barrington. Note the minimal landscaping around the building.

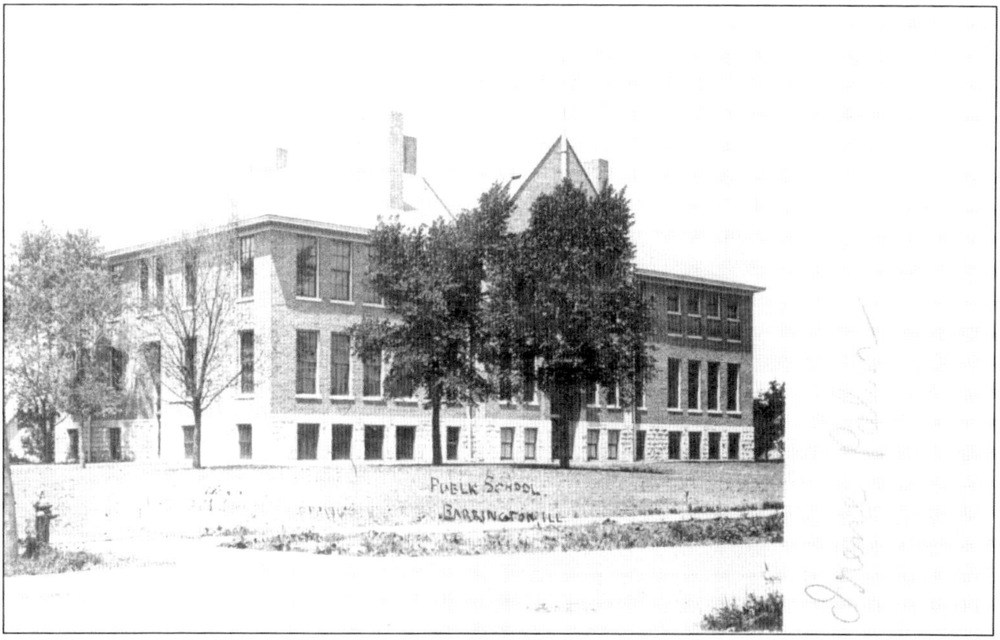

This photograph of the Hough Street School was taken from the corner of Lincoln Avenue and Hough Street. Note the numerous chimneys.

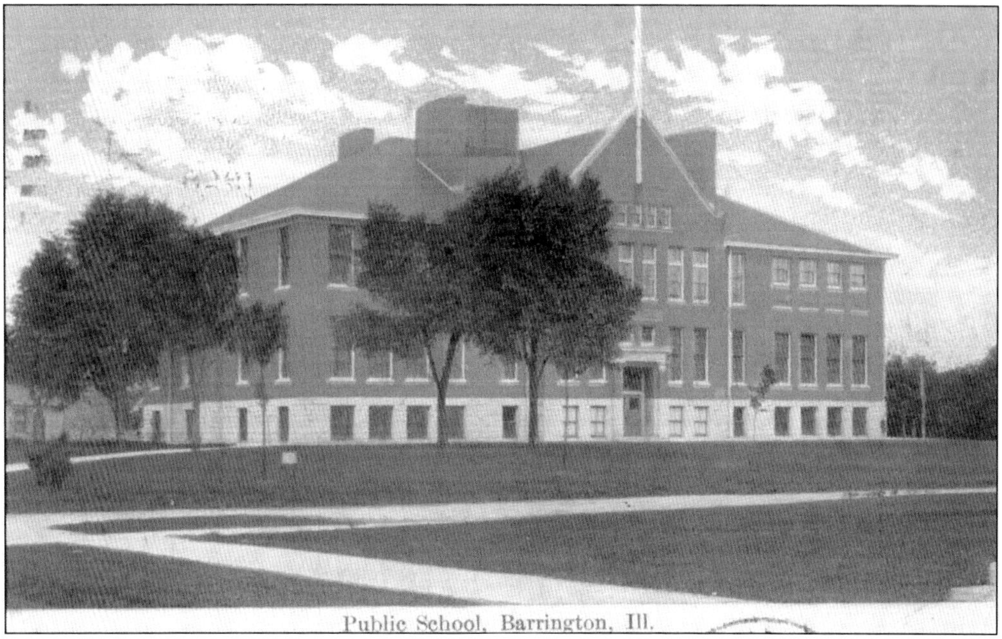

This 1908 colorized version of the Hough Street School showed the building in red brick with a blue-green roof. The sender of the card, Manie Mavis, noted that she would be seeing her cousins again very soon and added: "I have near a hundred postcards. I love these scenes, don't you?"

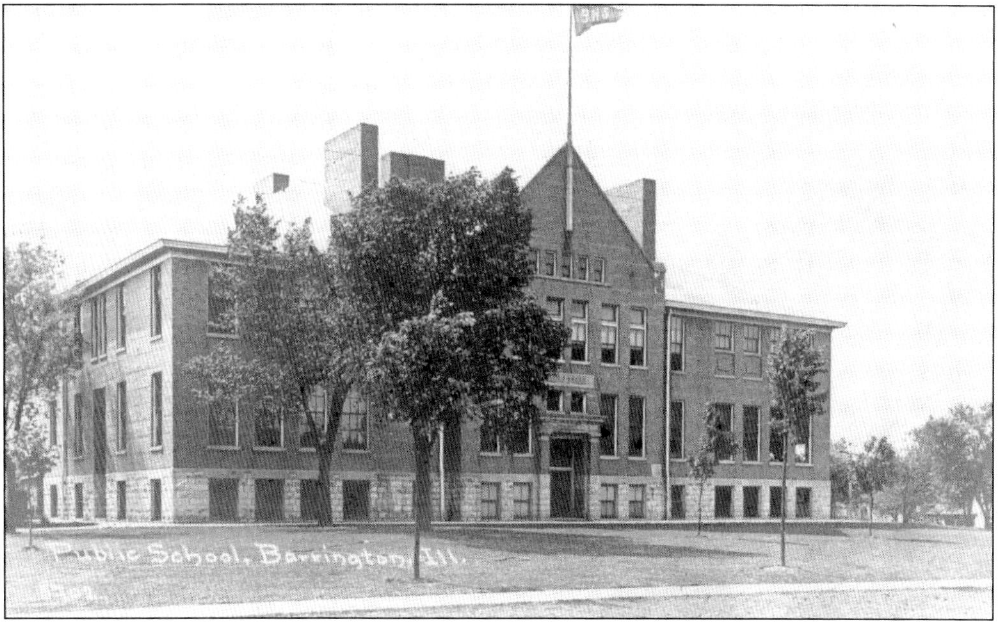

A real-photo postcard attributed to C.R. Childs shows Hough Street School after several years. The trees around the school building have matured and the flag, bearing the letters "BHS" (for "Barrington High School"), flies proudly above the school. There were no graduation classes in 1905 and 1906, and the first four-year class at Barrington High School graduated in 1907.

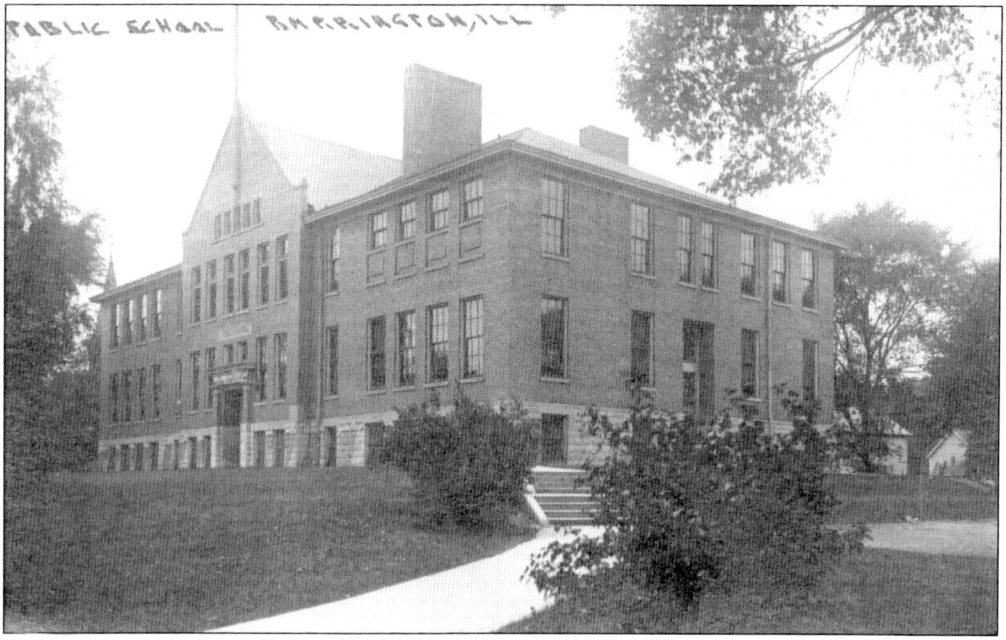

This photograph, by P.L. Huckins of Chicago, shows the combined grade school and high school. The landscaping around the building has matured and gives the school a different appearance.

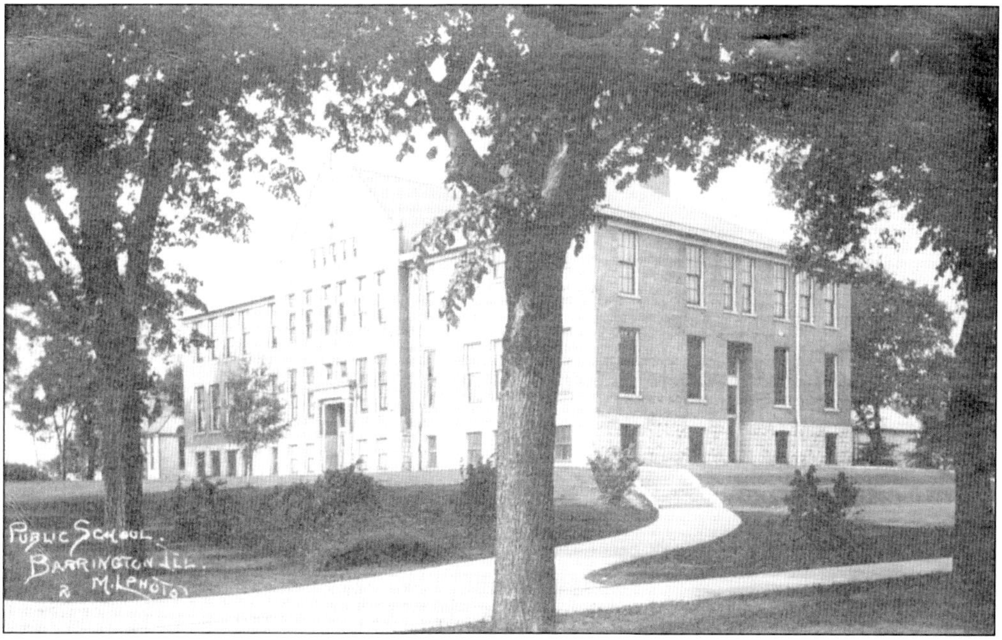

This image, by M.L. Photo Company, shows the school framed by the growing trees on the grounds. Hough Street School was probably one of the most-photographed buildings in Barrington.

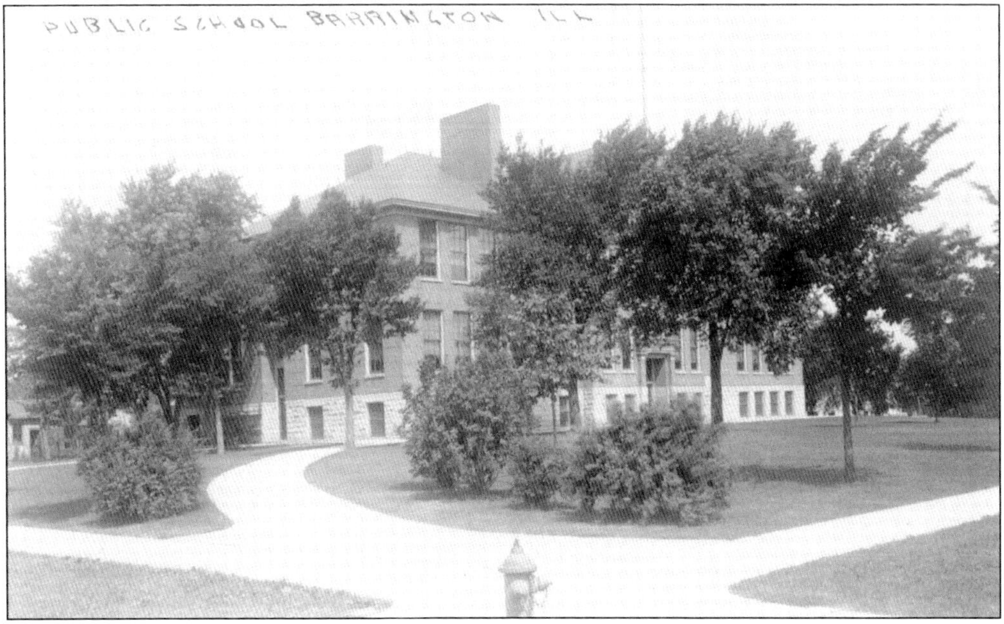

P.L. Huckins captured this 1914 image of Hough Street School from Hough Street facing northwest towards the business district. Note the close proximity of the fire hydrant to the school grounds.

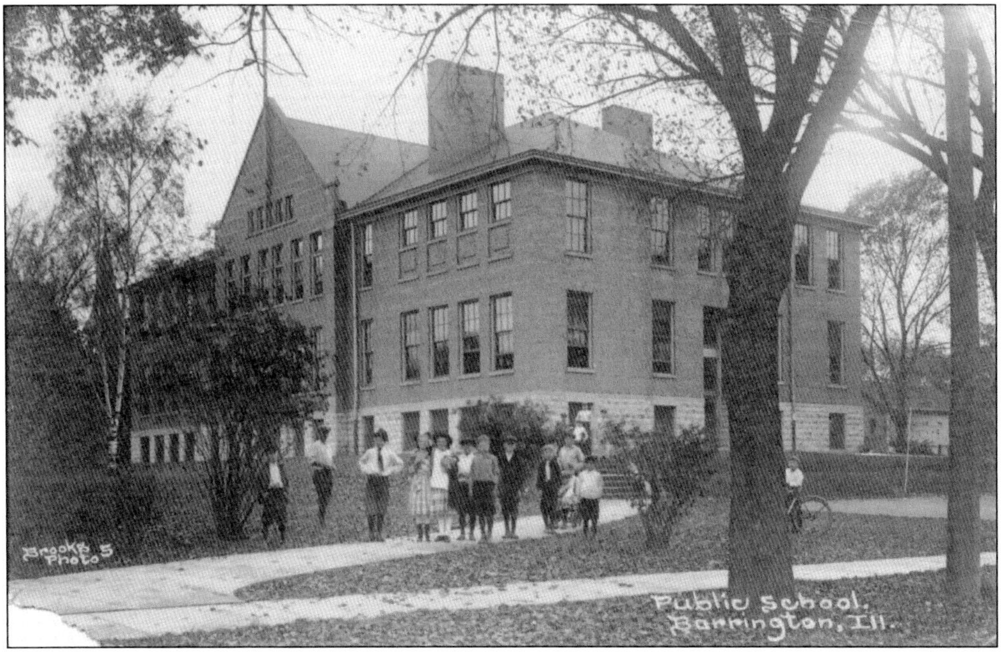

Children pose in front of Hough Street School in this picture from 1926.

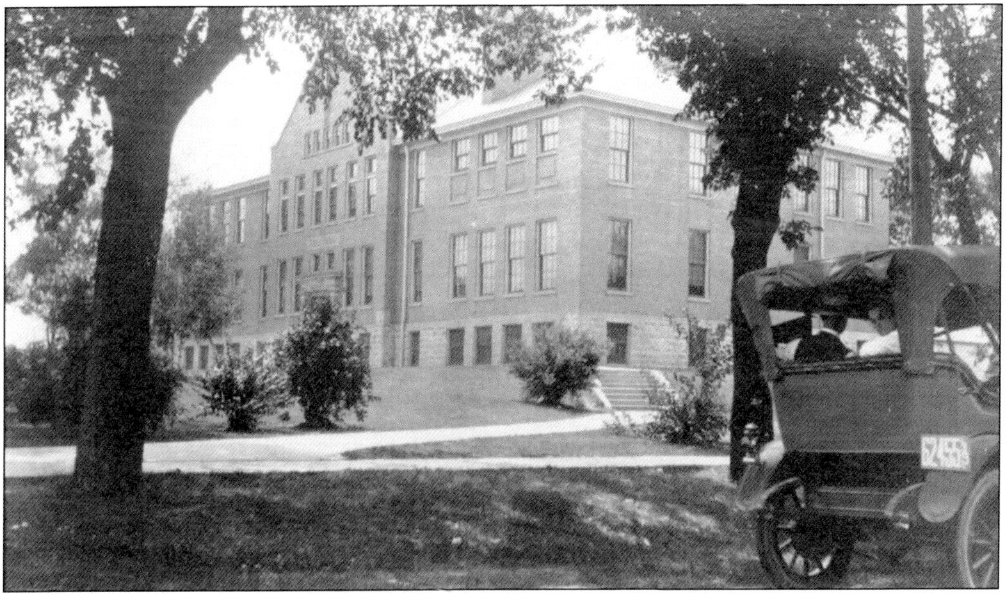

The school building was a popular place to bring visiting guests and relatives. Barrington residents were proud of their new school, as evidenced by the vehicle that has stopped for a view of this grand building.

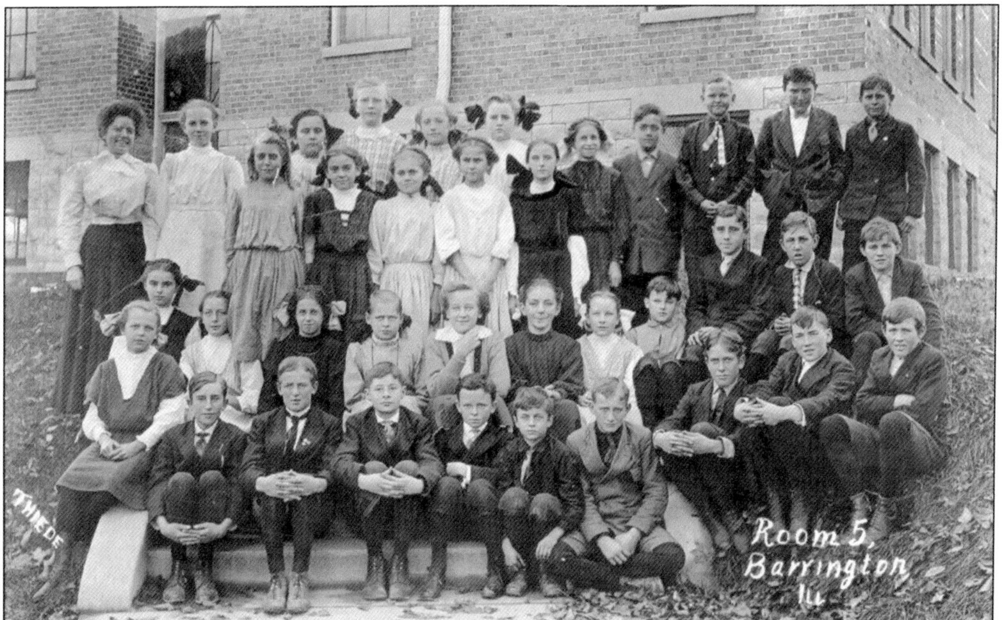

The children in room five were ready for photograph day in 1905. The girls wore their best dresses and ribbons and the boys donned their best suits and jackets.

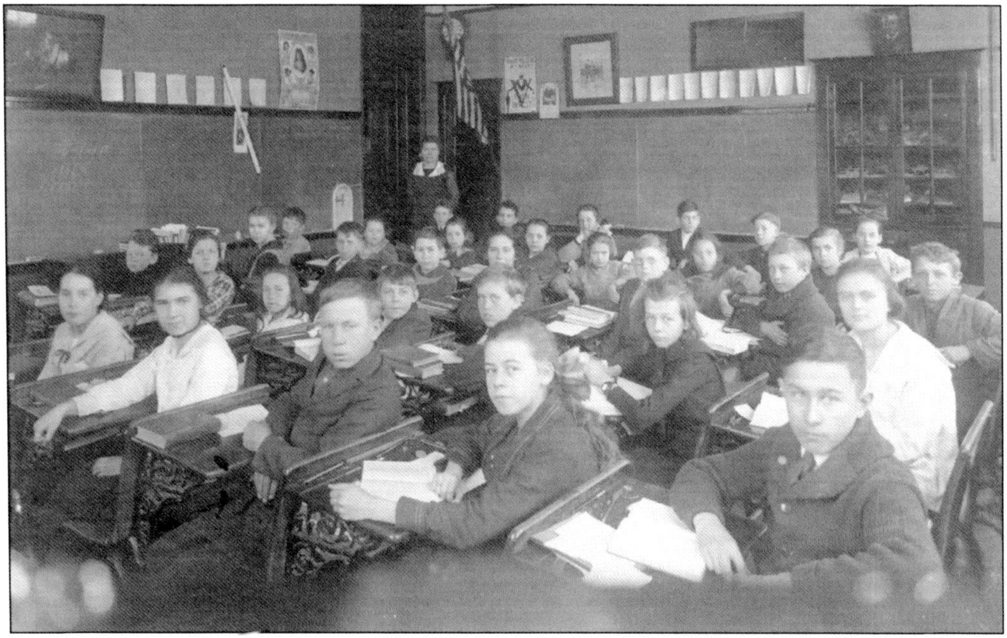

In this classroom at Hough Street School, President Roosevelt's picture hangs on the wall and most of the students have their books open for studying. Each individual desk has its own inkwell and the classroom even has its own drinking fountain.

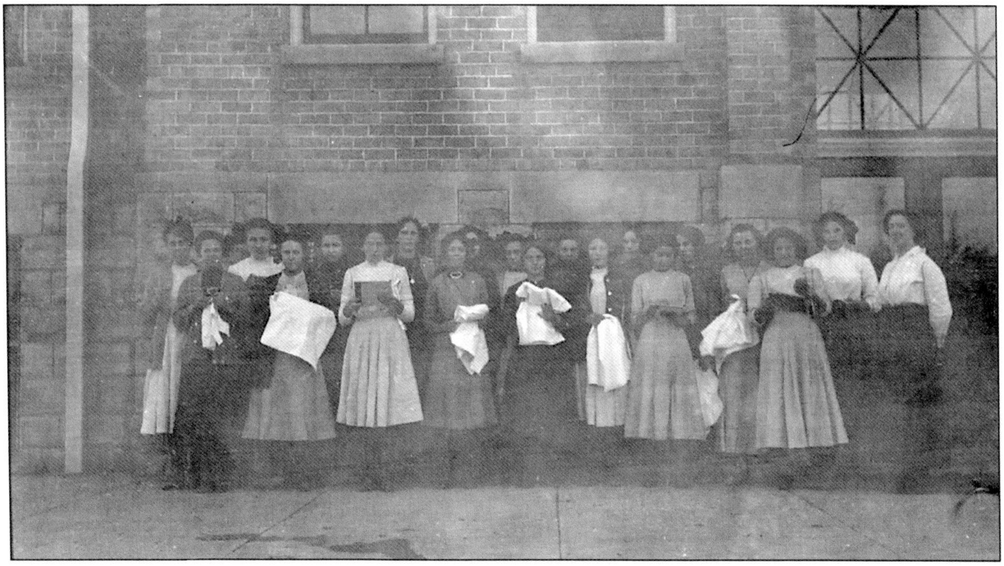

The individuals and instructor in this photograph are not identified. Could this have been a domestic arts or theater class at Hough Street School? The image was definitely taken at the school, as evidenced by the large stone blocks and bricks in the background.

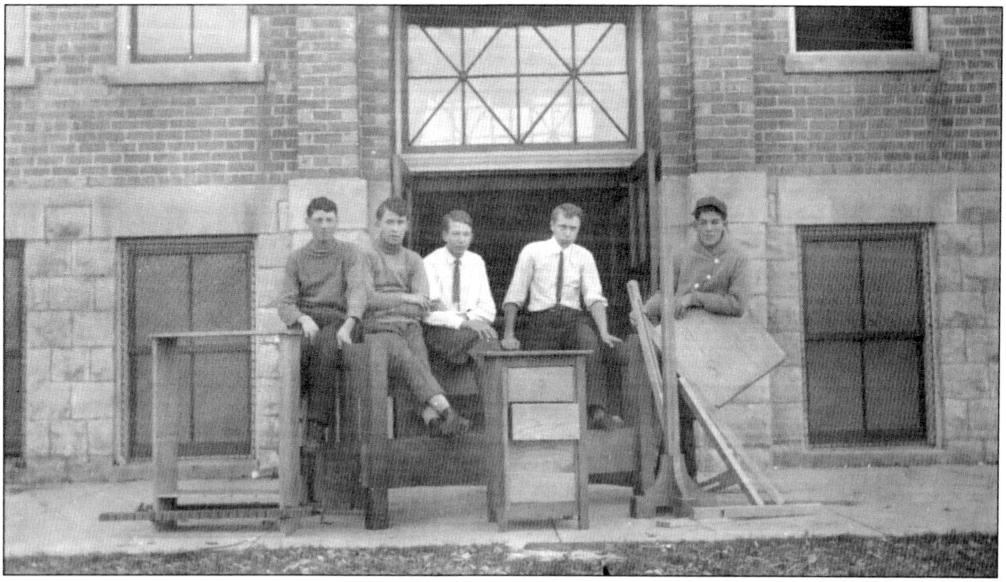

Students from the shop class at Hough Street School display their projects in this photograph, including a hall tree, a four-drawer stand, tables, and benches.

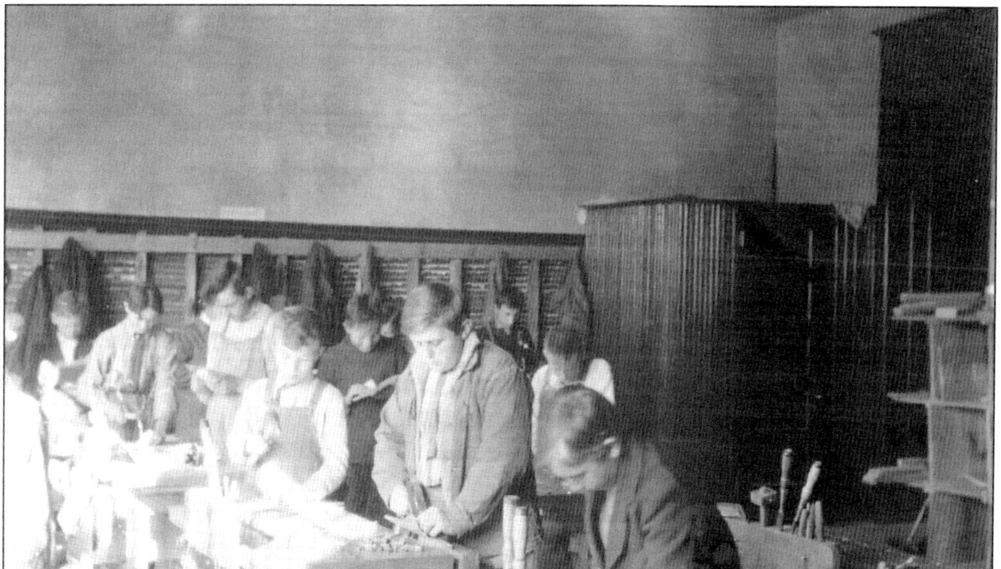

Young students at Hough Street School work diligently on their projects in shop class. They appear to be demonstrating the use of shop tools.

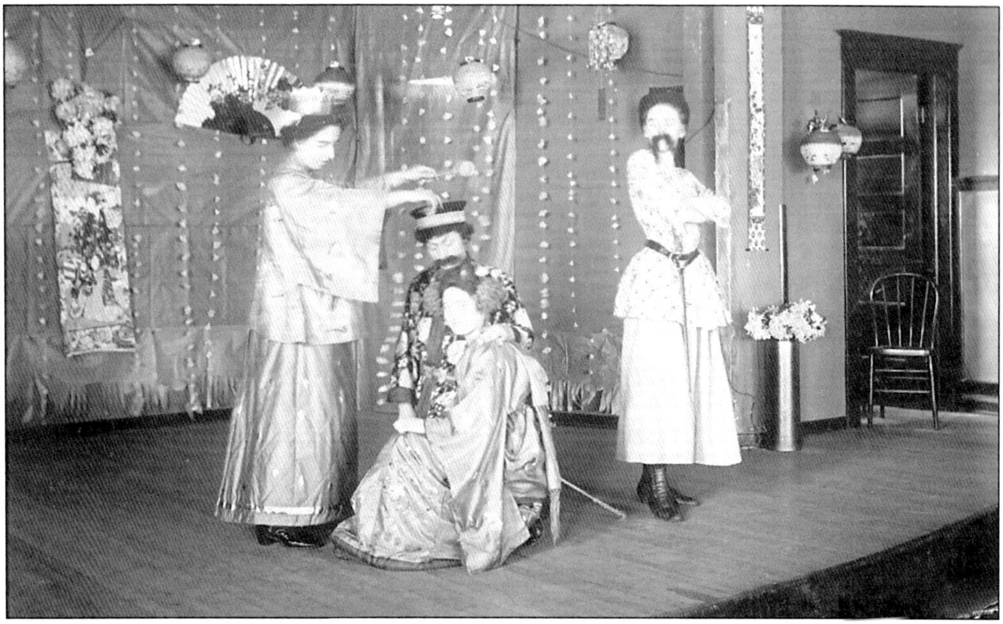

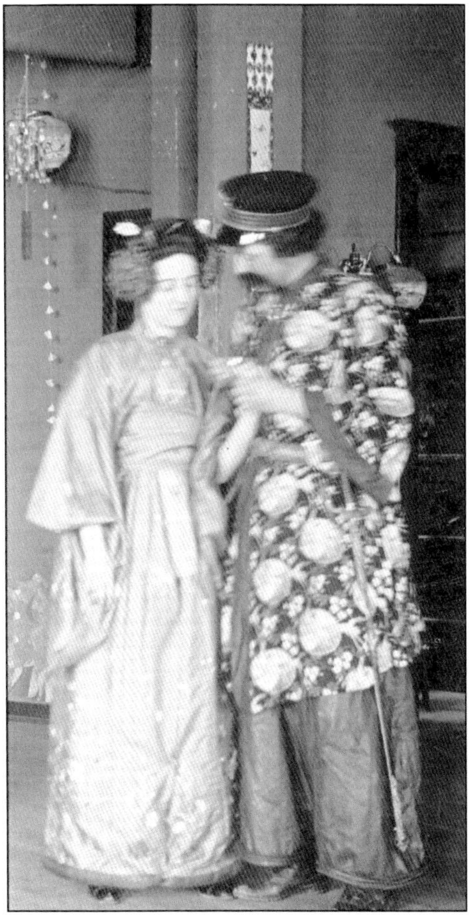

Theater was also an important part of a student's education at Hough Street School. Here, students present a scene from *Madame Butterfly* in 1910. Note the high button shoes on the actors and the special lanterns placed over the classroom lights.

This postcard image of the 1910 student production of *Madame Butterfly* was probably captured by the drama teacher, or perhaps a family member, and then printed on postcard stock to send to friends and relatives.

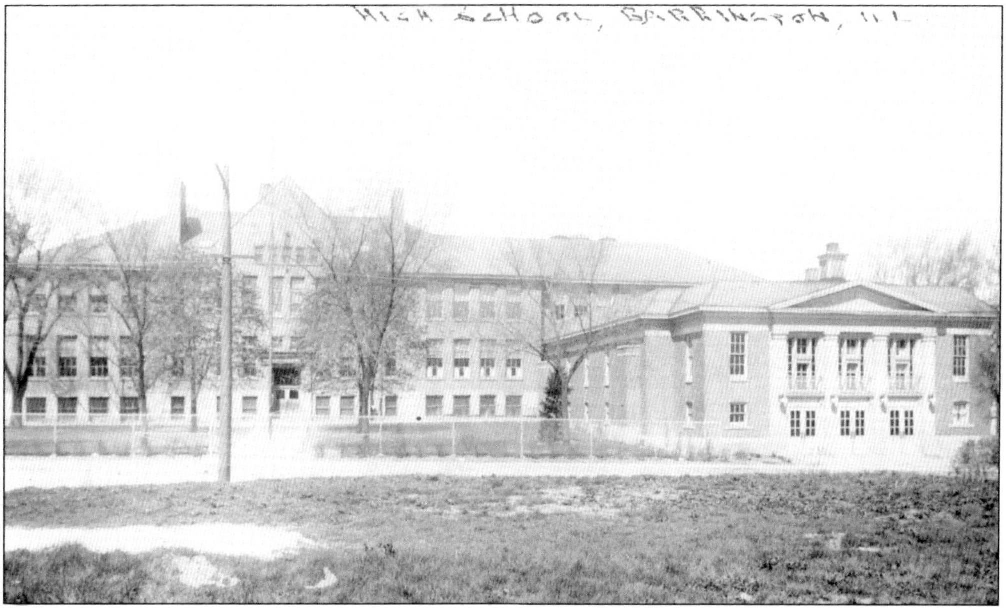

Continuing increases in the number of students attending the school created overcrowded conditions and, in 1937, a three-story fireproof south wing (not pictured) was completed. A gymnasium-auditorium (shown at the right) was also added to the original building to meet the needs of Barrington students.

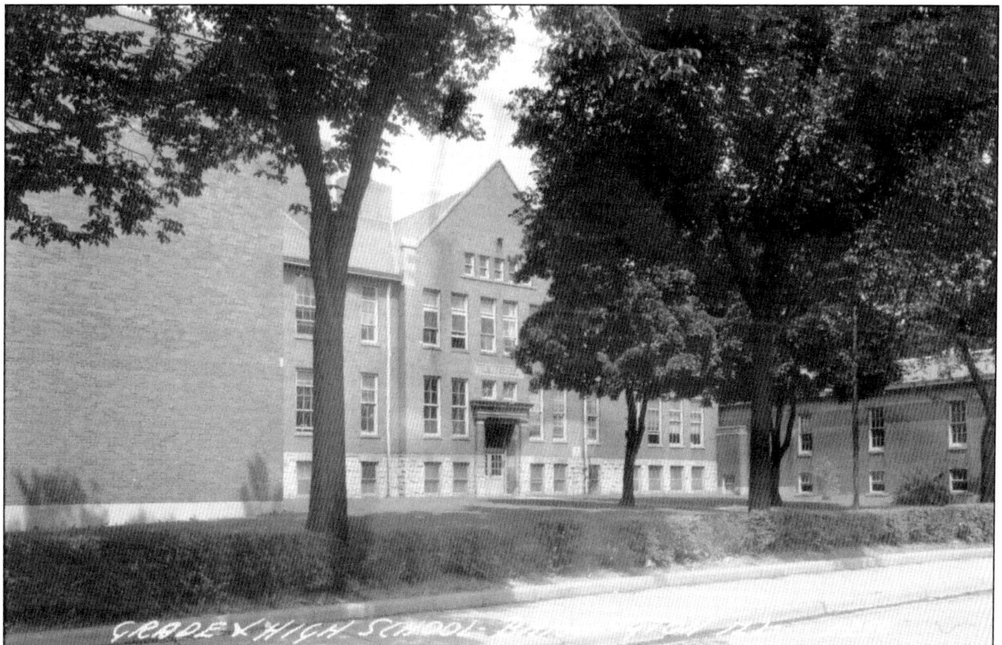

This image captures the Hough Street School building as it looked in 1947. The three-story 1937 addition is at the left, and the gymnasium-auditorium is at the right of the main building.

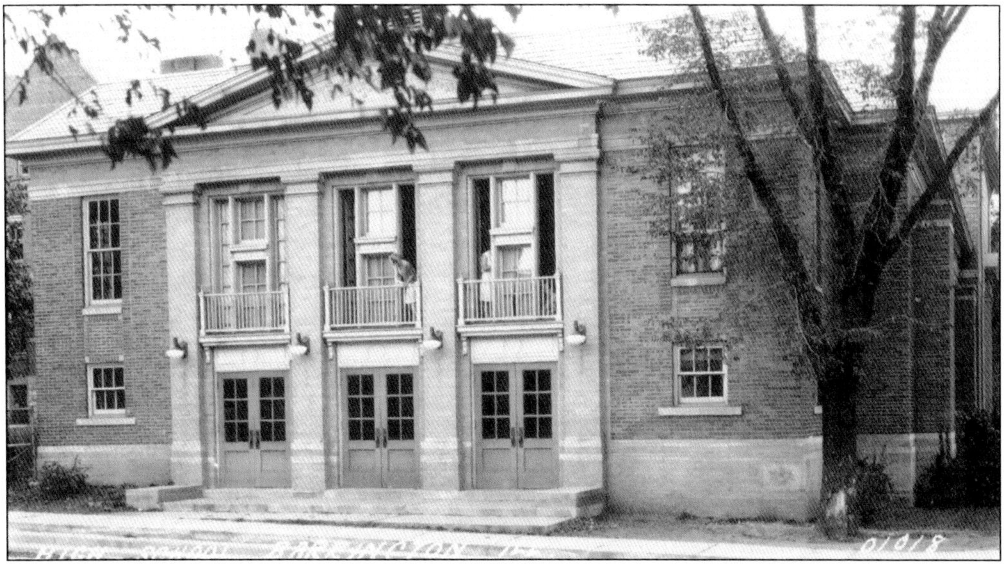

This postcard offers a close-up view of the gymnasium-auditorium at Hough Street School, where many plays and sporting events took place. Each graduating class purchased an item that was left with the school in perpetuity. In the early years, graduating classes donated marble busts of famous authors and writers, while later classes purchased items such as a new scoreboard or new theater equipment. Unfortunately, many of these historic items were lost when the original building was demolished in 1967 to make way for a new elementary school.

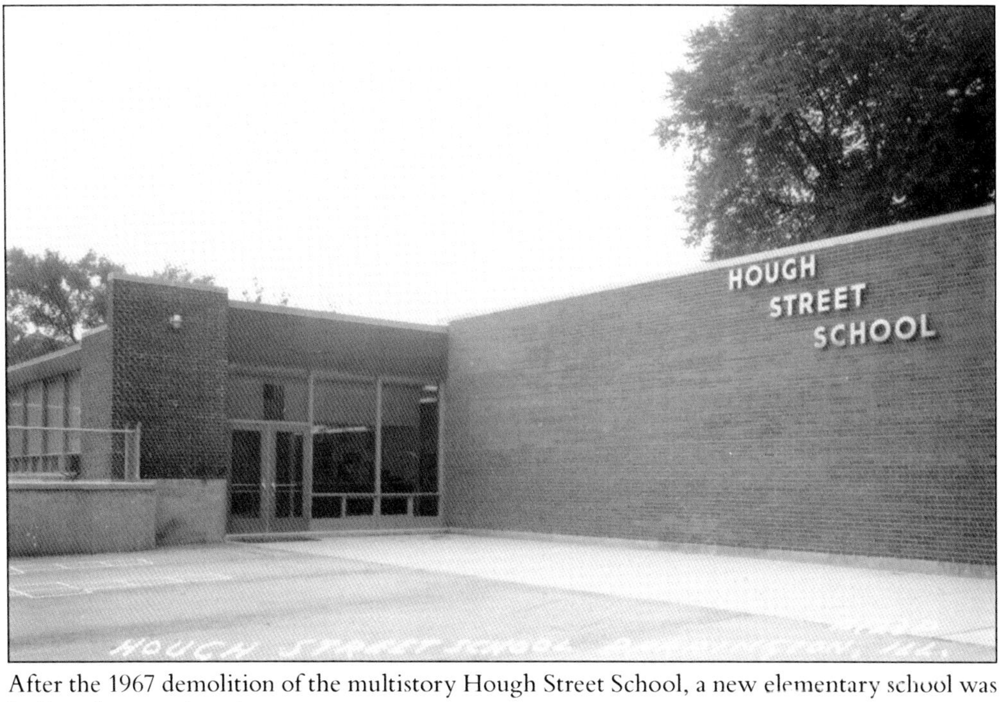

After the 1967 demolition of the multistory Hough Street School, a new elementary school was built at the same location.

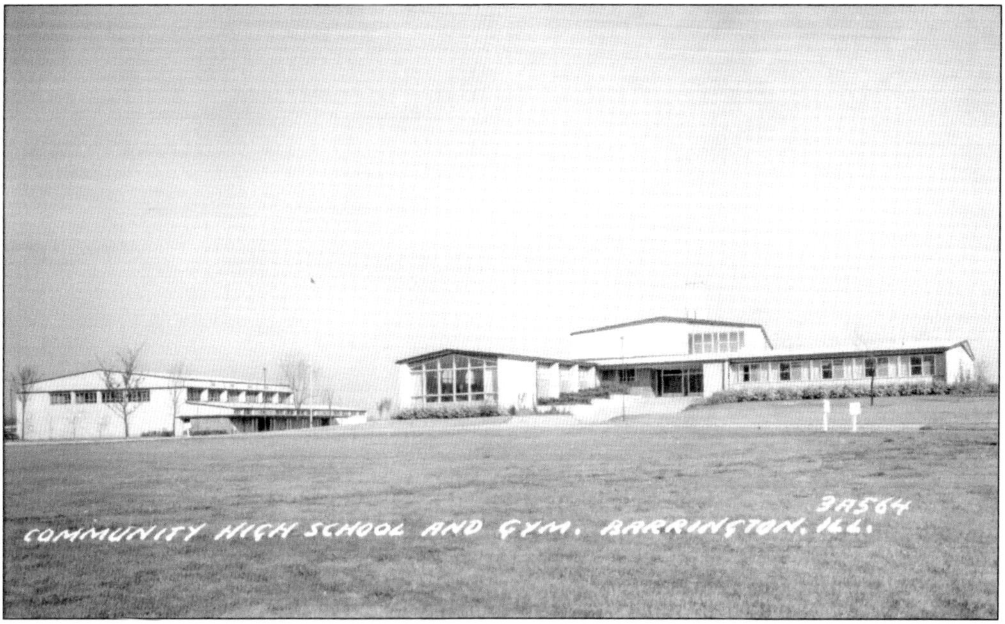

In 1947, Barrington needed a larger high school and a 70-acre site was purchased for $37,000. The extra acreage afforded the school space for future expansion and the addition of athletic fields and parking lots.

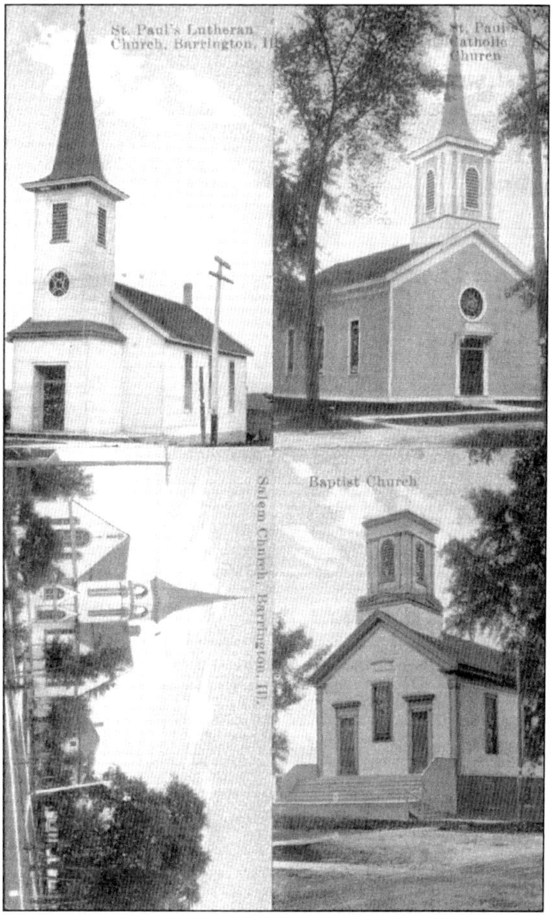

This multi-image 1909 colored card shows four Barrington churches: St. Paul Lutheran Church, St. Anne Catholic Church (incorrectly identified on the card as St. Paul Catholic Church), the Salem Church, and the Baptist Church. This card was published by William G. Hoffman of Chicago.

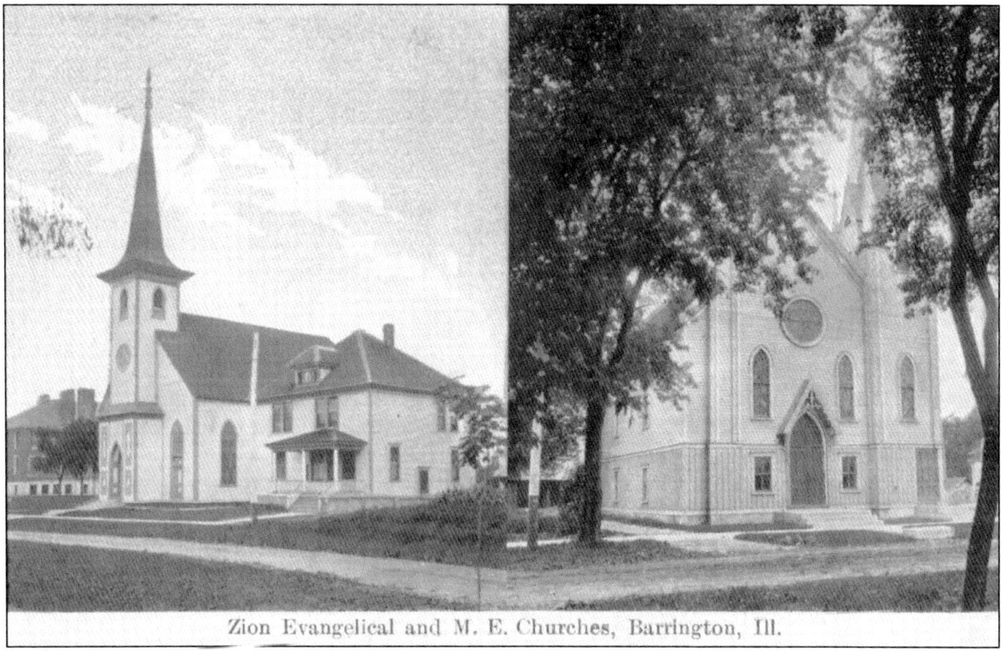

Another William G. Hoffman multi-image colored card contains images of the Zion Evangelical and M.E. churches in Barrington. The reverse side contains a 1918 postmark and a note from Vincent Porter that wishes Dora Termensen a happy and prosperous new year.

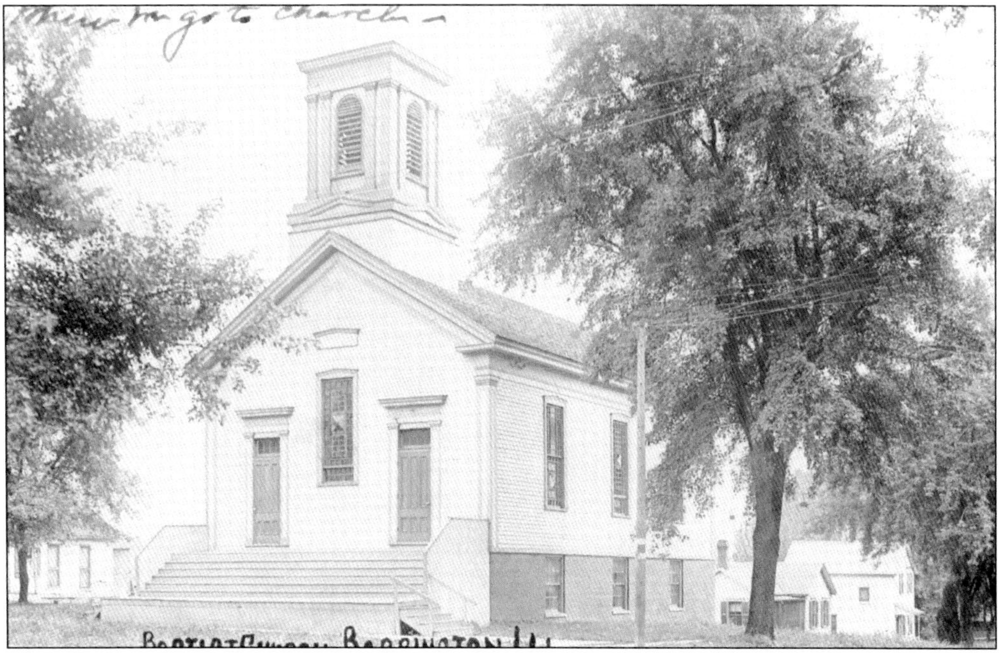

The Baptists of Barrington had been organized as a church congregation since September 1847 by a group of 20 individuals who were previously members of the Baptist church in Dundee, Illinois. When the railroad came to Barrington in 1854, people began to move closer to town. It was determined that a Baptist church within the village limits was a necessity. The Baptist church building was erected in 1859. This image is attributed to George Froelich Jr.

In later years, the exterior of the church was altered. The Baptists celebrated their golden jubilee in 1897, their diamond jubilee in 1934, and their centennial in 1947. This building was demolished in 1949 to make way for a larger building.

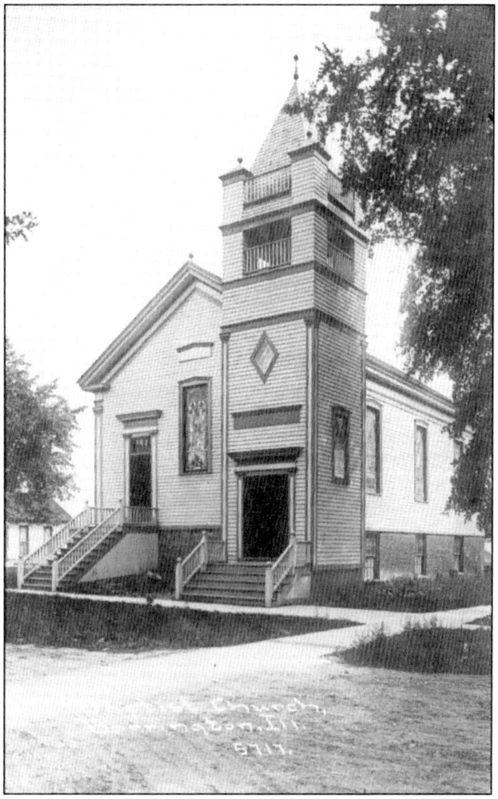

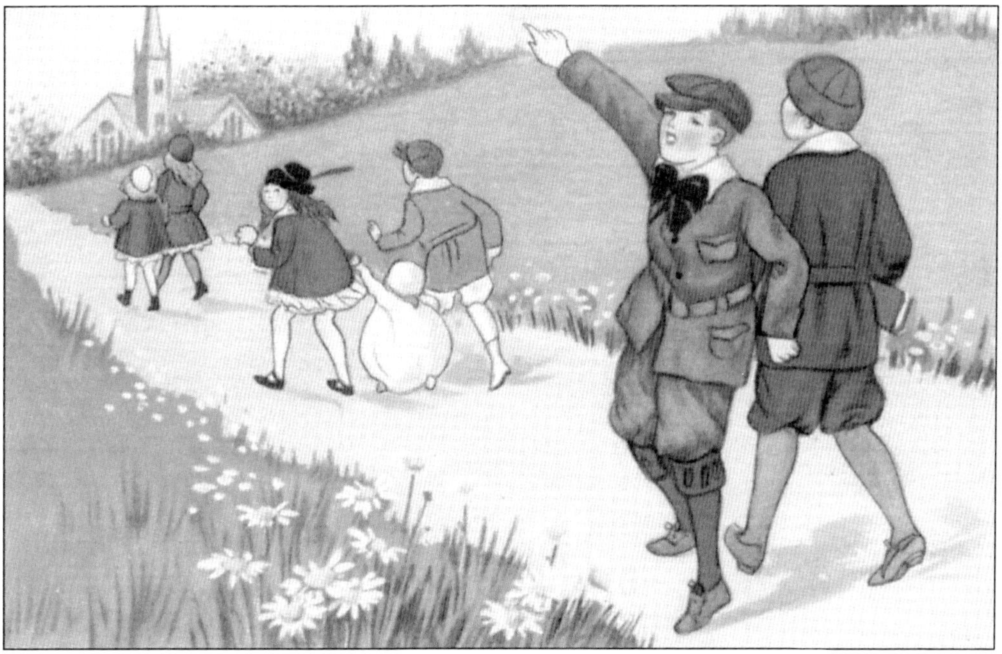

Once a year, Sunday school teachers mailed a postcard to every child within each church family to encourage attendance at a special service called Rally Day, an event meant to strengthen family bonds and boost the importance of the church within the community.

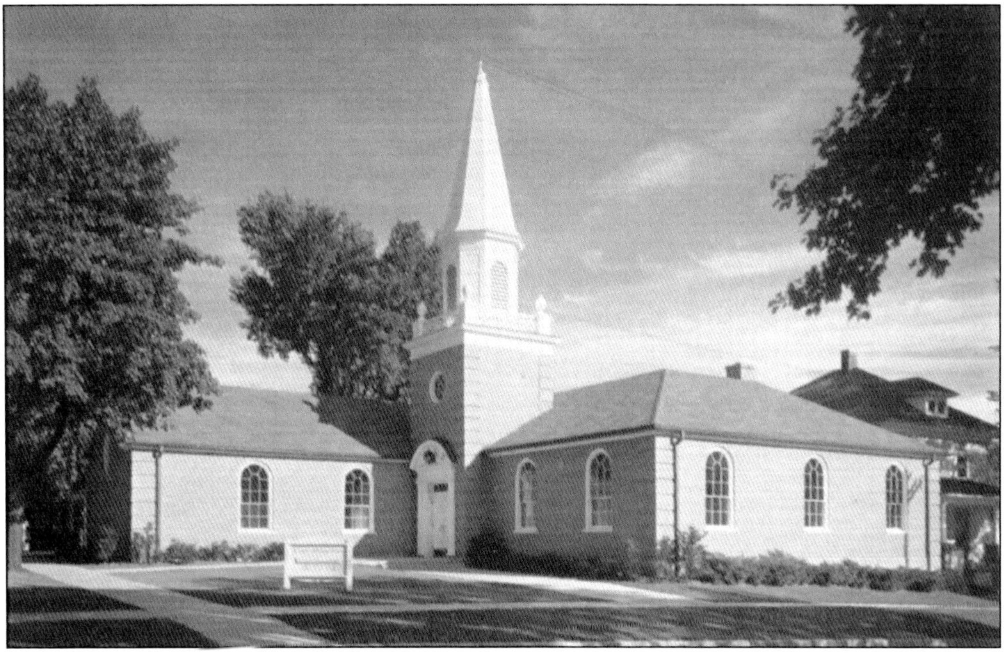

The new Baptist church, dedicated on November 26, 1950, was built by George Etters and Sons for $75,000 and was located on the corner of Lincoln and Grove Avenues. The new building offered more space for Sunday school classes and a larger sanctuary.

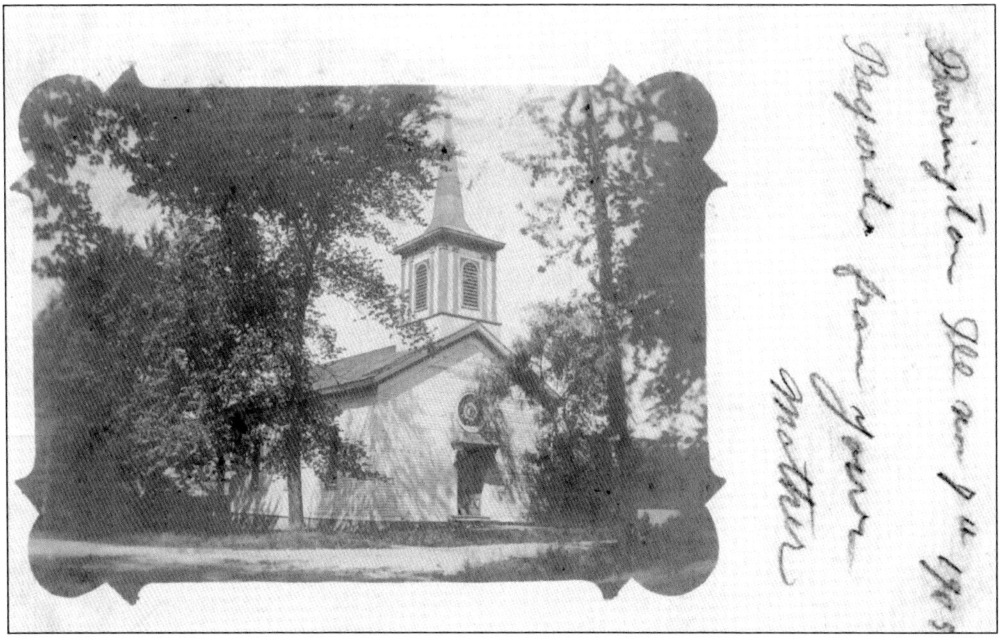

This 1905 image depicts St. Anne Catholic Church, located at Ela and Franklin Streets. The church was organized as a mission around 1871.

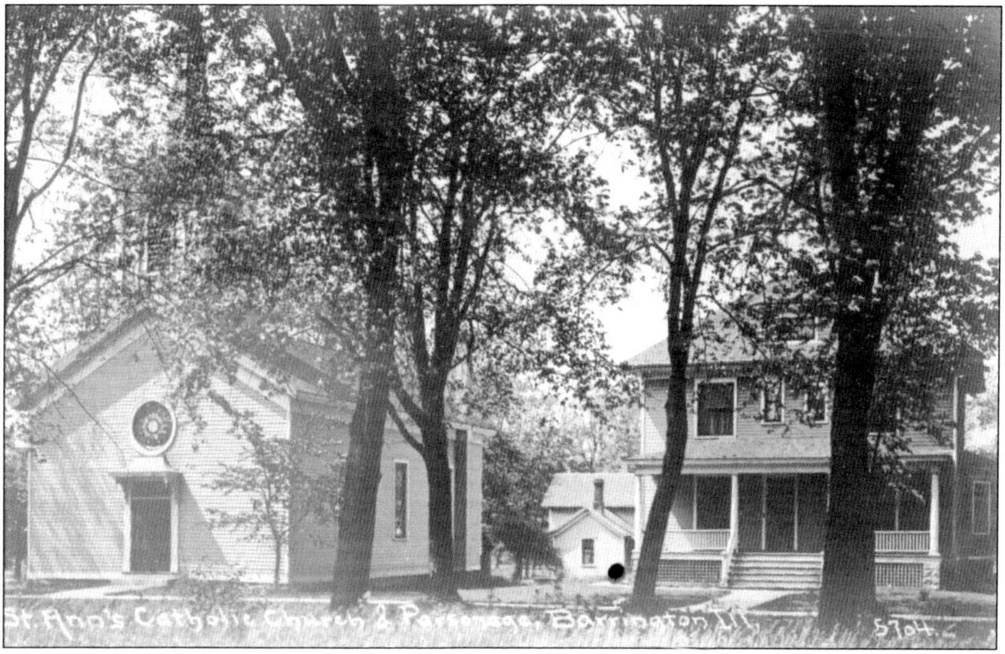

In 1906, Fred E. Lines and A. Gleason began building a rectory on Franklin Street, east of the church. It was first occupied by Father Fox. This image is attributed to C.R. Childs.

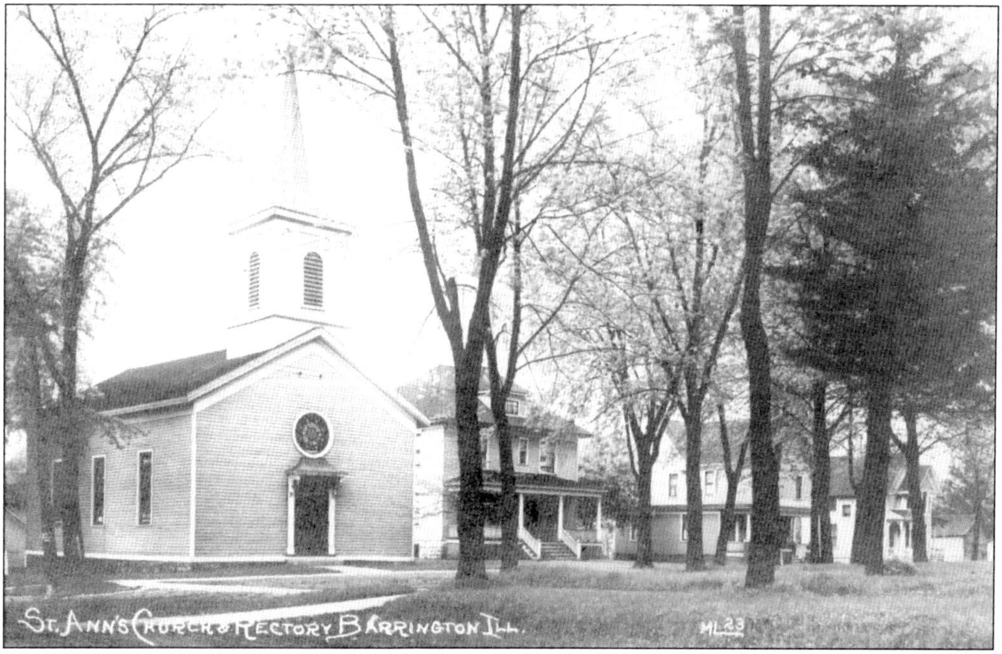

A 1912 streetscape view of St. Anne Catholic Church and rectory shows the beautiful tree-shaded grounds. This image is attributed to M.L. Photo Co.

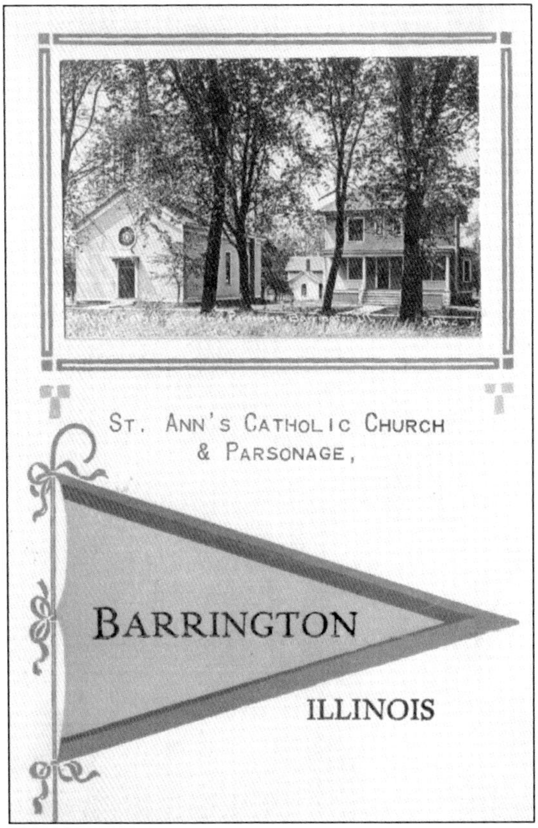

A smaller image of the St. Anne property was printed and attached to a souvenir postcard in 1916 by C.R. Childs.

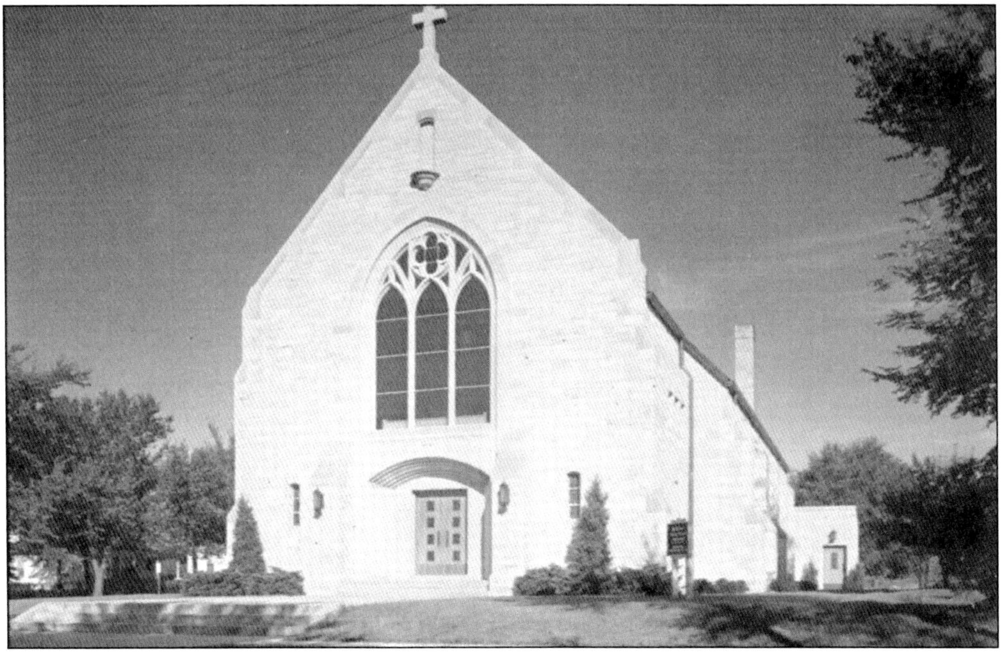

The parish of St. Anne continued to grow in the 1930s and 1940s. A larger church building was constructed in 1950–1951 and dedicated in June 1951.

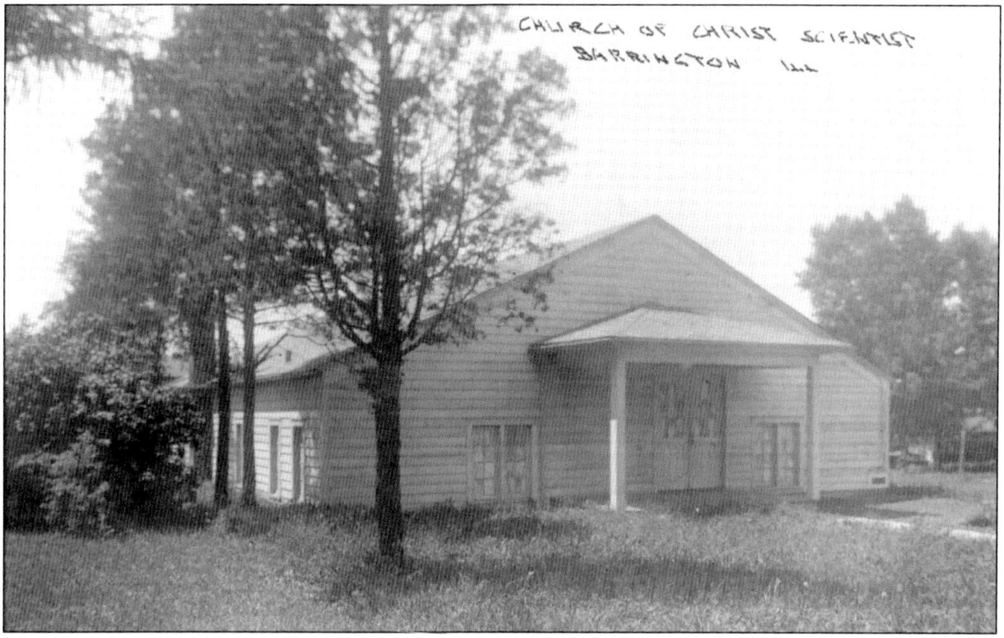

The First Church of Christ Scientist in Barrington started in 1910 and was organized in 1915. Early records show that the group first met in Stott's Hall.

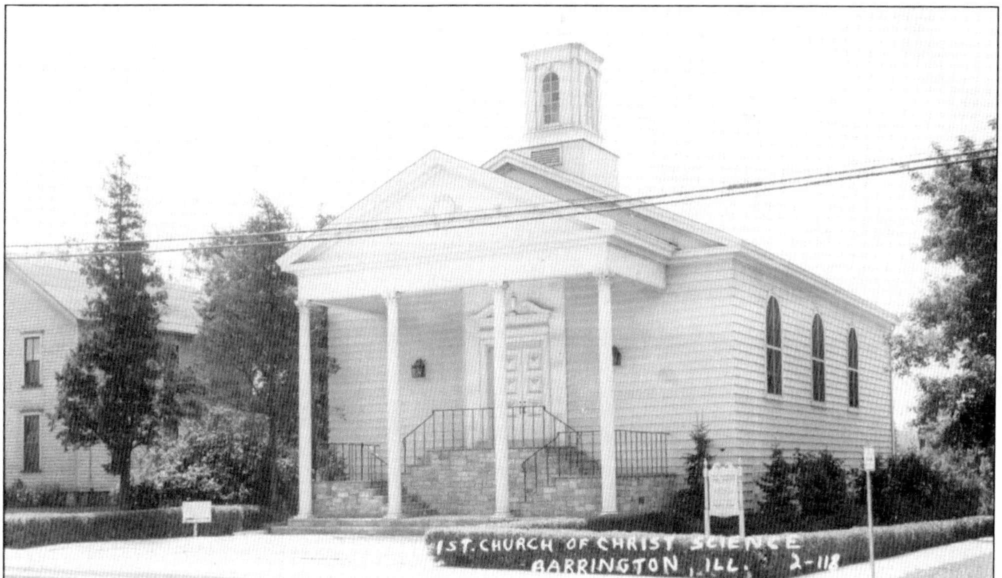

This image of the First Church of Christ Scientist building, located on East Main Street within the downtown business district of Barrington, was available as a real-photo postcard in local stores in 1953.

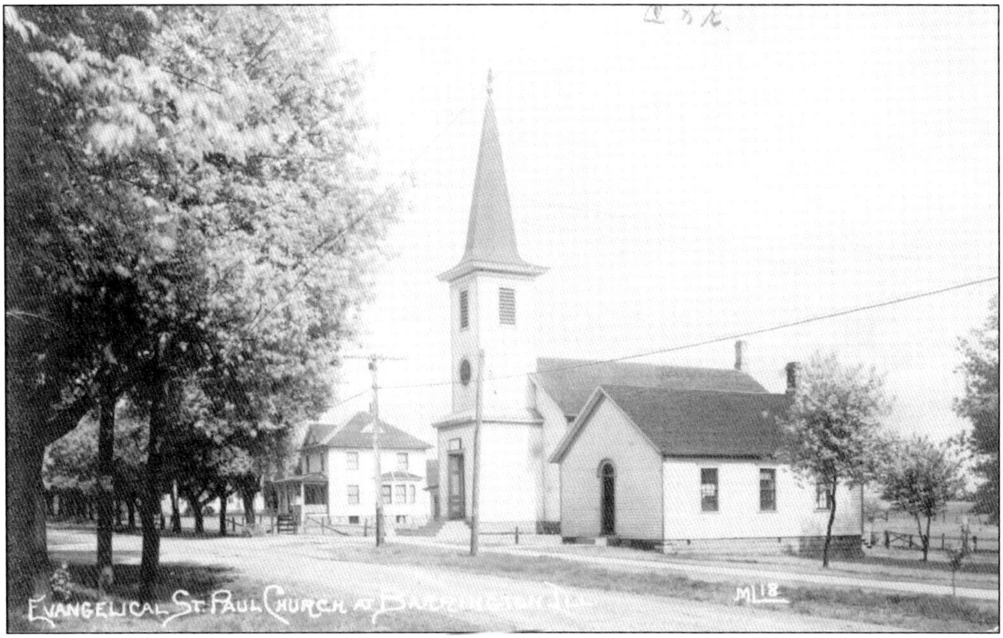

St. Paul United Church of Christ, located on East Main Street, was organized in 1863 with 20 members; the first official congregation meeting took place in 1864. In 1866, the resident pastor left Barrington, and the church was closed until a new pastor arrived in 1868.

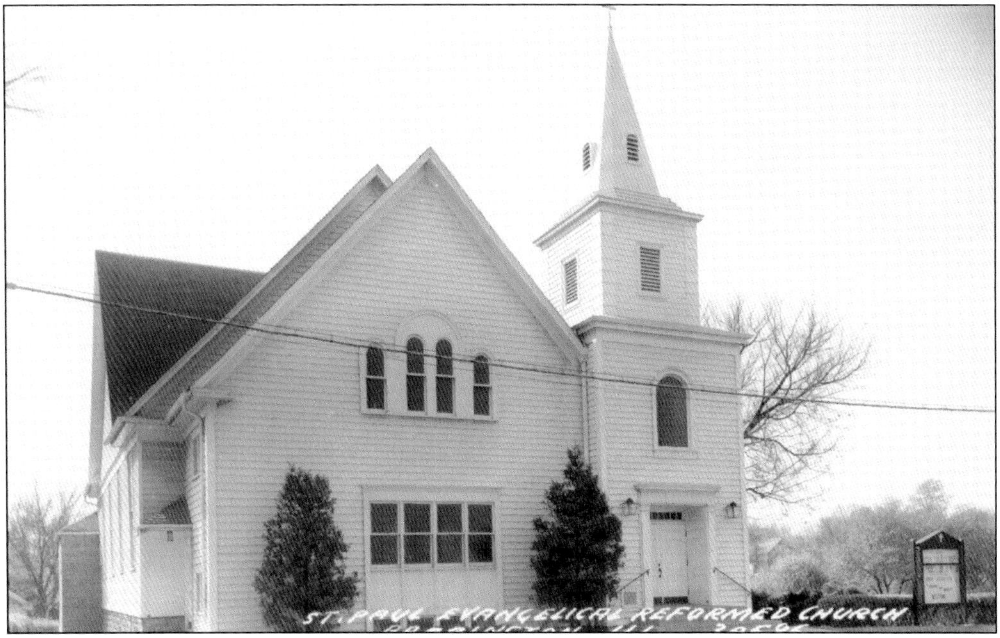

This photograph shows St. Paul Church on East Main Street. A brick addition to the southwest of the church was dedicated and opened in 1956.

The Zion Church was originally built on Ela Road in 1854. As the railroad moved the depot to Barrington Station (as it was called at that time), the group moved to downtown Barrington and built a village Evangelical church in 1866.

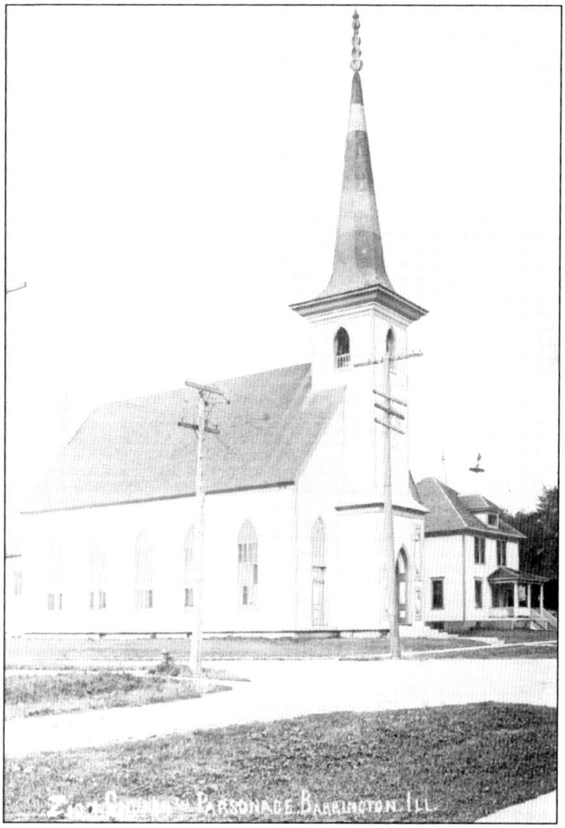

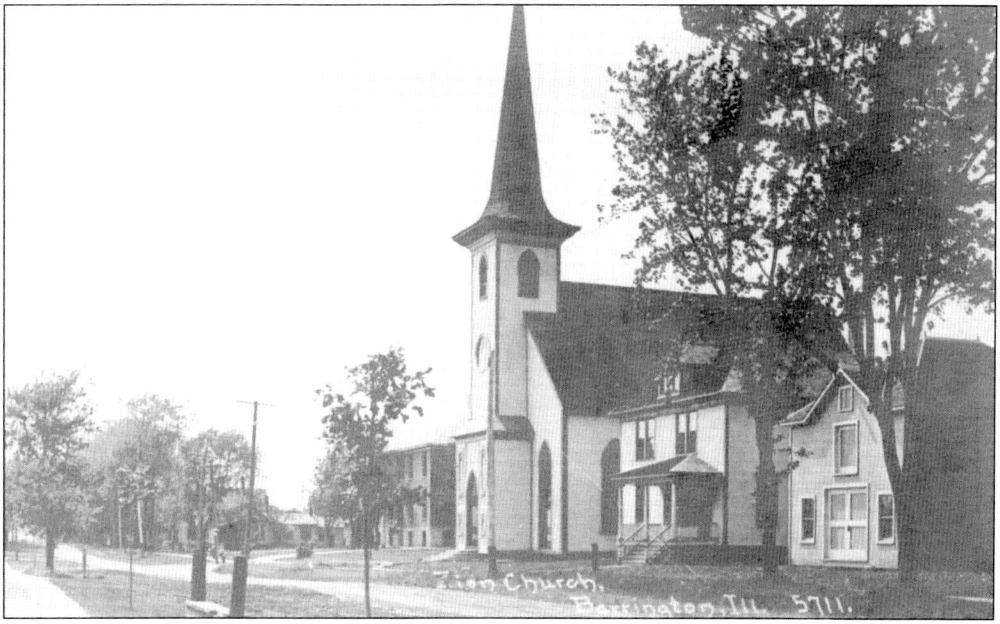

This streetscape view of the Zion Church offers a clue as to its location within the community, as the Hough Street School building's south wing is visible. This image is attributed to C.R. Childs.

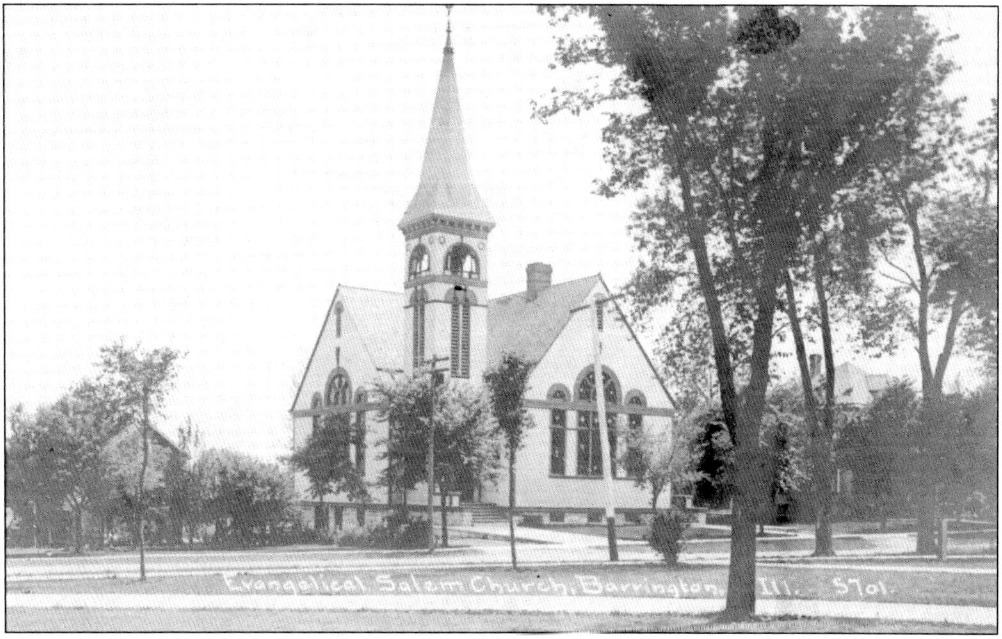

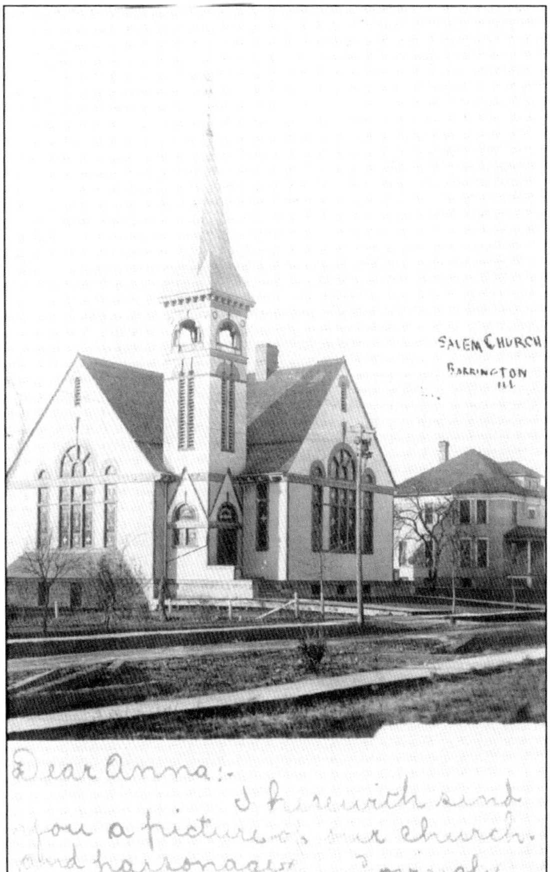

The Salem Evangelical Society was established under Bishop Dubs. The group's June 1893 charter lists trustees Fred H. Frye, Fred A. Lageschulte, Henry J. Lageschulte, John L. Meiners, and Bernhard H. Landwer as the founding members. The congregation's church was built in 1893 and services were held in German until World War I. This image is attributed to C.R. Childs.

This image of Salem Church, with the new parsonage built in 1899, clearly displays the architectural details of the buildings. On the reverse side, the sender of this postcard noted: "I heard the town hall burned down. Tell us all about it."

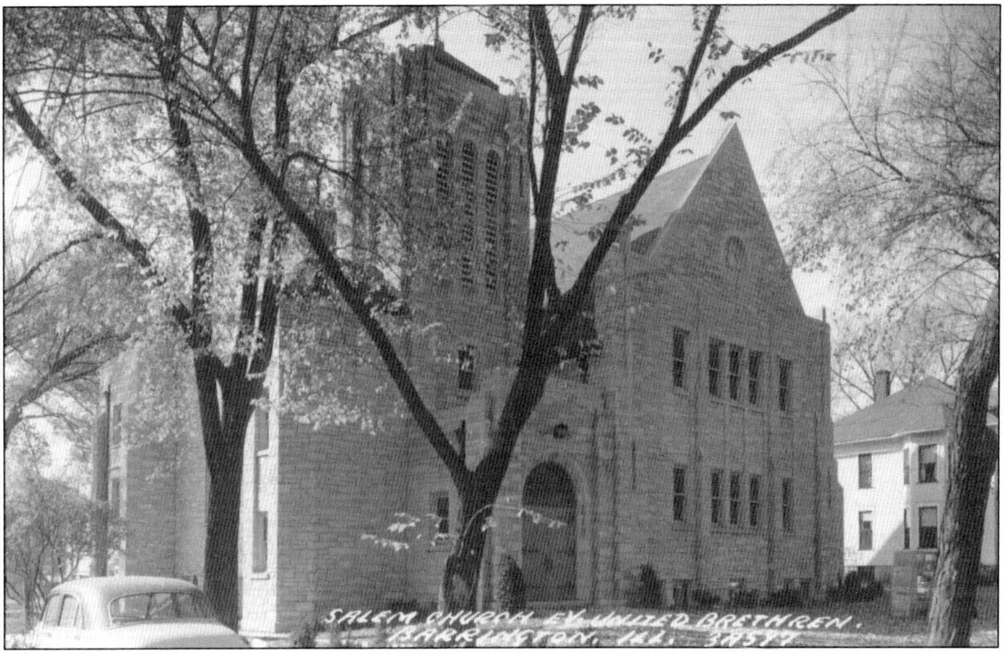

The Salem United Methodist Church is shown on this postcard mailed in 1956. The church is still located at 115 West Lincoln Avenue, across the street from Hough Street School.

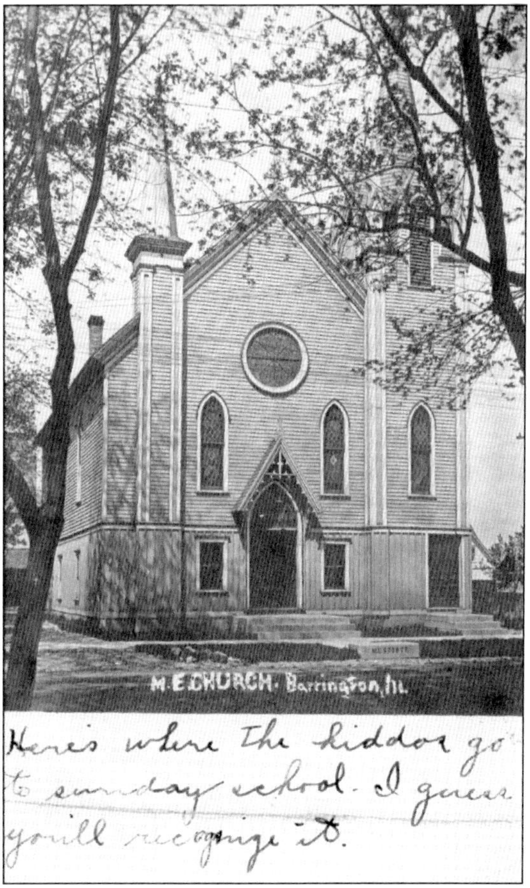

In 1872, the Methodists constructed a new worship center on South Cook Street at a cost of $4,000. The congregation, consisting of members from Methodists who had previously formed a Bible class at Olcutt White's home, joined with some members of the Barrington Center Methodist Church to become the congregation of the M.E. Church.

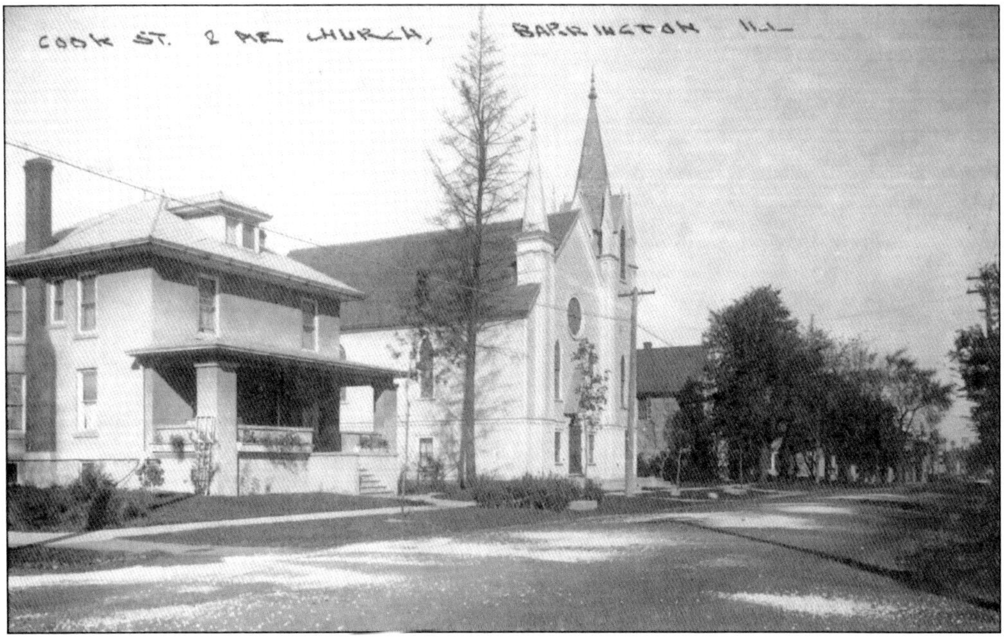

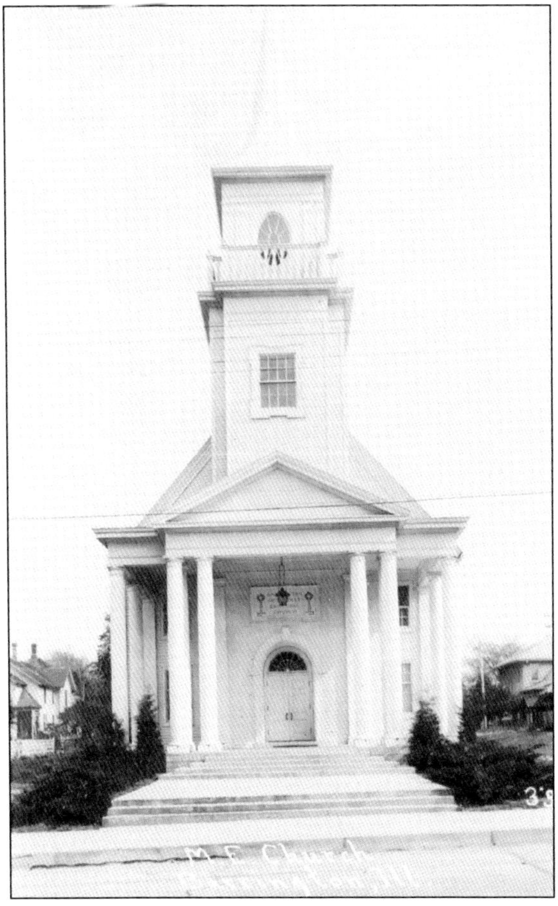

A 1926 real-photo postcard shows the M.E. Church on Cook Street. Barrington had numerous tree-lined streets throughout the downtown area. This building was sold to the Lounsbury Masonic Lodge in 1931.

As the Methodist congregation continued to grow, it needed a larger building. A campaign was initiated to raise money for a new building, only to be brought to a halt by the Depression. Nevertheless, members of the congregation were determined to acquire a larger structure. The former Zion Church building was vacant and for sale; the structure was purchased for $700 and remodeled into a new Methodist church by architect Robert Work.

This postcard offers a different perspective of the new Methodist church, redesigned by Robert Work in the Colonial style. The church was dedicated in 1931.

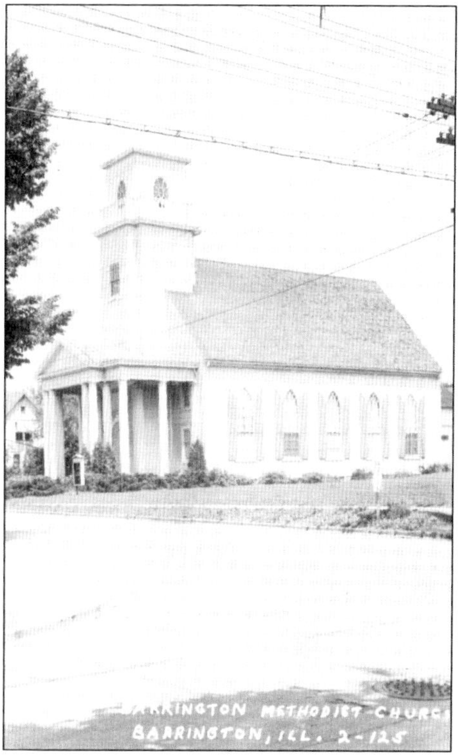

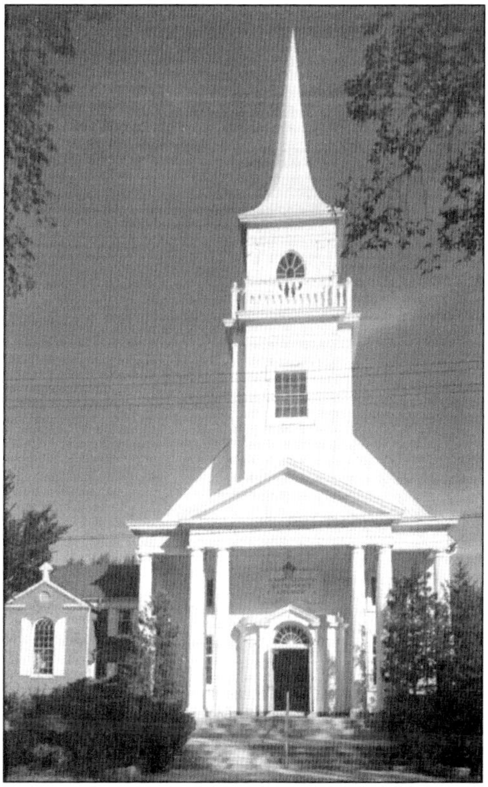

A new brick addition to the north of the church was dedicated in 1953. The Methodist church faced west and was located across from the Hough Street School building.

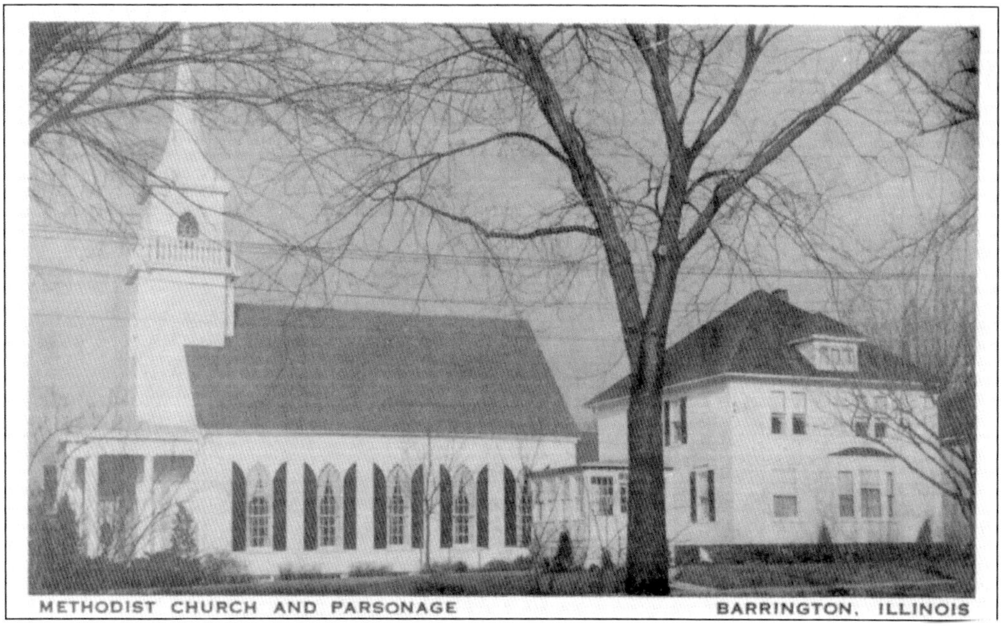

This postcard offers a view looking north from Lincoln Avenue toward the Methodist church and parsonage. The parsonage was later removed to make way for the church's expansion. In 1959, more than $200,000 was pledged to build an addition on the south side for the church's activities.

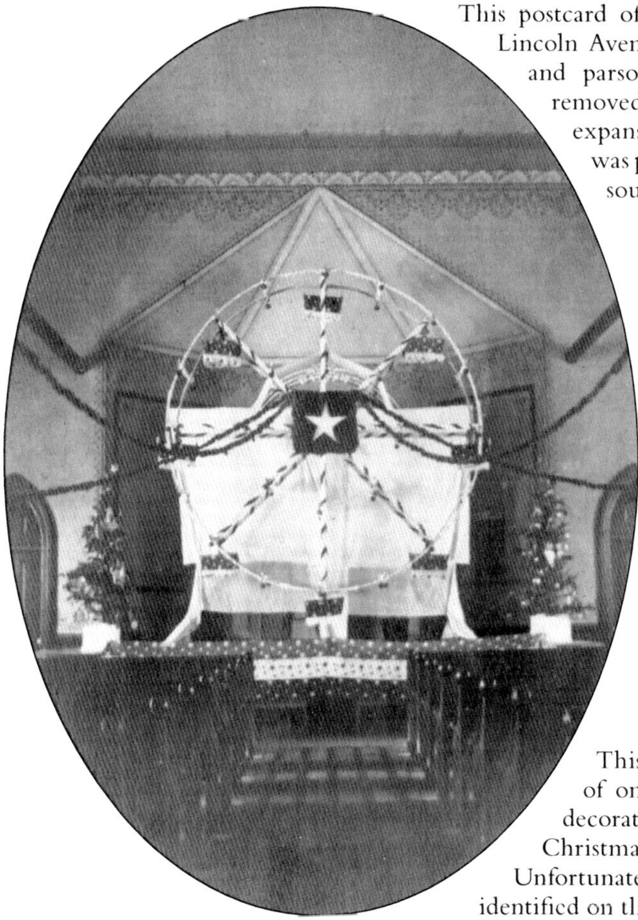

This 1908 image shows the interior of one of Barrington's early churches decorated at Christmastime, with two Christmas trees at the front of the sanctuary. Unfortunately, the church location was not identified on the photograph.

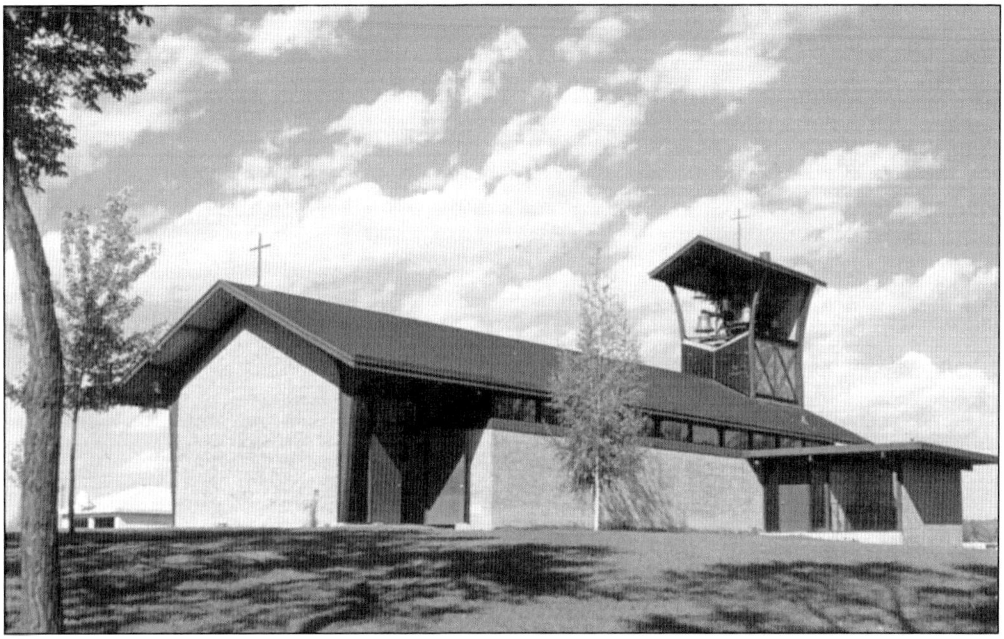

This 1950s color postcard depicts St. Michael's Episcopal Church at the corner of Hillside and Dundee Avenues. St. Michael's was organized in 1948 and originally met in the Masonic Hall on Cook Street. In 1949, property was purchased at Hillside and Dundee Avenues for the new church building.

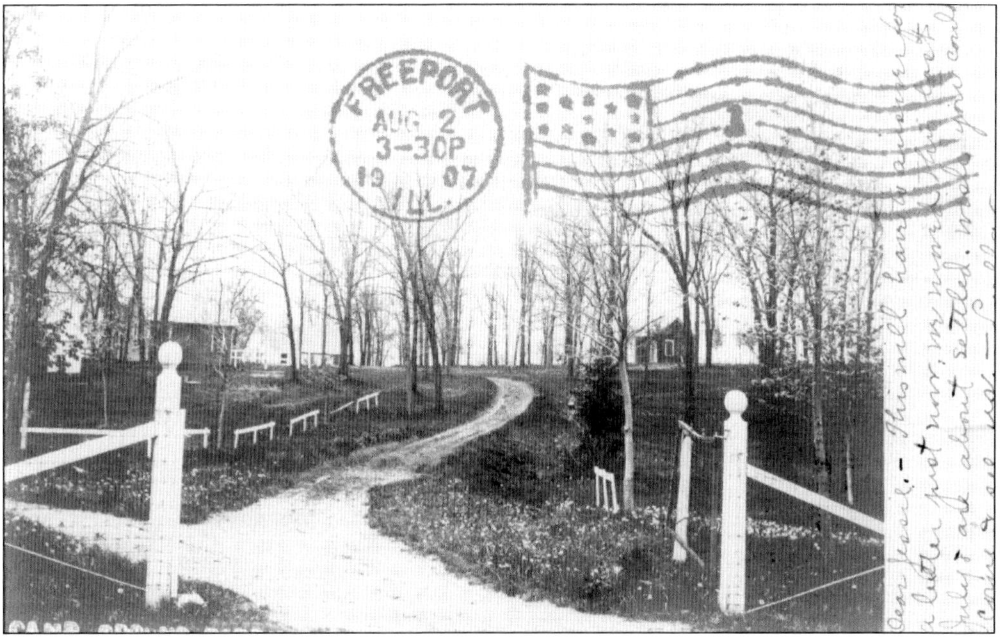

The Evangelical Society established a summer camp meeting association. In early years, they met in the wooded area behind the Louis Elfrink farm on Ela Road. In 1874, after 25 years, it was decided that the camp meeting would move to B.H. Landwer's woods on East Hillside Avenue. This very early view of the entrance to the campground meeting area was captured for a postcard in 1907, probably by photographer George Froelich Jr.

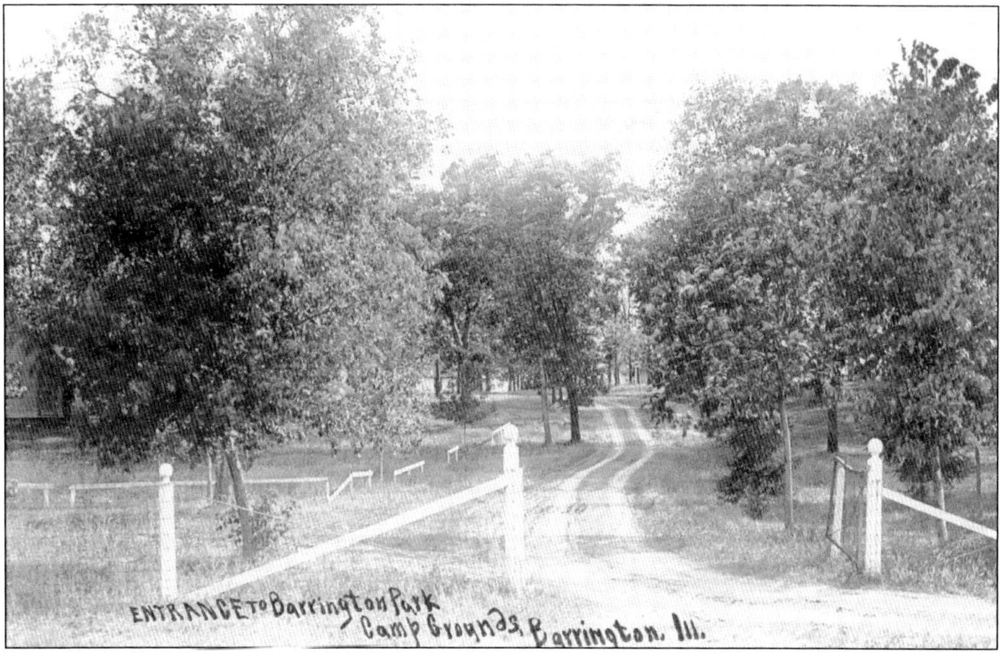

This 1908 postcard, with a photograph by George Froelich Jr., shows the entrance to the campgrounds and offers insight into the welcoming nature of B.H. Landwer's woods.

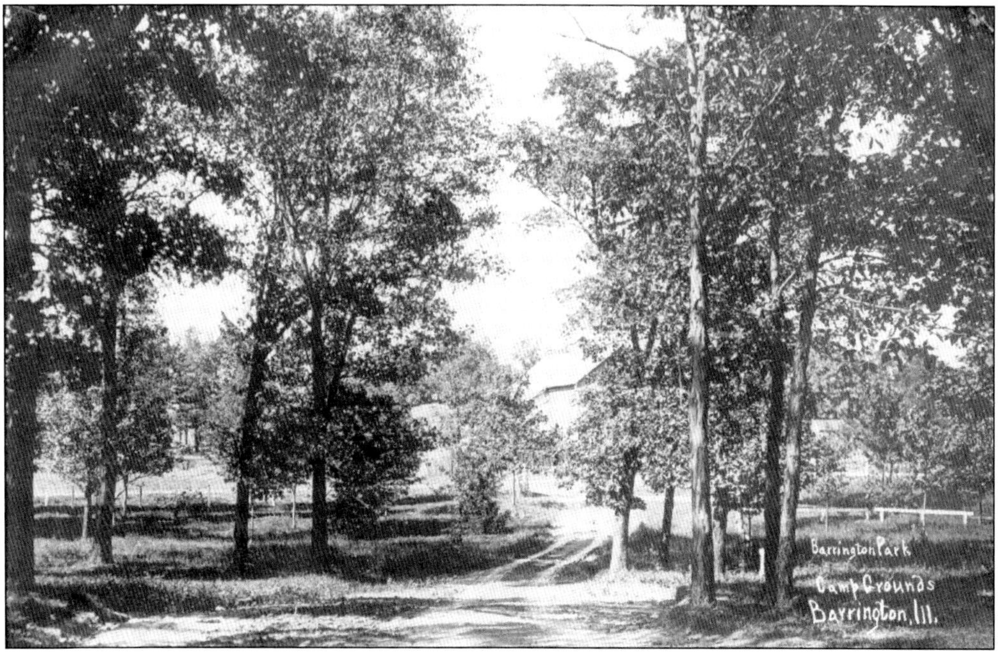

In 1898, the Camp Grounds Association was formally organized and eight acres were purchased. The association had plans to acquire more acreage in later years. The wooded acreage offered an inviting retreat from its members' busy lives, as shown in this 1908 postcard.

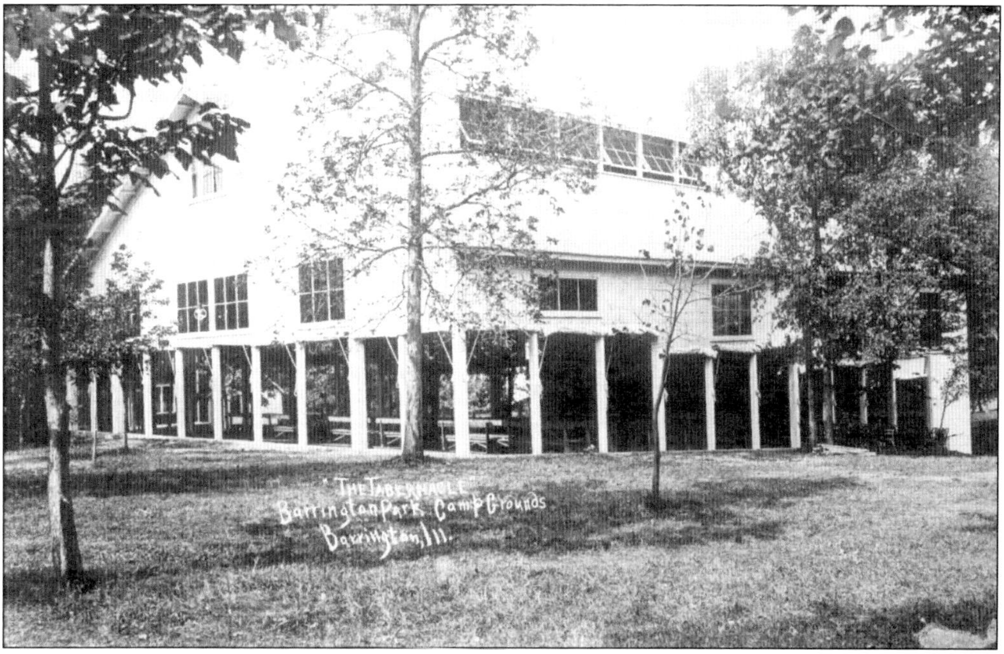

Services at the campgrounds were originally held in the open air or a tent. In the early months of 1908, a large tabernacle building was constructed to protect the members from inclement weather, at a cost of $2,800. It was officially dedicated in late summer 1908. This image is attributed to George Froelich Jr.

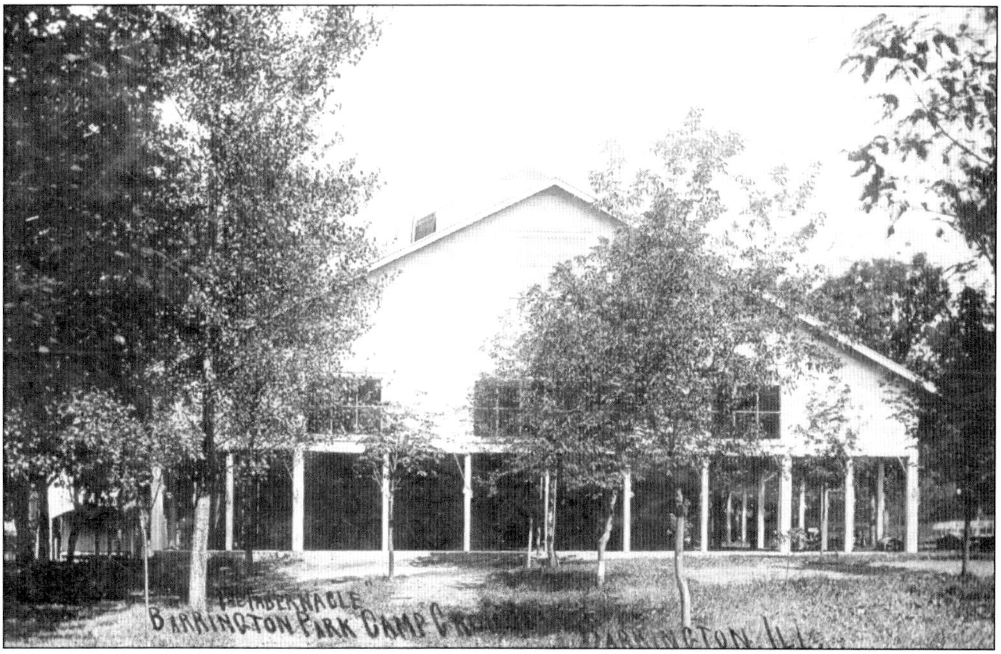

The tabernacle at the Barrington Campgrounds is shown in this different perspective of the building. Laura Naeher sent this postcard to Stella Wolthausen in Duluth, Minnesota, in 1908 with the following message: "This is a picture of our tabernacle. Isn't it nice? School has started. I like my teacher. Please send me a card. Laura Naeher."

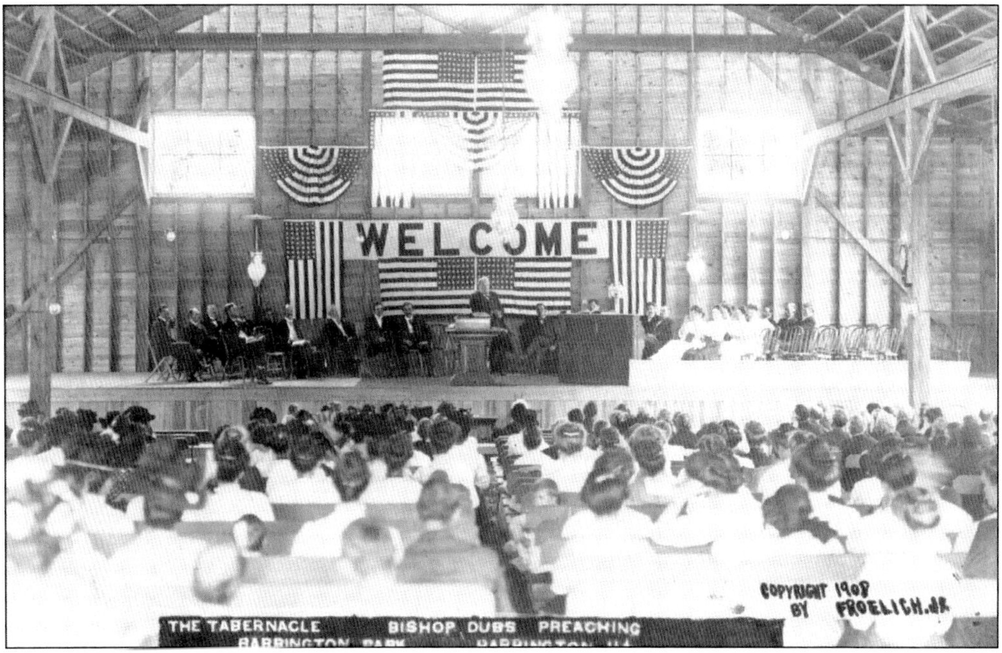

Bishop Dubs preaches before the association members in this 1908 interior view of the tabernacle photographed by George Froelich Jr. The revival meetings were well attended and offered an opportunity for local residents and friends to socialize after the tabernacle events, although the building does not appear to have any kind of cooling system.

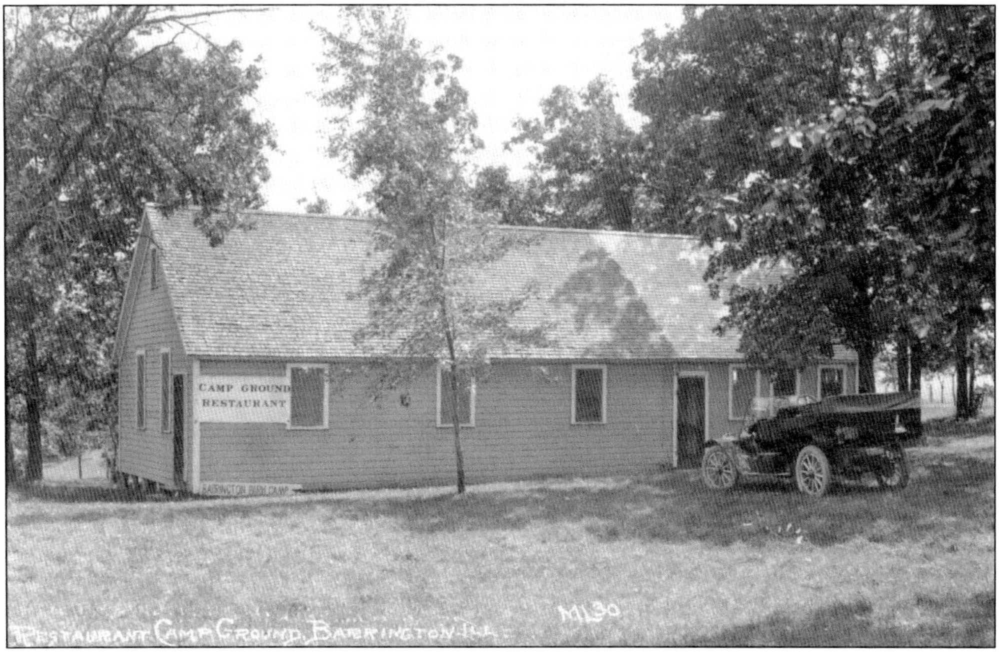

Along with being able to reside on the campgrounds during the revivals, local association members also had access to a restaurant for daily meals. This 1922 postcard is attributed to C.R. Childs.

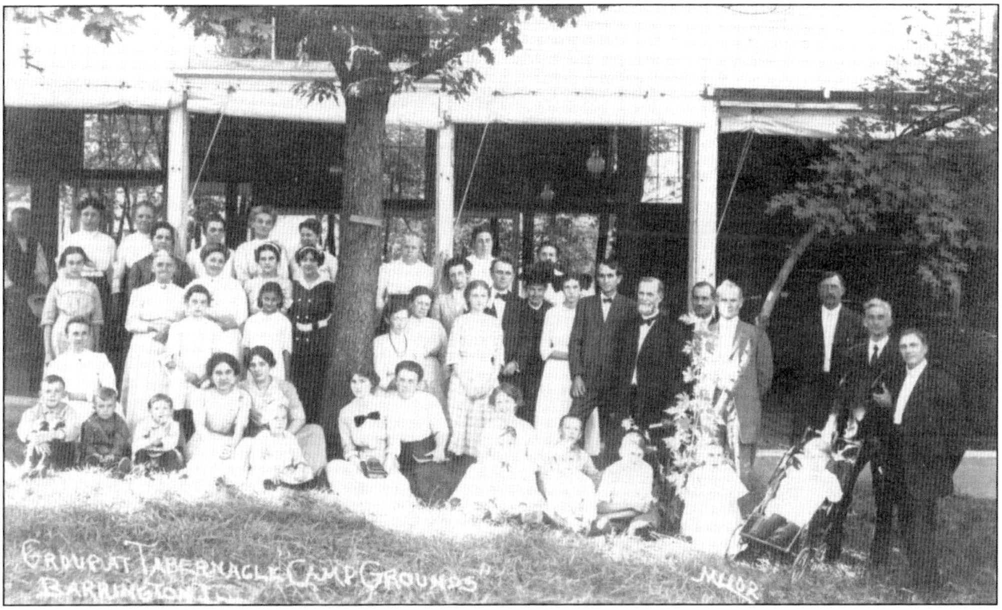

Campground association members take time from their camp meeting activities to pose for a photograph outside of the tabernacle building. The ladies wore white dresses to stay cool during the warm summer days. Unfortunately, the men had to wear suits and ties throughout the duration of the revival meetings. M.L. Photo Company produced this image for sale as a memento.

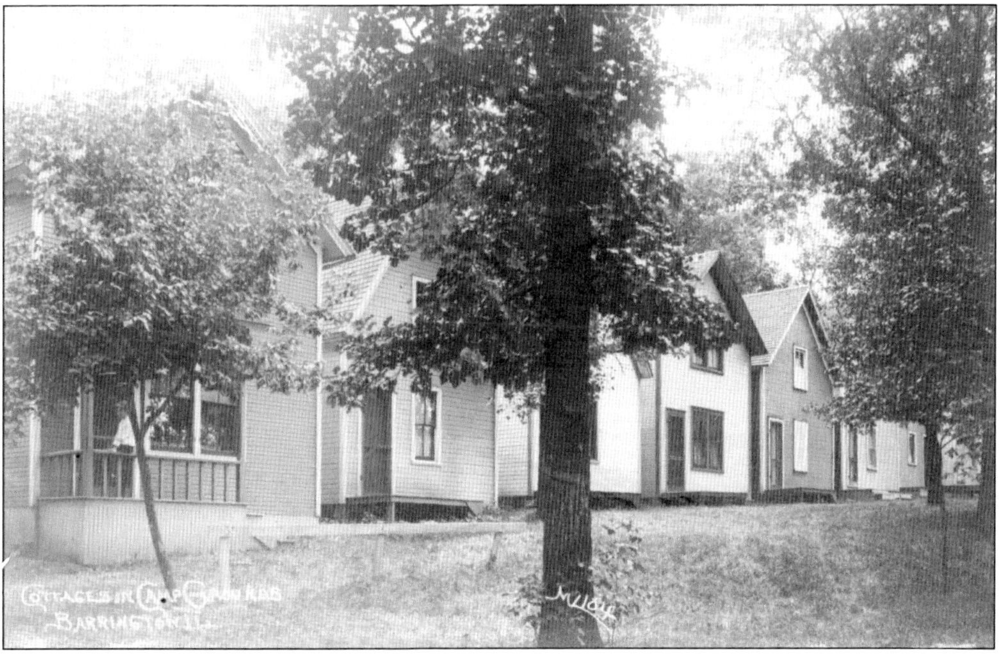

M.L. Photo Company photographed this section of small cottages used as living quarters during events at the campgrounds on Hillside Avenue. This June 1913 photograph shows how shaded the grounds were, offering some respite from the summer heat.

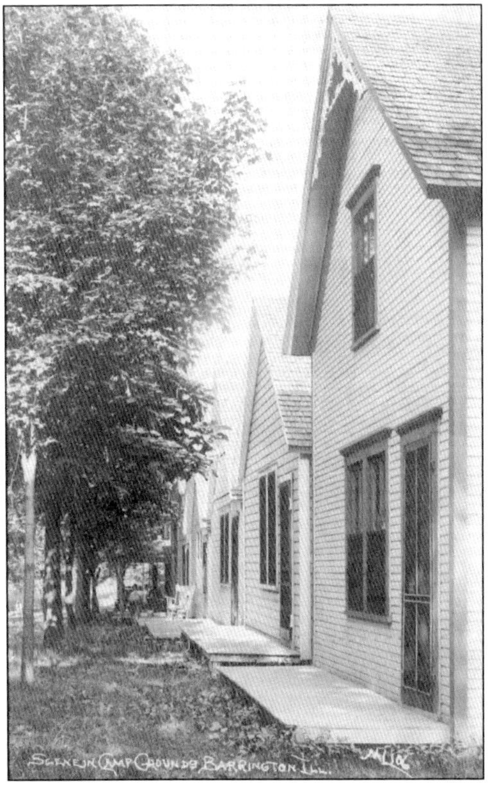

Many of the small cottages at the campgrounds had a second story for sleeping, with the main floor used for reading and relaxing. There were no concrete sidewalks and the cottages were not insulated. In the distance of this August 1913 image, the photographer caught one of the campground members doing some painting between meetings.

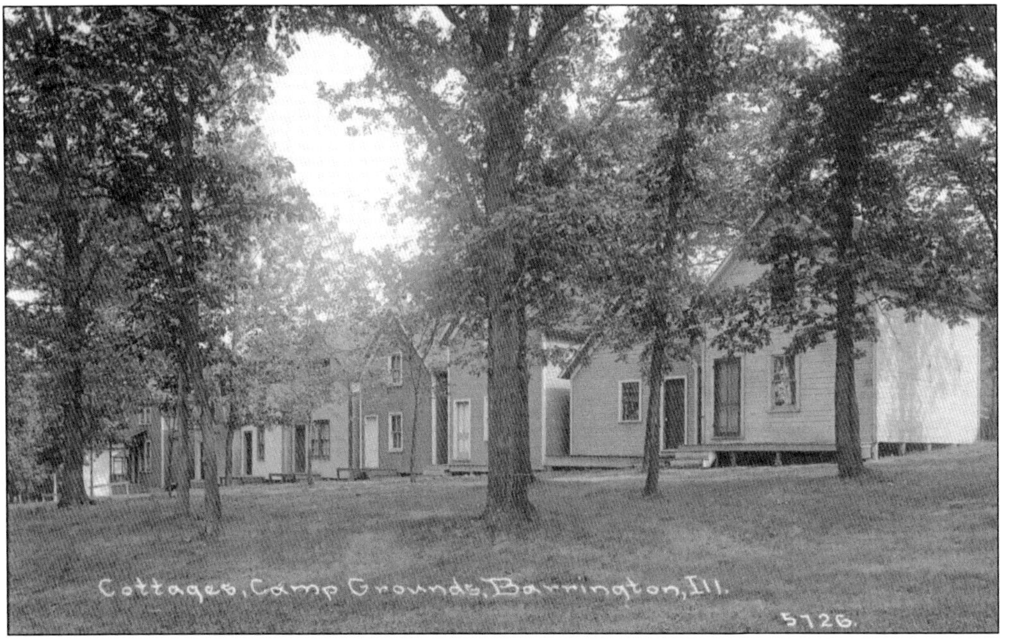

Photographer C.R. Childs offers a closer view of one row of cottages at the Barrington Campgrounds in 1947. Many of the cottages had two front or side steps for access to a wooden porch and the front door. Some of the cottages even had wooden gingerbread trim. The cottages usually required painting on an annual basis.

Four

Residences and Street Scenes

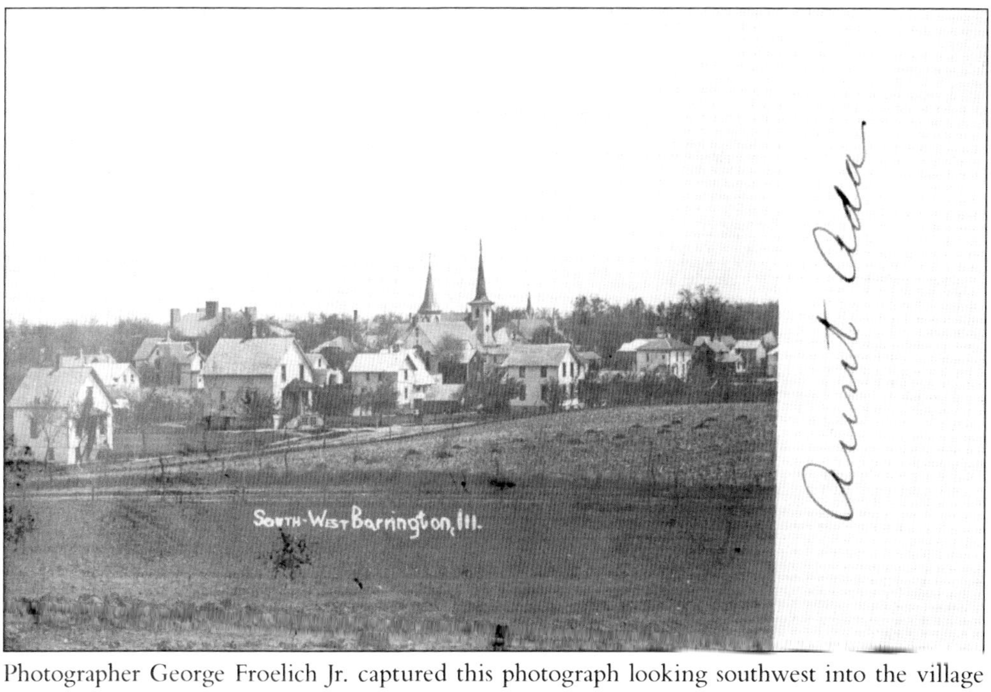

Photographer George Froelich Jr. captured this photograph looking southwest into the village around the beginning of the 20th century. New trees have been planted along the streets, and the roof and prominent chimneys of Hough Street School can be seen in the distance at the left.

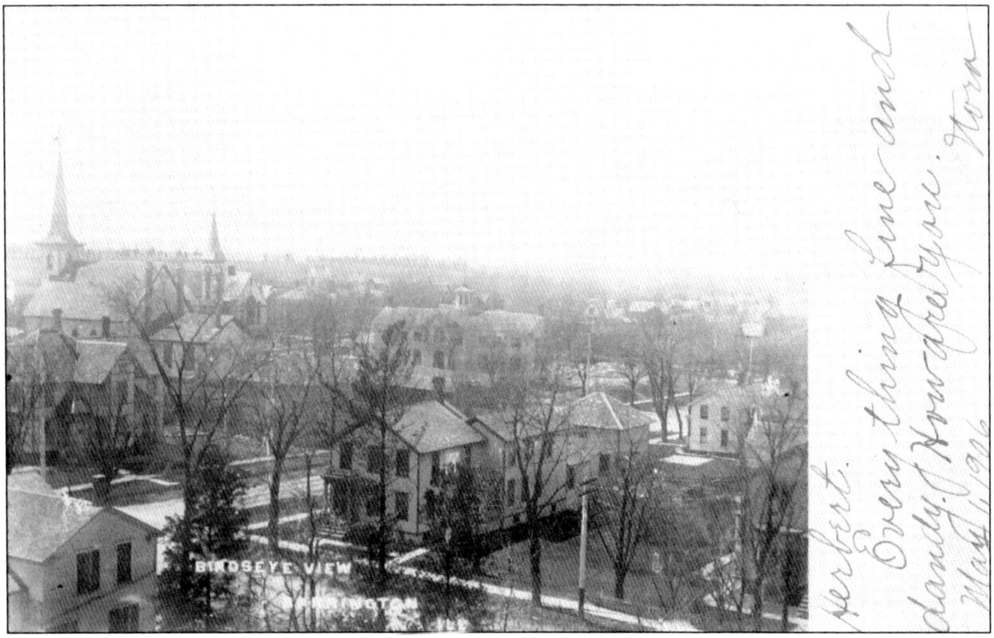

A bird's-eye view of a residential area in Barrington looks across the streetscape toward the old frame schoolhouse on Hough Street. This 1906 photograph was taken by George Froelich Jr. Many of the homes pictured were sizeable and offered a fine quality of living.

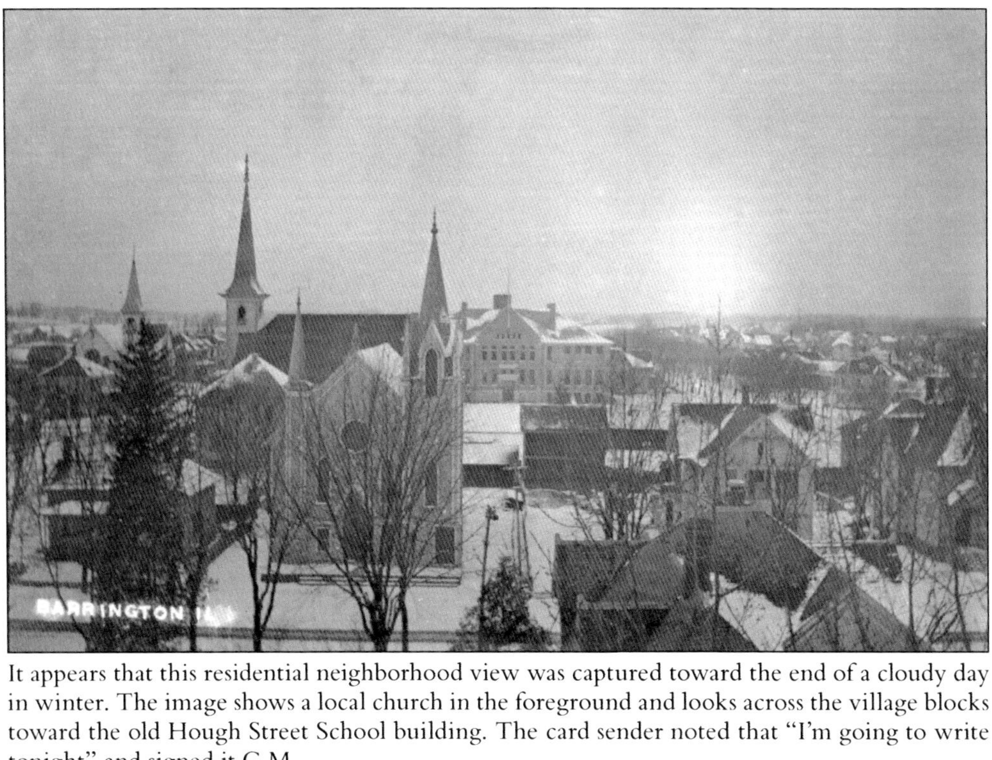

It appears that this residential neighborhood view was captured toward the end of a cloudy day in winter. The image shows a local church in the foreground and looks across the village blocks toward the old Hough Street School building. The card sender noted that "I'm going to write tonight" and signed it C.M.

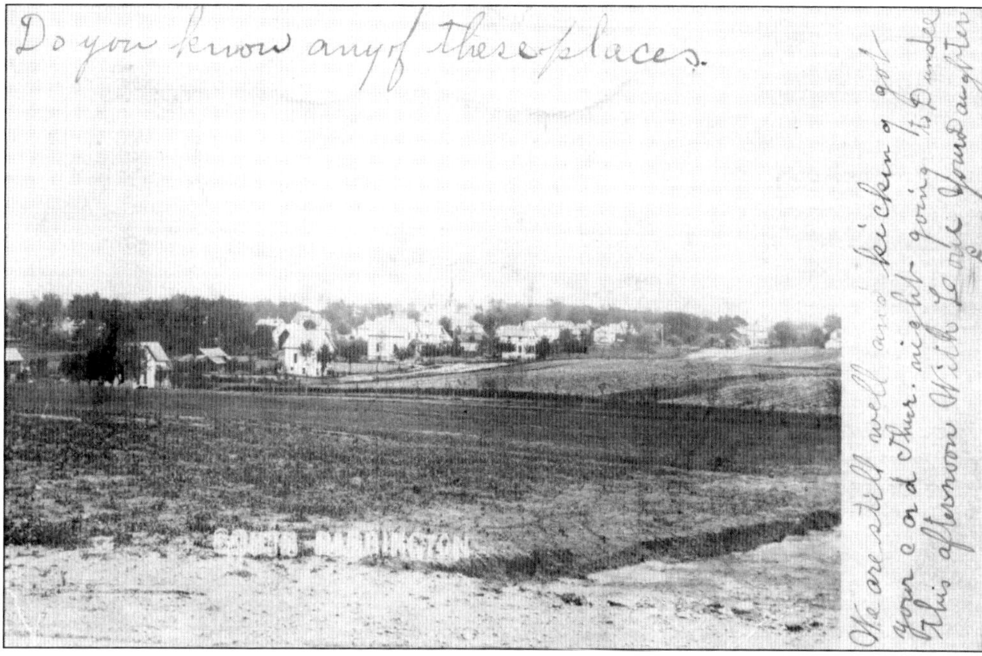

The sender of this card asks, "Do you know any of these places? We are still well and kicking and got your card Thursday night—going to Dundee this afternoon. With Love, Your daughter Emma." This image was taken from the location of the monument in Evergreen Cemetery at Dundee Avenue and Coolidge Avenue. The church steeples in the distance are the Salem and Zion churches.

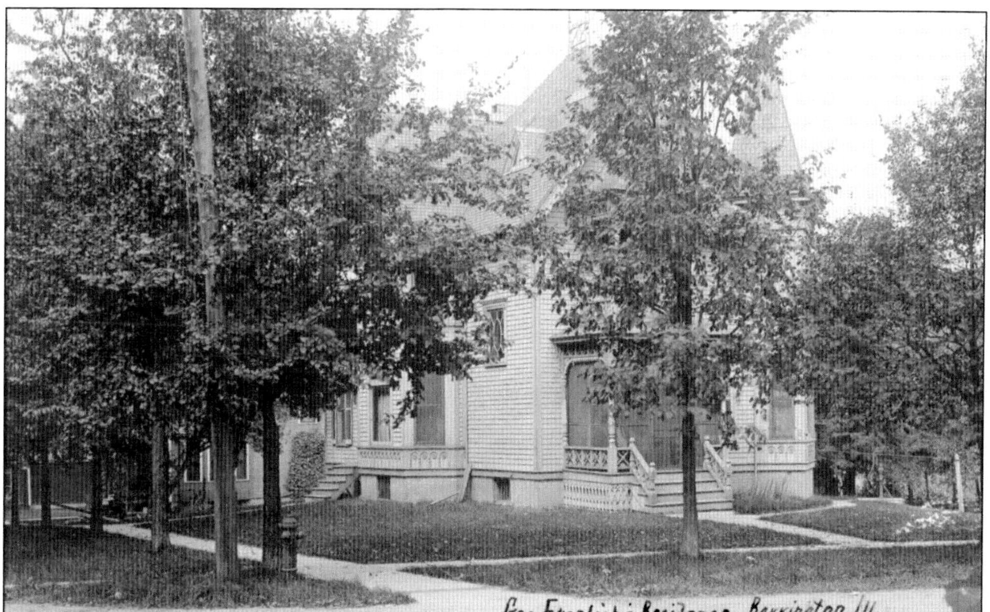

Local photographer George Froelich Jr. captured this image of George Froelich Sr.'s residence at the beginning of the 20th century. Barrington was known for its beautiful tree-lined streets. Note the intricate and elaborate railings on the porches of the home and the water pump to the right of the house.

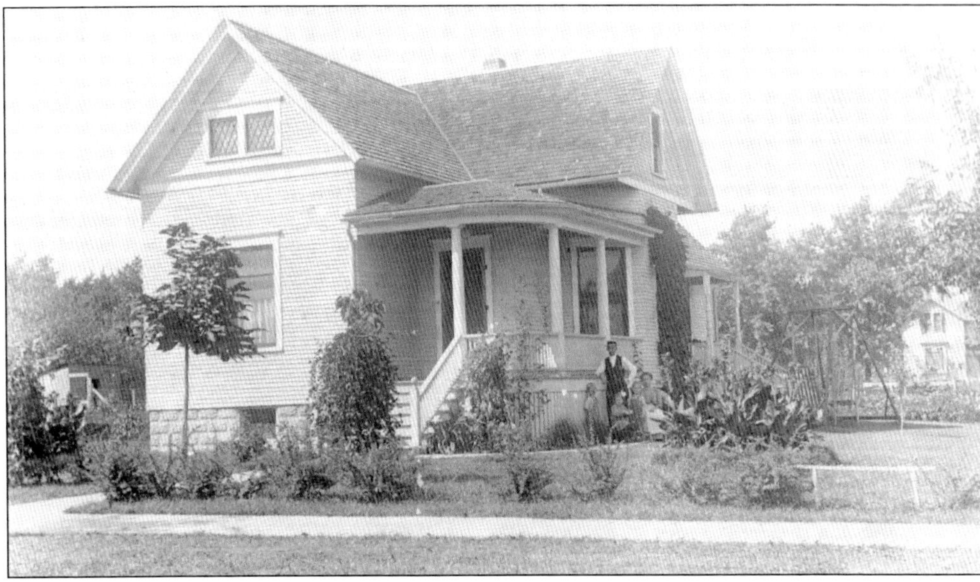

The Herman Ahrens residence, located at 212 West Russell Street, was built in 1908 by John Brasel. In 1923, the home was remodeled and a second-floor apartment was added. The backyard is complete with a swing and a large garden with tomatoes, green beans, and raspberry bushes. The Ahrens are standing with their three children to the right of the porch.

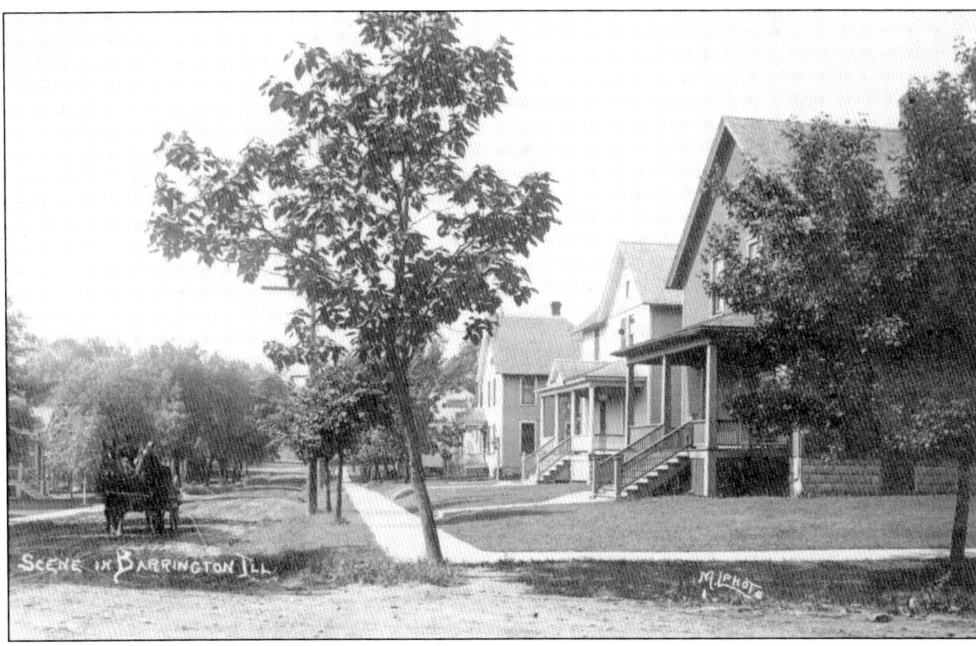

This 1912 image depicts an unidentified street with concrete sidewalks, young trees planted along the roadway, and a dirt road with two horses pulling a wagon.

A June 1912 image of the MacRaes farmhouse shows the property—previously owned by William Klingenberg Sr.—on Oak Knoll Road. A horse is harnessed to the wagon on the dirt road.

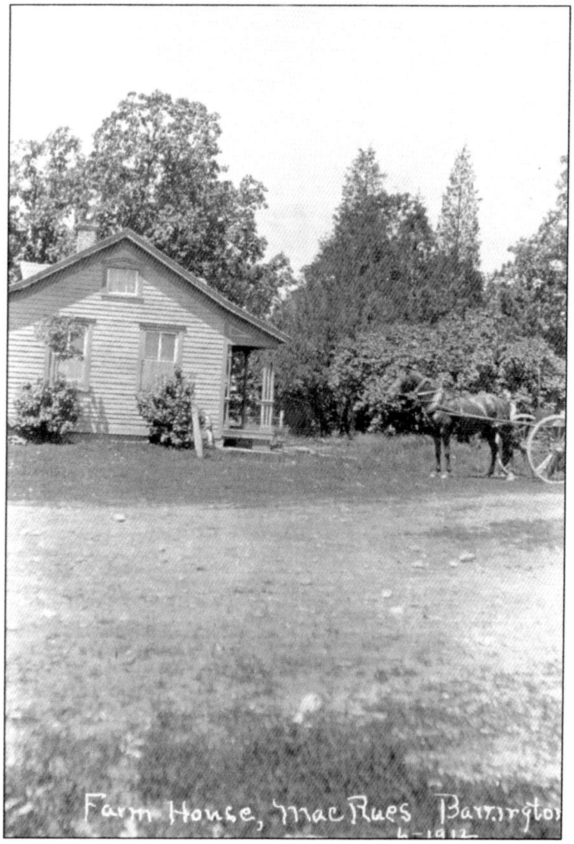

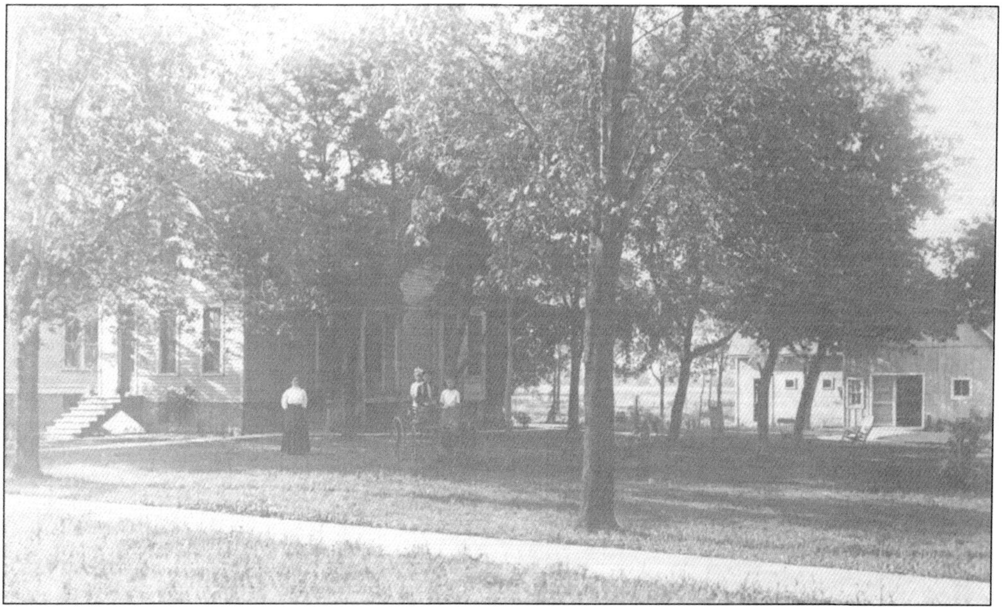

This clear and detailed image depicts an unidentified local residence with family members posing in the yard. The children are proudly seated in the pony cart while their mother poses by the house. Note the rocking chairs under the numerous shade trees.

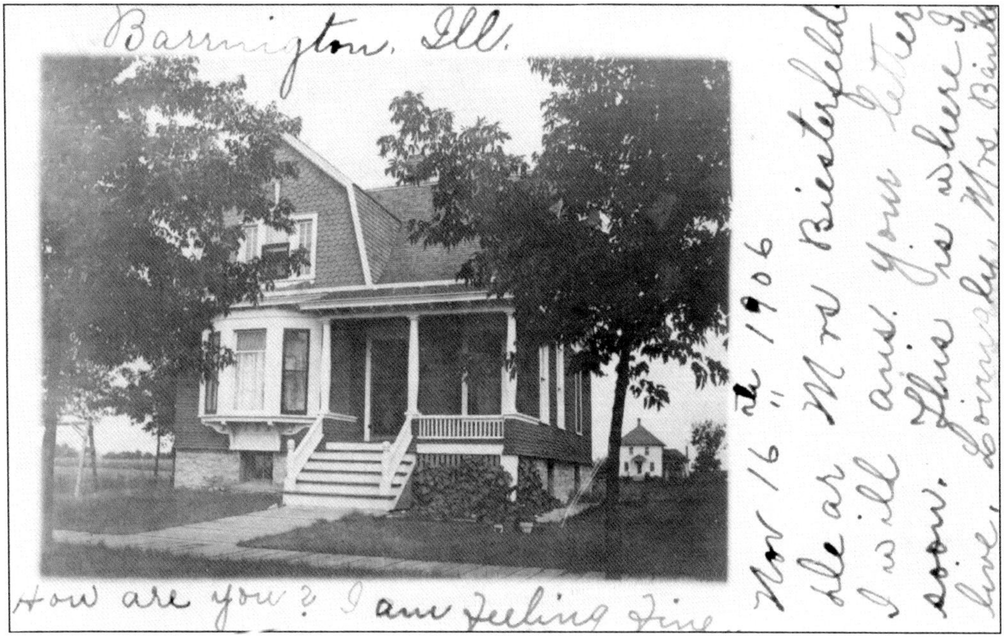

This postcard shows an unidentified residence in the village with minimal plantings and landscaping. The postcard sender writes "Dear Mrs. Bresterfeld, I will answer your letter soon. This is where I live. Lovingly, Mrs. Binils. How are you? I am feeling fine." The card was addressed to Mrs. C. Bresterfeld in Crete, Illinois.

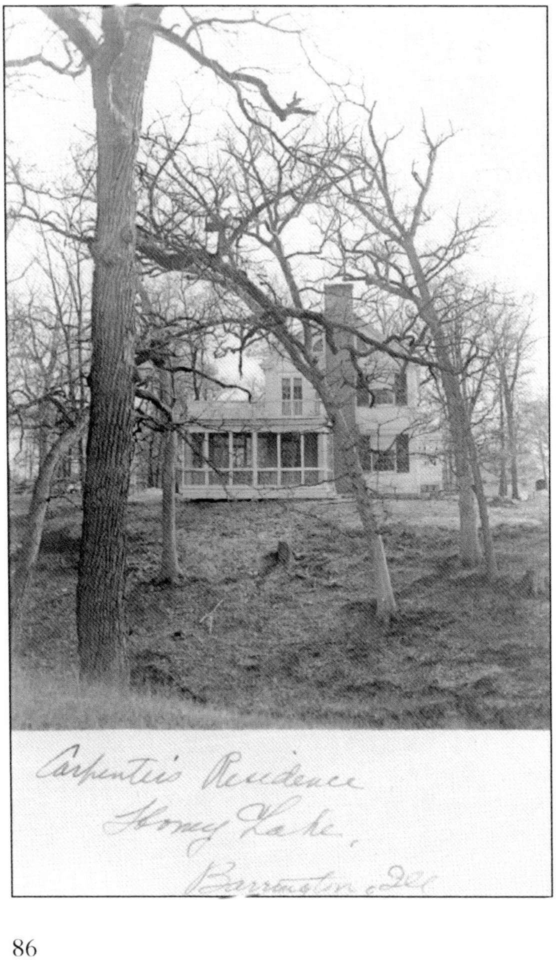

This 1917 postcard depicts a local residence noted as the Carpenter's Residence, Honey Lake. The message on the reverse side of the card, mailed to Pennsylvania, notes that the image was recorded by George Froelich Jr.

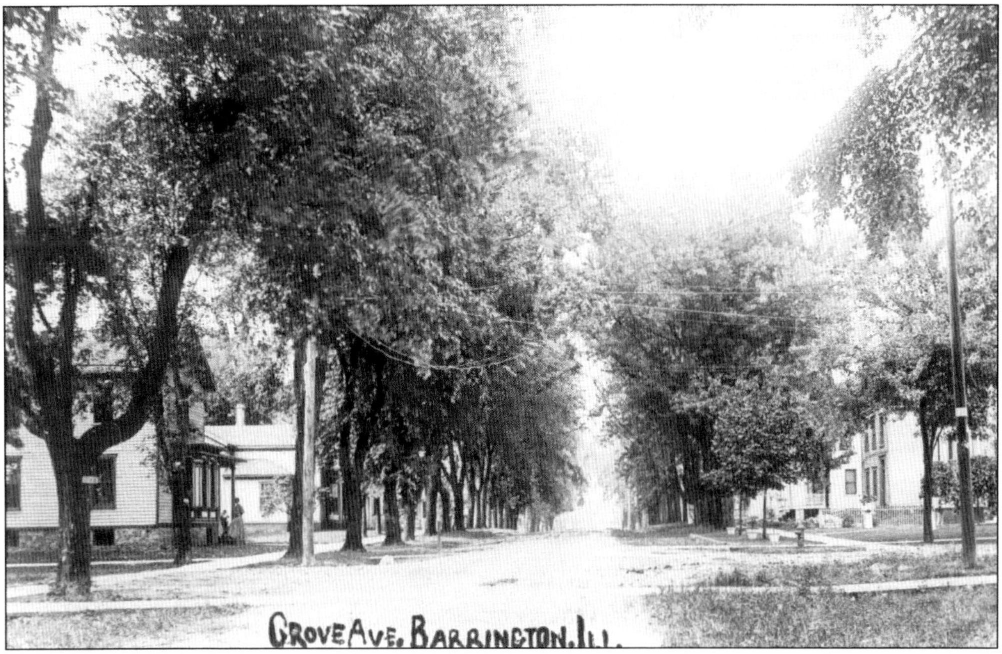

This streetscape perspective of Grove Avenue is a fine example of the beautiful tree-lined streets and quality homes in the Barrington area. The postmark is not clearly shown, but this postcard appears to date from the early 1930s.

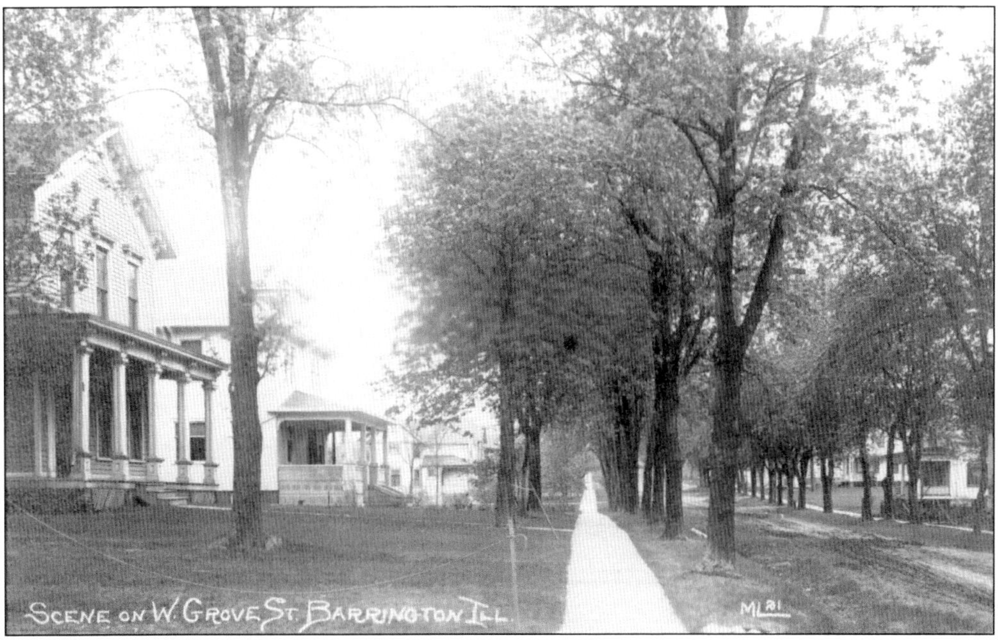

An M.L. Photo Company streetscape view of Grove Avenue captures Victorian-style and turn-of-the-century homes on this shaded street.

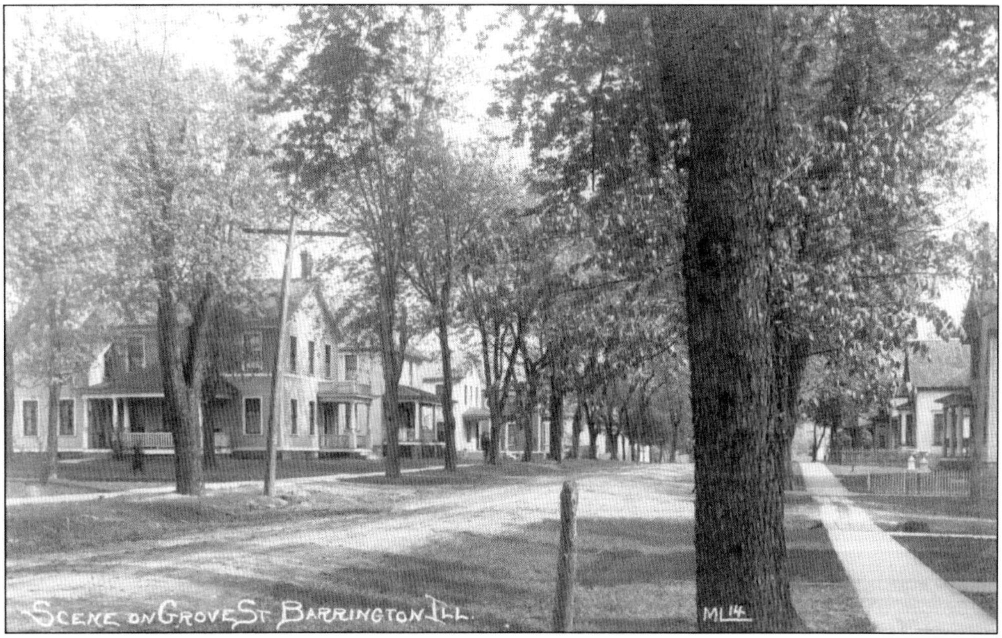

This M.L. photograph offers a wider street perspective of Grove Avenue in 1913. Sidewalks had been laid, but the community still had dirt roads. On the reverse side, the sender of this card wrote, "Dear Helen, I am having a fine time. Some beautiful scenery here."

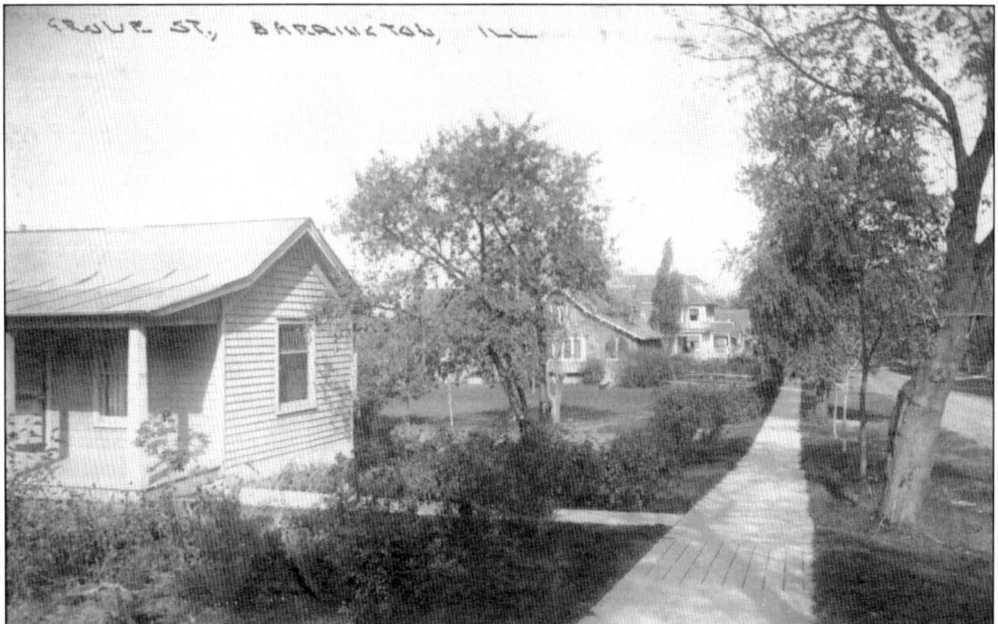

This image, recorded by an unknown photographer, captures some of the smaller homes in Barrington around 1925. Many photographers referred to the location as Grove Street as opposed to the correct identification of Grove Avenue. Note the abundant shrubbery around the perimeters of the yards.

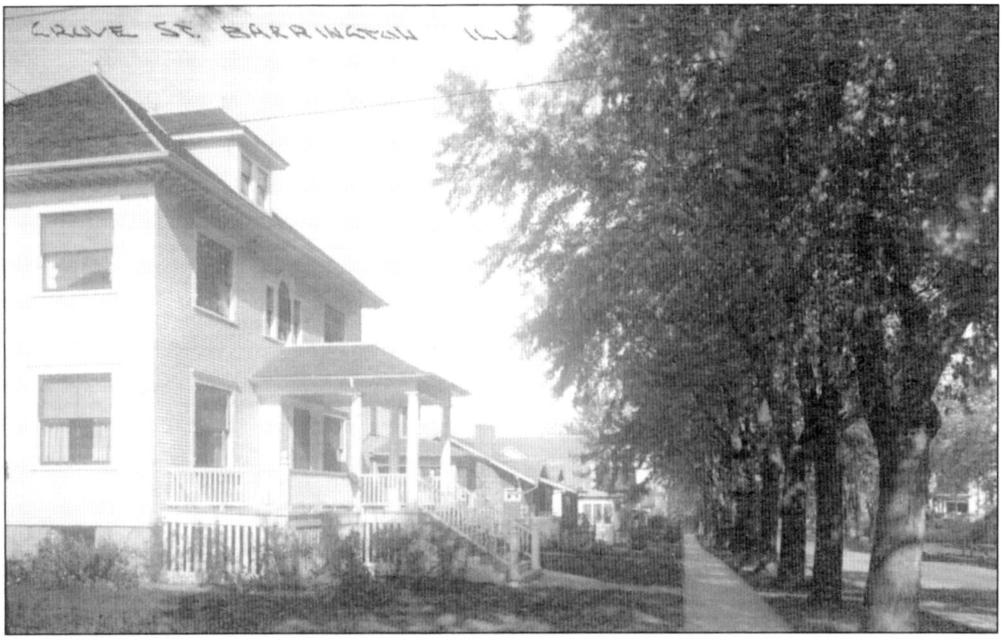

Photographer P.L. Huckins captured this photograph of Grove Avenue. It is difficult to date this card as it was never mailed. Perhaps it was added to a collector's album to remind someone of a visit to Barrington.

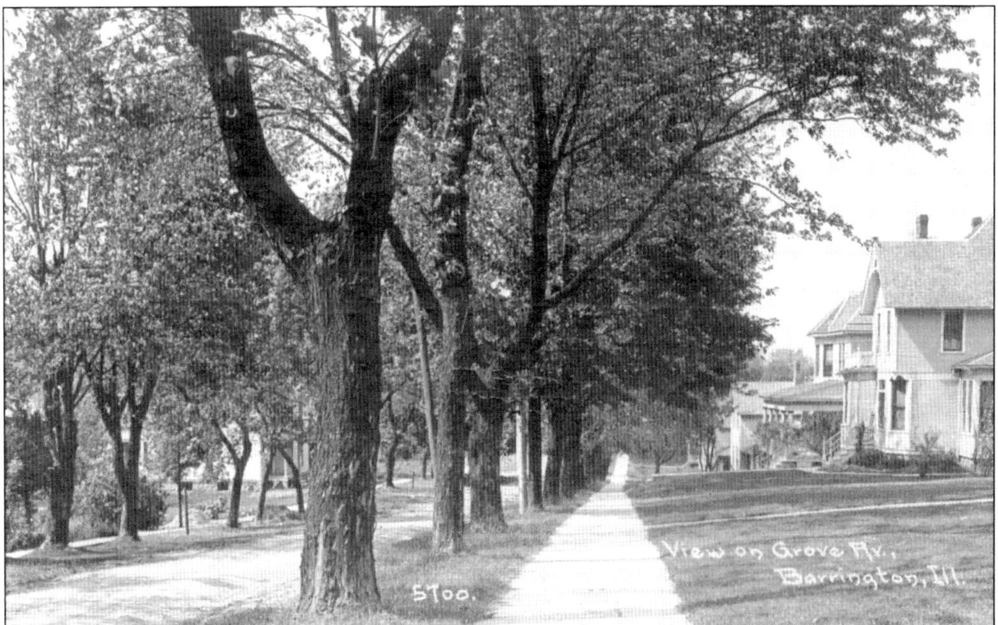

C.R. Childs captured this image of Grove Avenue that shows the street running downhill toward downtown Barrington. Hitching posts are still visible in some of the front yards.

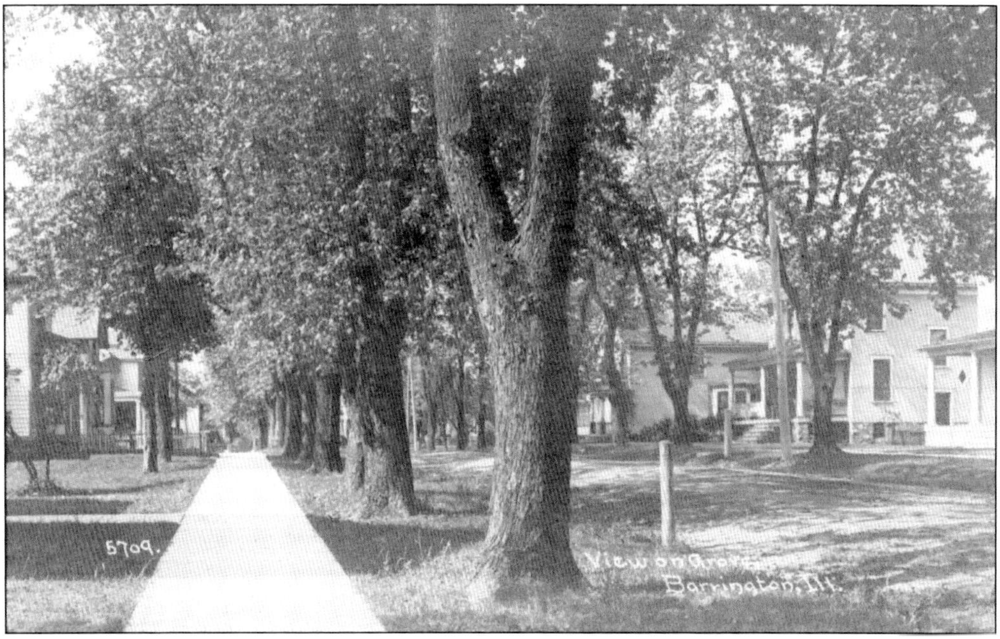

C.R. Childs must have been fascinated with the homes on Grove Avenue, as he captured numerous images of the neighborhood, adding to the selection of real-photo postcards offered in local stores at the time.

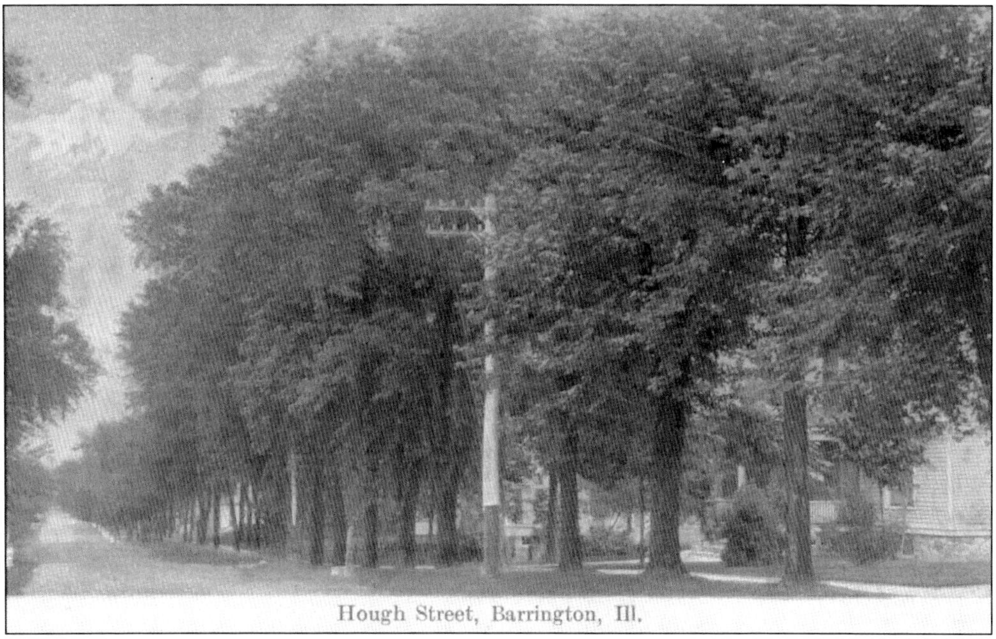

Photographer William G. Hoffman of Chicago offered a more generic color postcard showing tree-lined Hough Street. It is difficult to identify any of the homes on this card as they are obscured by the dense tree growth. The author has found very few real-photo postcards of the homes along Hough Street.

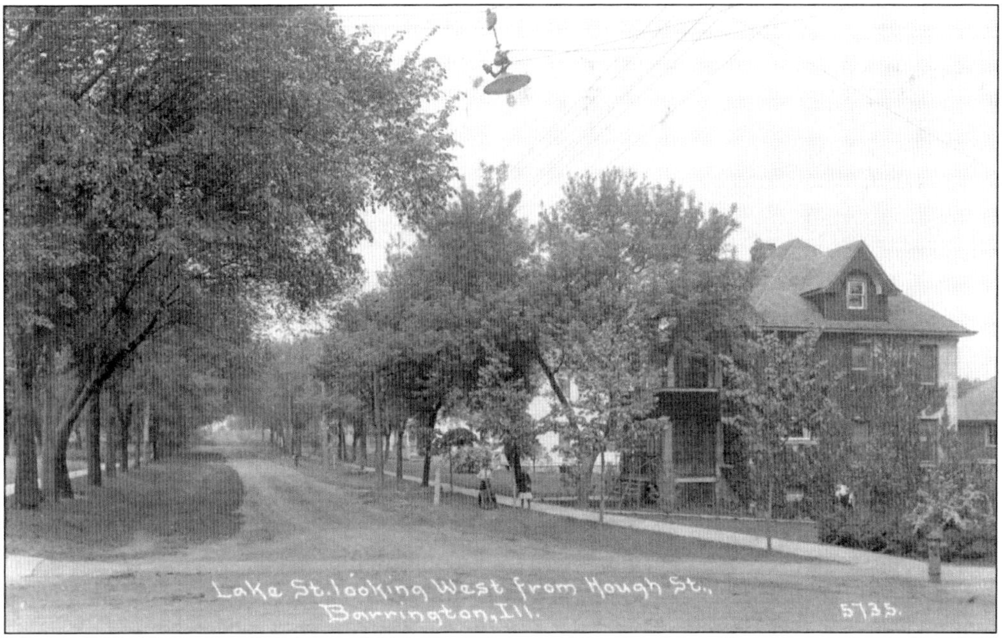

C.R. Childs captured this view of Lake Street looking west from Hough Street in the 1920s. A boy and girl are in a front yard, with the boy pushing the lawn mower and the girl standing nearby. Note that the two children are not dressed for yard work; perhaps the photographer made prior arrangements to pose them for this real-photo postcard.

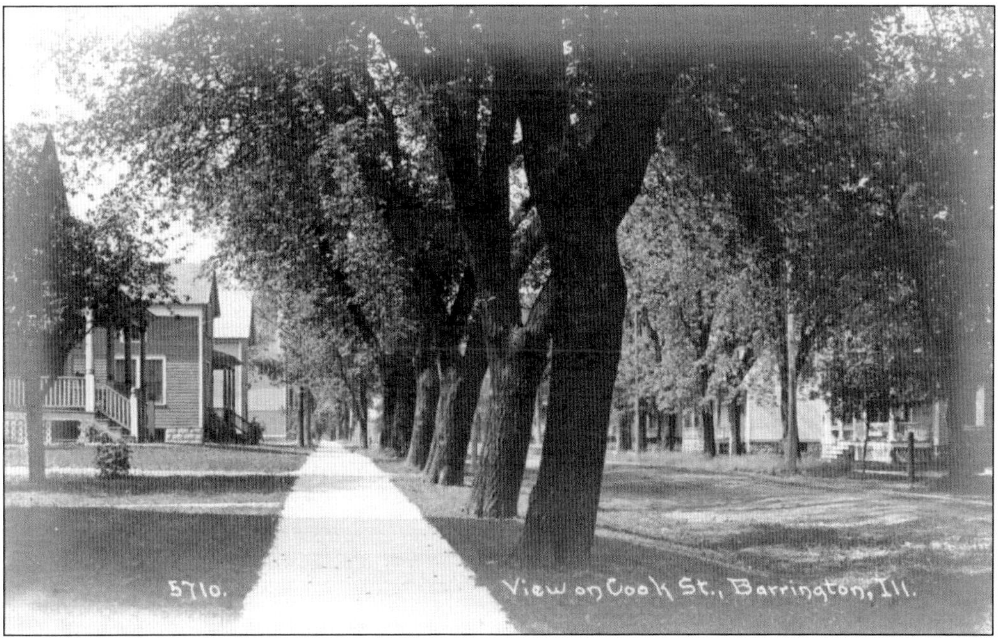

Photographer C.R. Childs photographed this view of the homes on tree-lined Cook Street. This card was never sent, so it is difficult to date. It is apparent from the sidewalks in this photograph that it was taken sometime after 1907, as Barrington passed an ordinance that year requiring cement walkways.

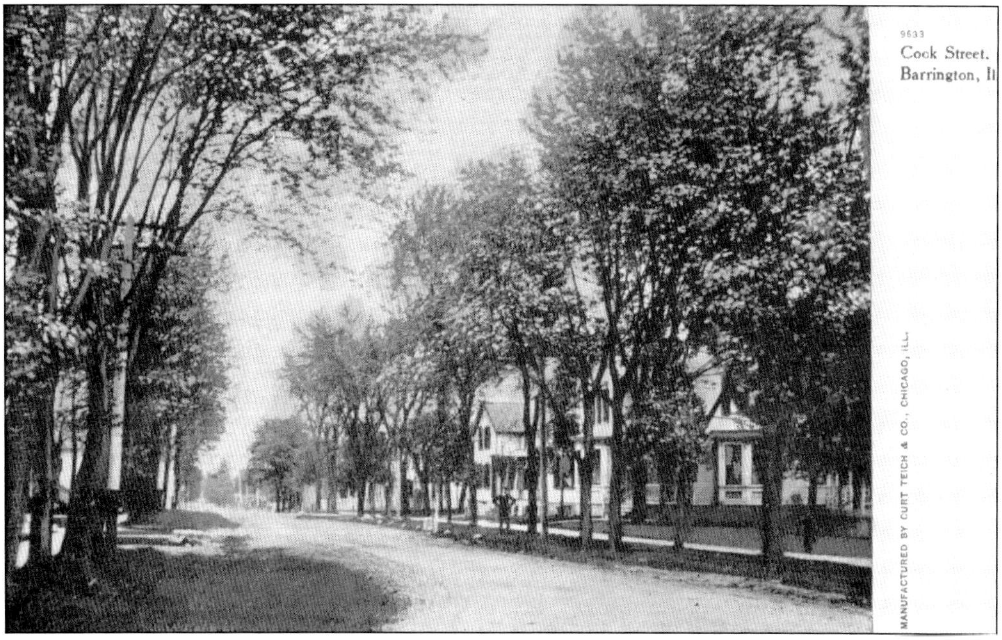

In 1908, A.L. Cudahy sent this colorized postcard of Cook Street to Emma Meyer in Rockefeller, Illinois. Colorized cards were popular with both visitors and residents.

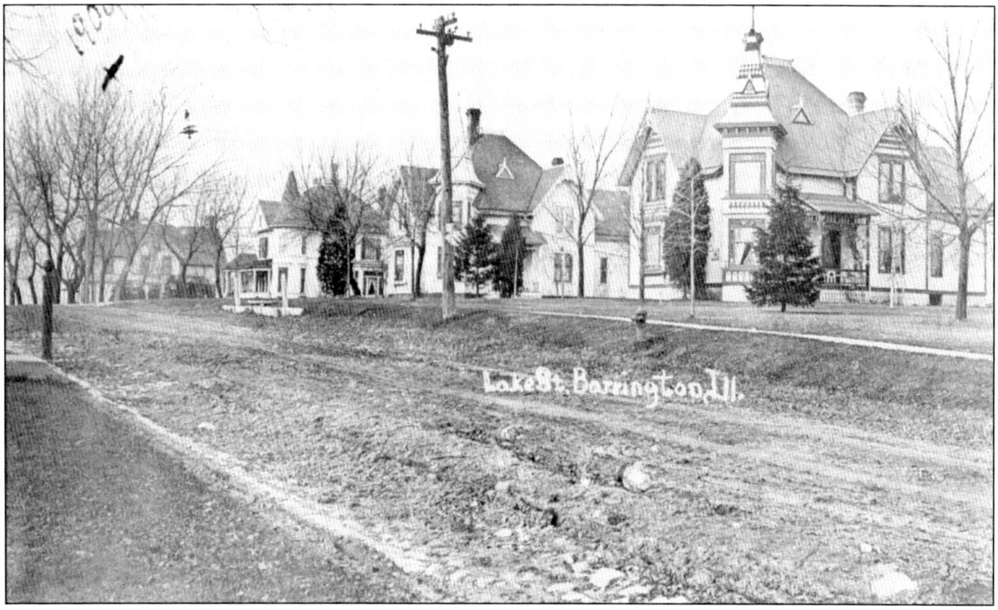

George Froelich Jr. photographed these residences on Lake Street. Many fine examples of Victorian architecture can be found in the residential areas of Barrington. The two homes at the right and in the center, with identical designs, are outstanding examples of Victorian Gothic architecture. One home was built in 1889 by Levi Higley and the other in 1891 by Dell Loomis—the men's wives were sisters (Elizabeth and Ellen Hawley). Note the fish-scale siding, square towers, and large windows with stained glass transoms.

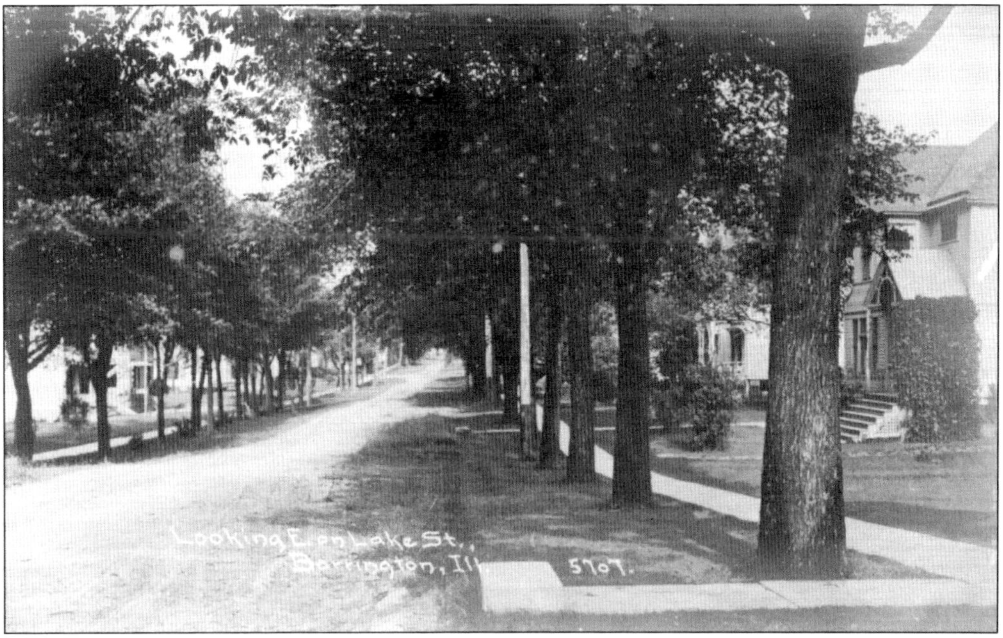

C.R. Childs captured this view looking east on Lake Street in 1911. The sender of this card, mailed to Walter Prehm in Lake Zurich, Illinois, wrote: "We are planning on going to that dance, but are not sure as yet. Say, send me a new pen will you. I haven't got a cent. May see you at Palatine. E.P."

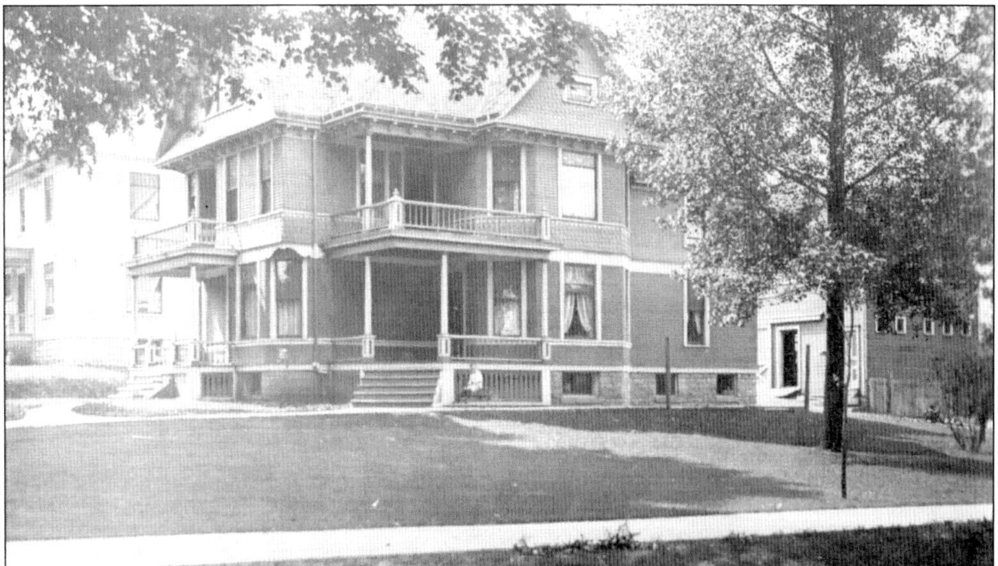

An unknown photographer captured this image of a grand home on the corner of West Main and Applebee Streets. The home still stands today and serves as a professional office building.

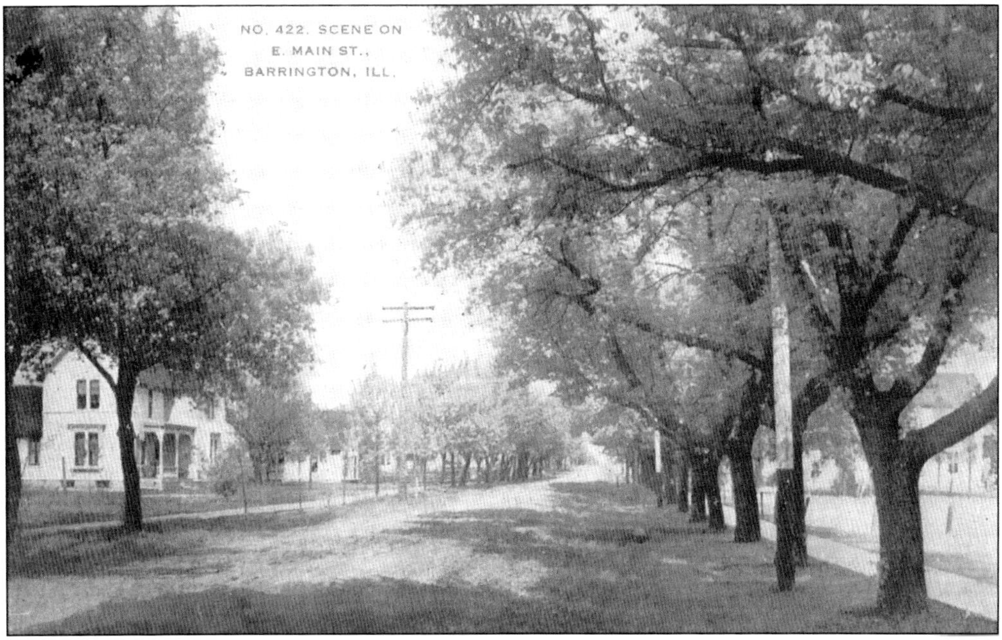

In 1909, William G. Hoffman photographed East Main Street looking east from the front of St. Paul Church at North Avenue.

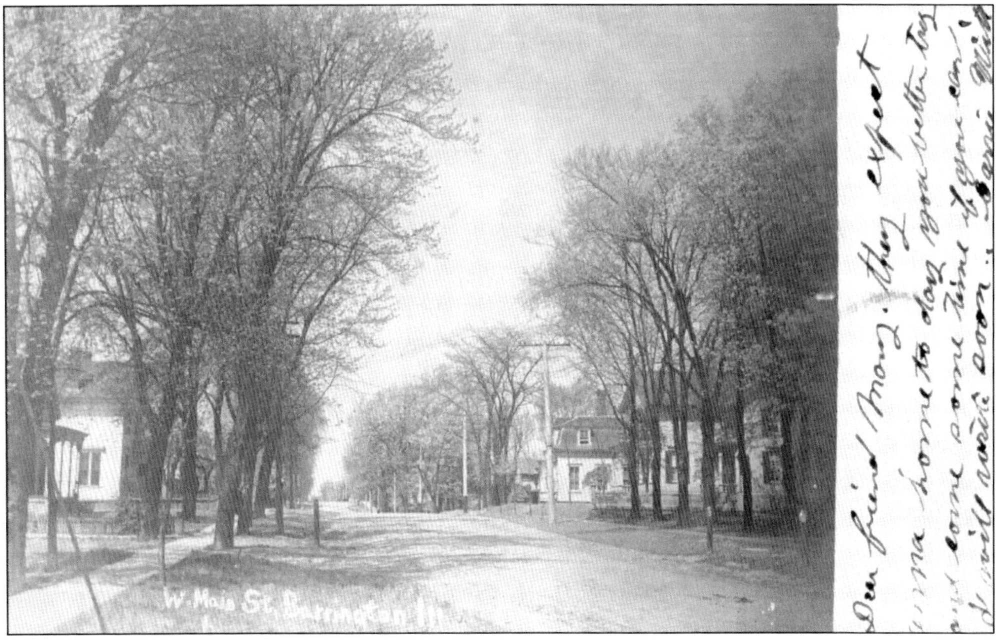

An unknown photographer snapped this image of West Main Street in 1909. Carrie Witt wrote on the reverse side of the card: "Barrington, July 1909—This is the street we live on, but you cannot see the house." Note the number of new trees planted along the street.

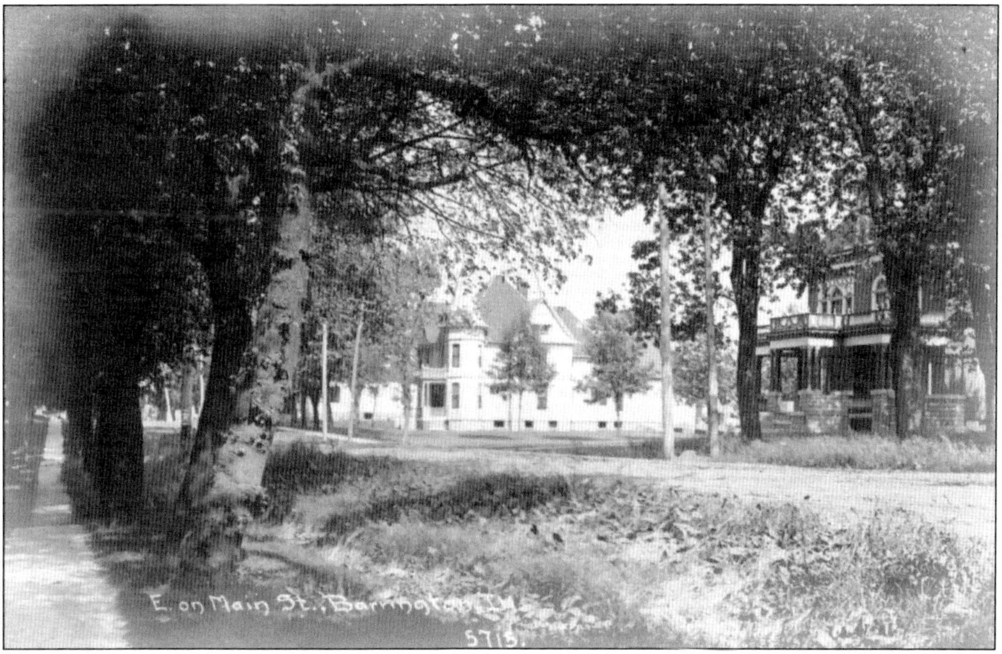

This 1910 image looking east on Main Street was taken by photographer Charles R. Childs. The sender noted on the reverse side: "Dear Aunt, Pretty little town and we are all enjoying ourselves. Babes thinks it's great. Plenty of green grass and good things to eat. El."

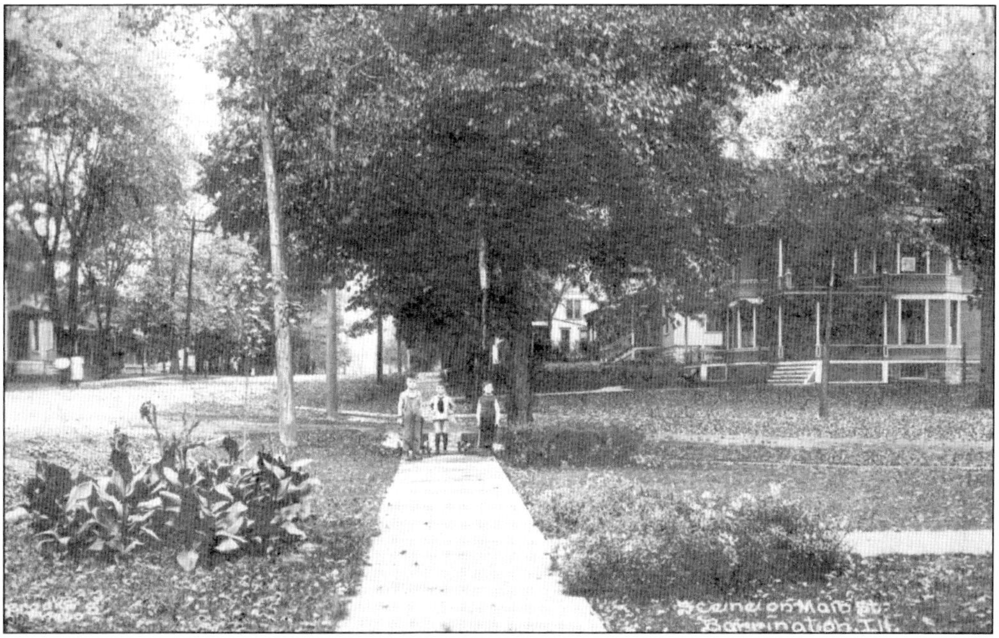

Photographer H.B. Brooks captured this image of Main Street, with three small boys standing with their two wagons on the sidewalk.

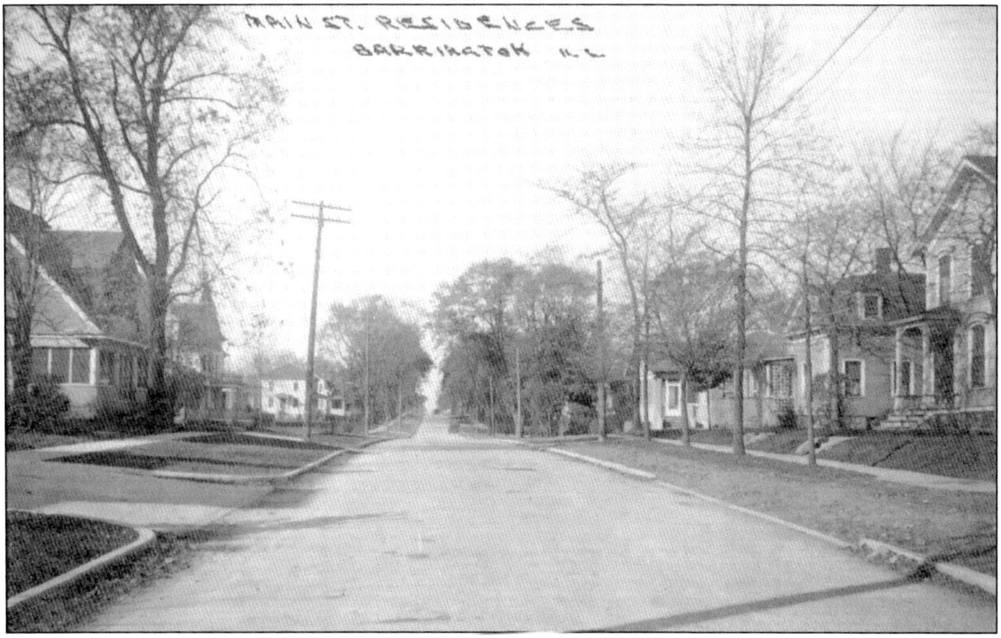

P.L. Huckins's photograph of Main Street residences captures wide, paved streets, with cars in the distance. The hitching posts that stood prominently in front of many of the local homes are gone; the horseless carriage was now in vogue and here to stay.

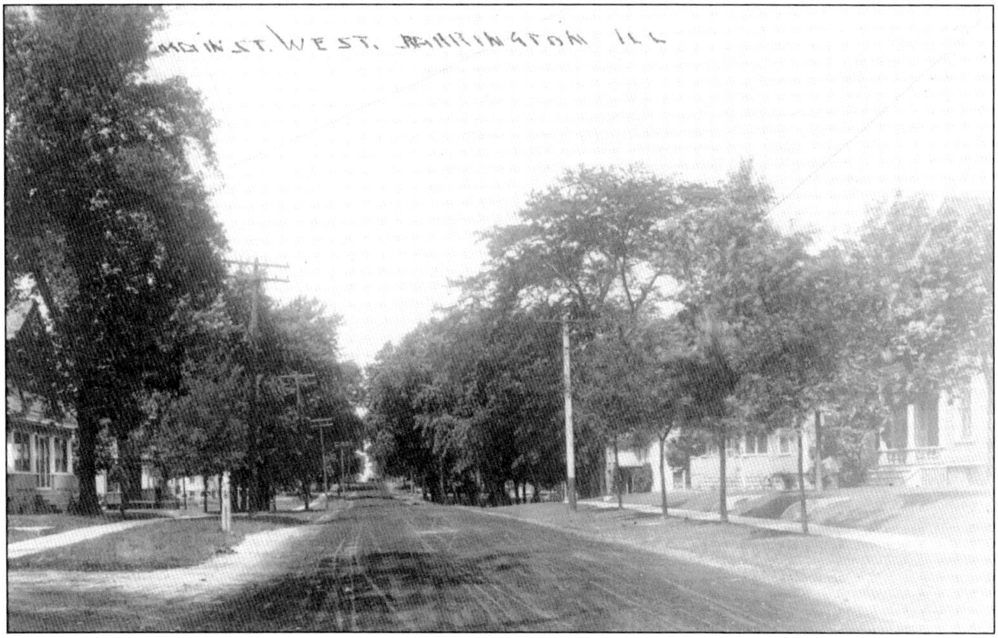

Huckins took this image of the residences along Main Street. It is difficult to determine the date of this postcard, as it was never mailed but perhaps placed in a photograph album.

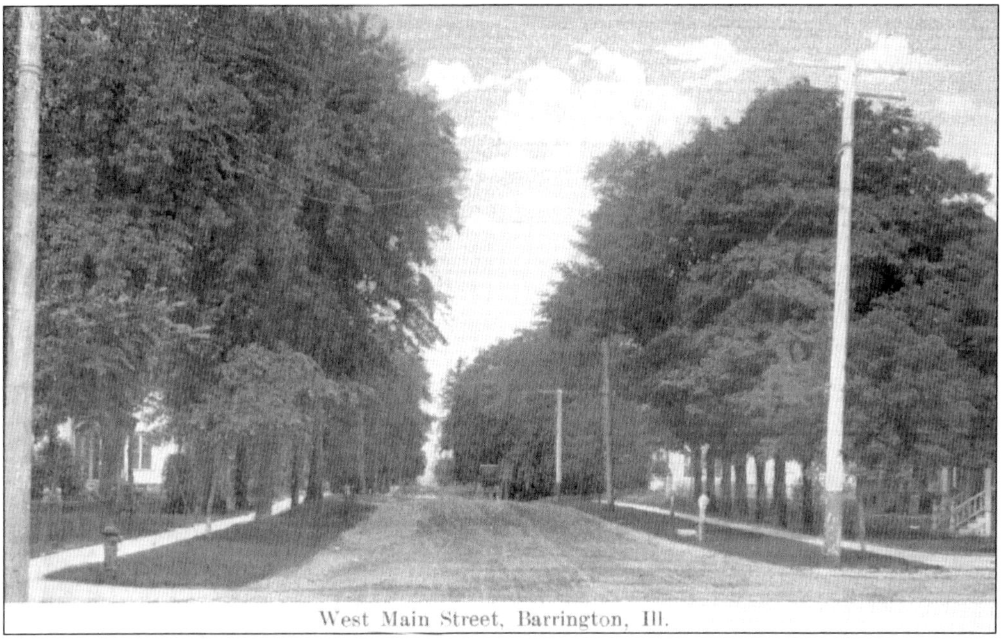

Photographer William G. Hoffman offered this colorized version of West Main Street in the early 1900s, showing the street and surrounding trees on either side of the road.

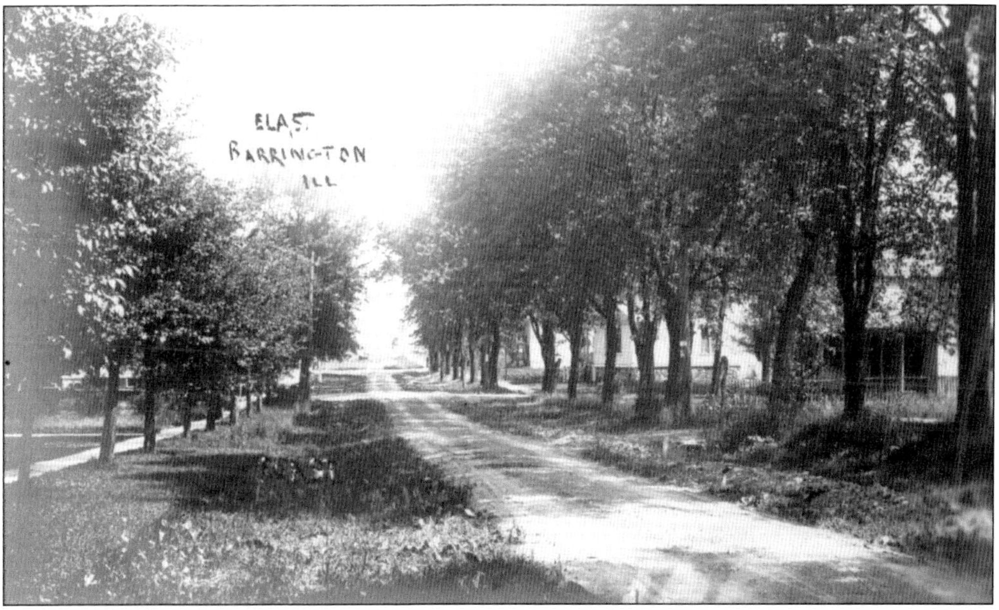

A real-photo postcard, probably taken by George Froelich Jr., shows Ela Street in 1908. Froelich resided in this area of the community and captured a good view of the green environment surrounding the homes. It is interesting to note that the identification of "Ela Street Barrington, Ill." faintly appears next to the road in the foreground and was lost when the image was printed. Therefore, the identification of this location was recorded directly above the tree line in the real-photo postcard.

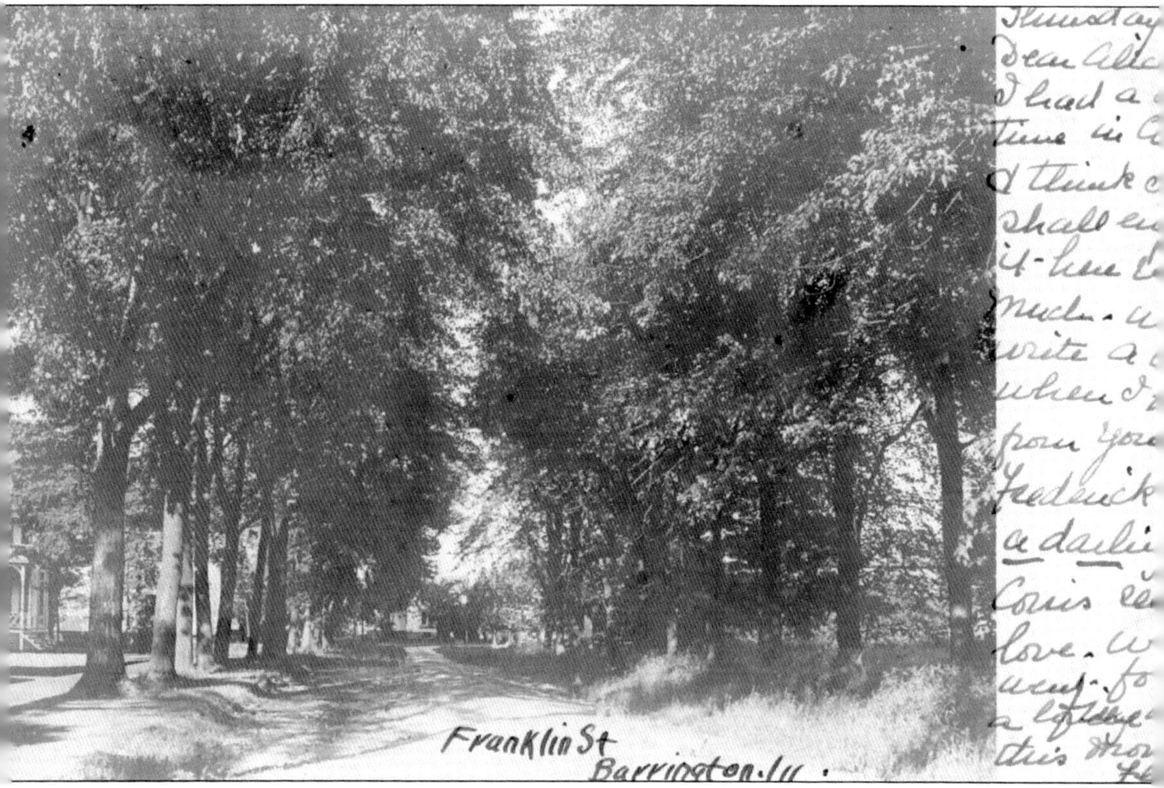

George Froelich Jr. brought his large camera and tripod to Franklin Street to capture this restful view of the residential area. The sender of this card, which was mailed from Barrington, wrote: "Dear Alice, I had a lovely time in Chicago. I think I shall enjoy it here very much. Will write a letter when I hear from you. Frederick is a darling and Coris sends love. We went for a lovely drive this morning. Flo." Local residents found it very convenient to reach "the windy city" within a couple of hours by train on the C&NW.

Five

Around Town

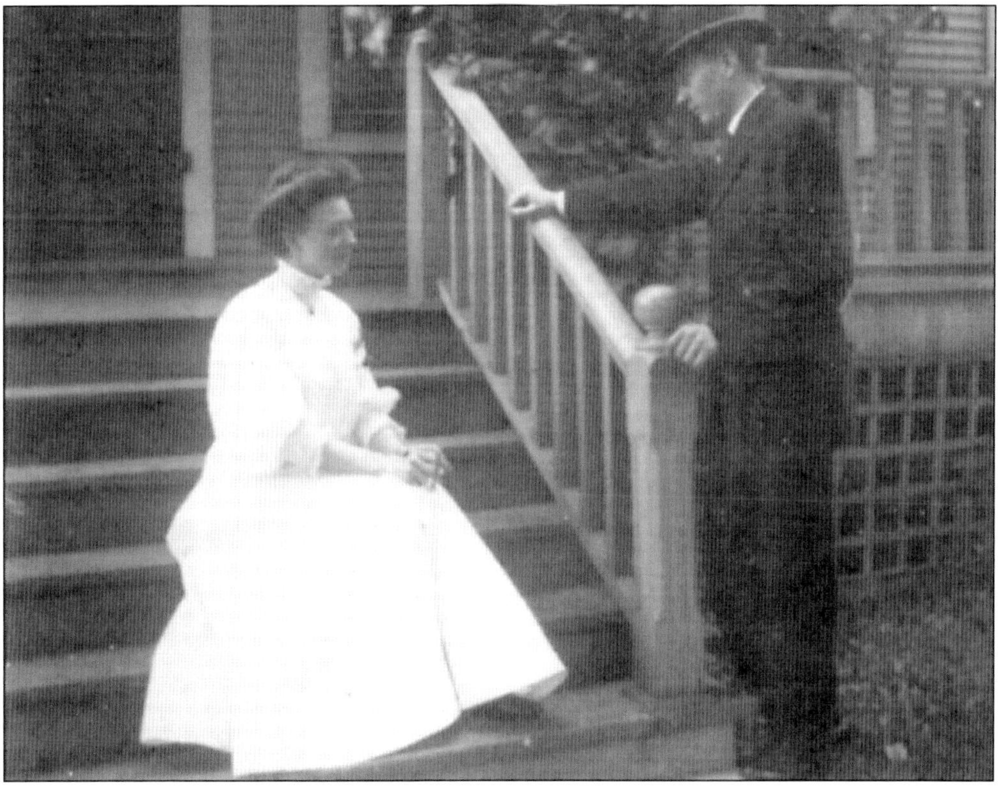

Photographer and Barrington resident George Froelich Jr. visits with an unidentified lady on the porch steps of a Barrington home in an unknown year. Froelich (1888–1972) captured many interesting and finely detailed photographs of Barrington during his lifetime. He left a legacy of important photographs for future generations.

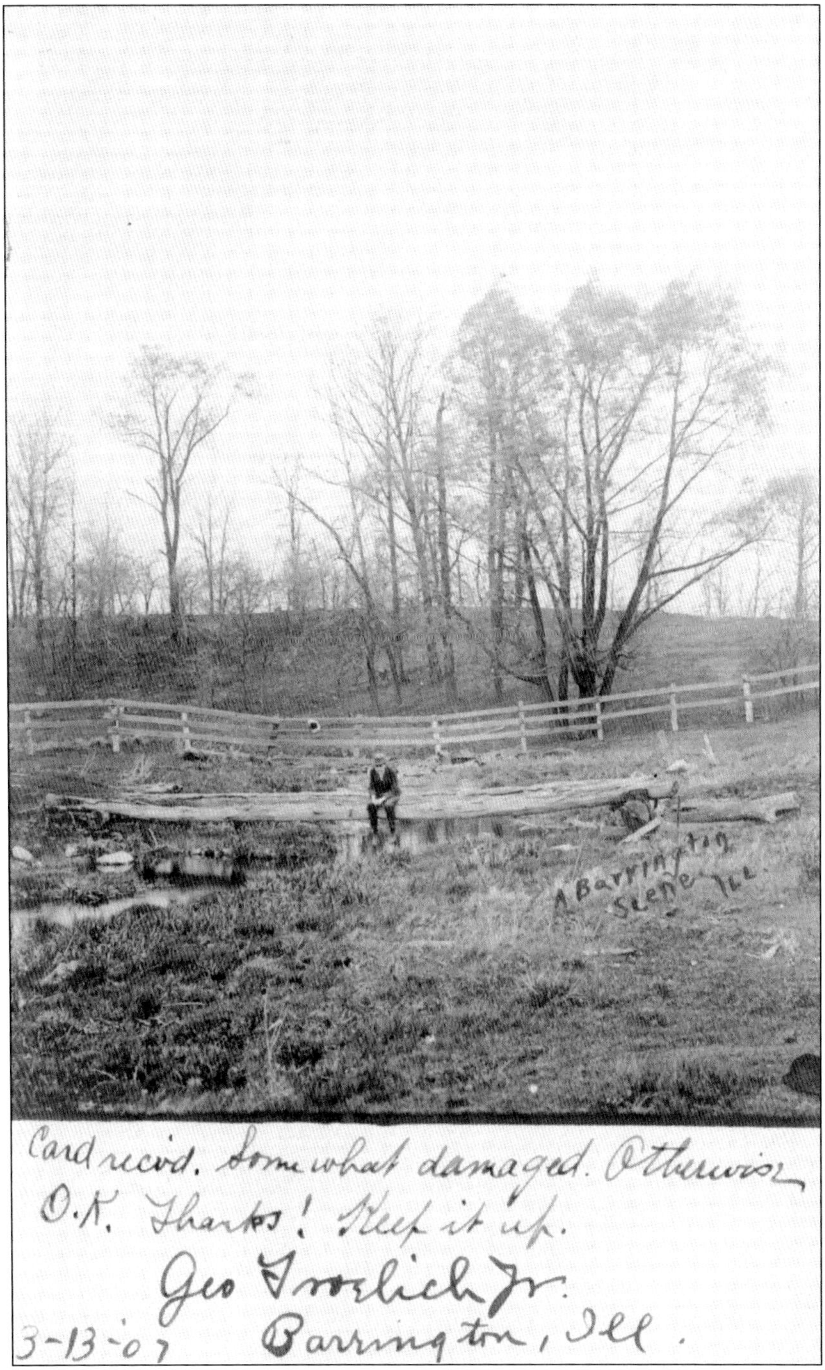

George Froelich Jr. tried experimenting with different views, angles, and perspectives when he started his postcard business. He even tested the durability of his postcards by sending them to friends to determine the condition of the cards when they reached their destinations. As shown at the bottom of this card sent to Kutztown, Pennsylvania, it arrived somewhat damaged but otherwise okay. Froelich simply titled this card "A Barrington Scene, Ill." Each day, Froelich noted specific listings of the subjects he photographed in his diary.

Evergreen Cemetery was organized in 1867, with the cemetery designed in 1868 by J.W. Powers. In 1869, a charter was granted to lot owners of the cemetery, including such prominent Barrington names as McIntosh, Ela, Creet, Applebee, Waterman, Abbott, Howarth, Spunner, and Clark. The Thomas W. Sweeney Woman's Relief Corps No. 85 worked to erect a monument in Evergreen Cemetery to honor soldiers and sailors. A color postcard by an unknown manufacturer recognizes this important monument.

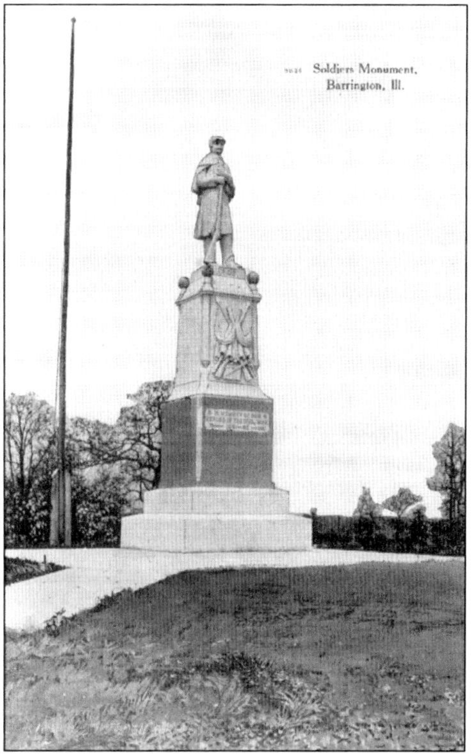

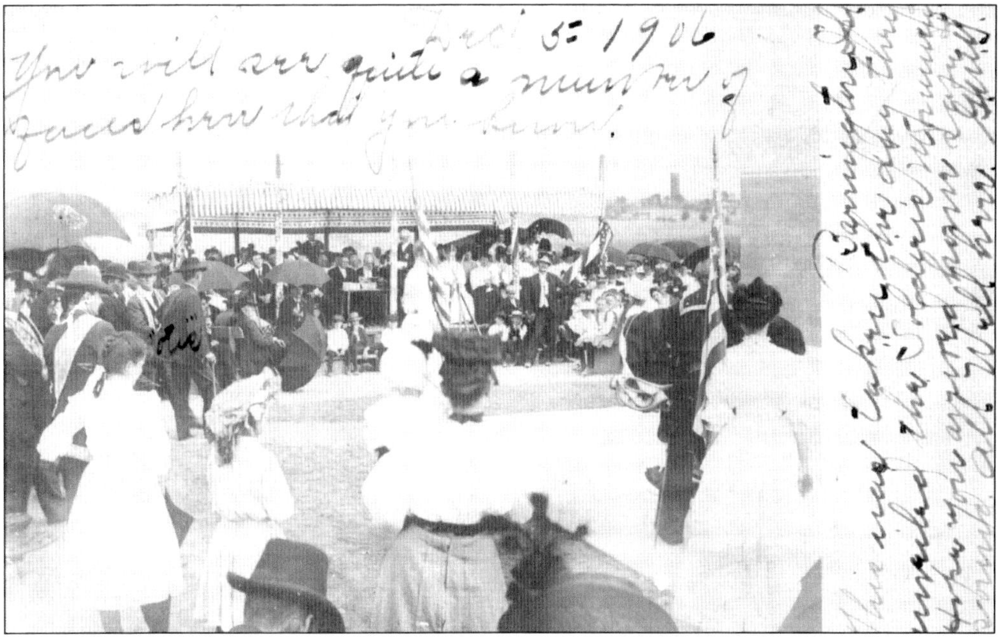

An unidentified photographer captured this dedication event at Evergreen Cemetery on September 6, 1906. The Soldiers and Sailors Monument is on the right side of the photograph, with the audience seated around the perimeter. Residents young and old gathered to celebrate this momentous day and, based on the number of umbrellas present in the picture, the weather was either rainy or hot.

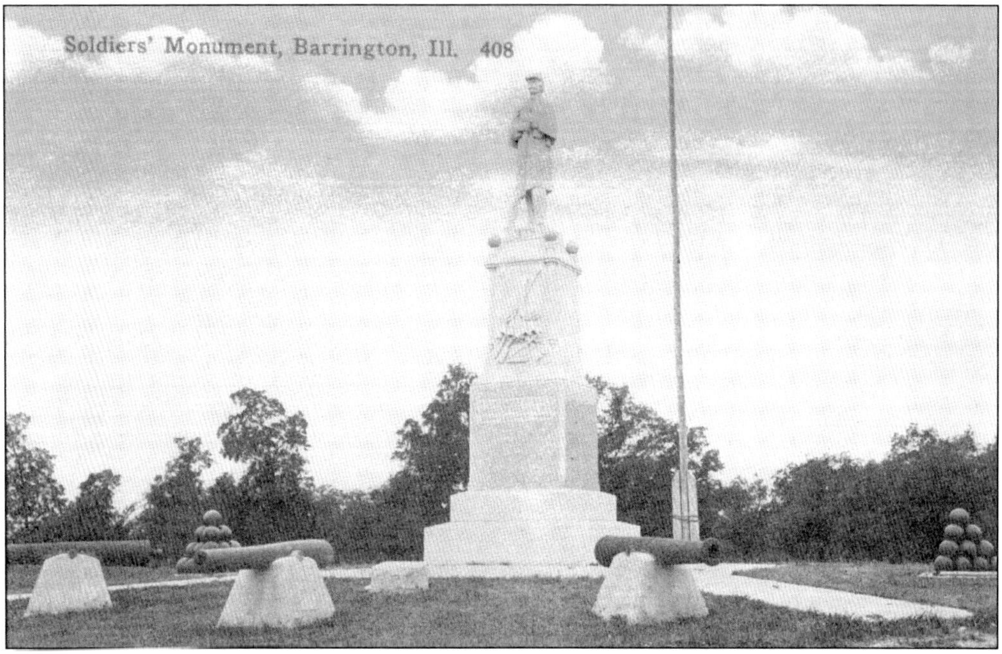

Photographer William G. Hoffman of Chicago created this postcard showing the Soldiers and Sailors Monument complete with cannons and cannon balls. The monument still stands today and plays an important role in Barrington's Memorial Day celebrations—a parade starts downtown and ends at Evergreen Cemetery, where local residents gather around this monument to honor those lost in past wars.

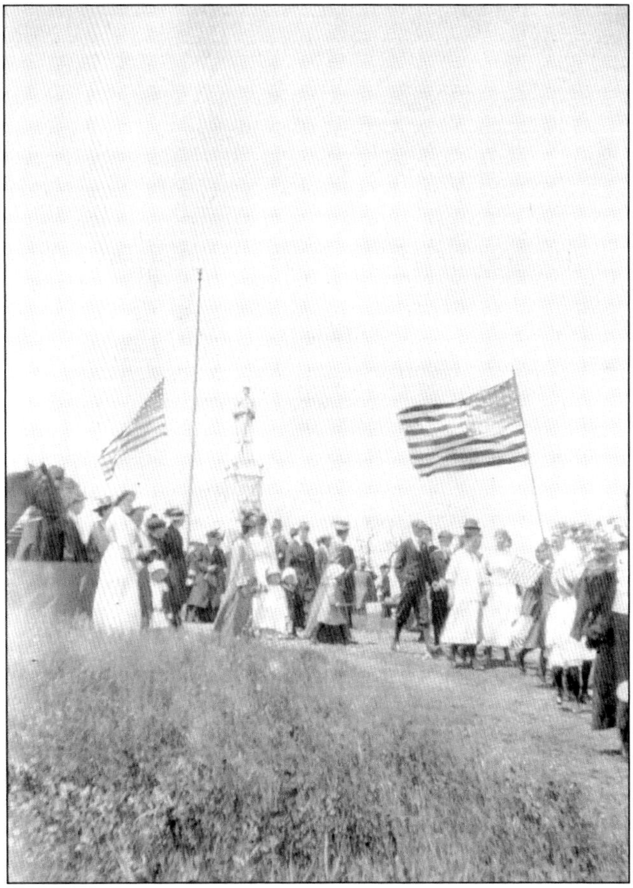

An unknown photographer captured this 1916 image of residents following the parade route as they leave Evergreen Cemetery following completion of the ceremony. Note the horse at the left and the 48-star flags held by participants.

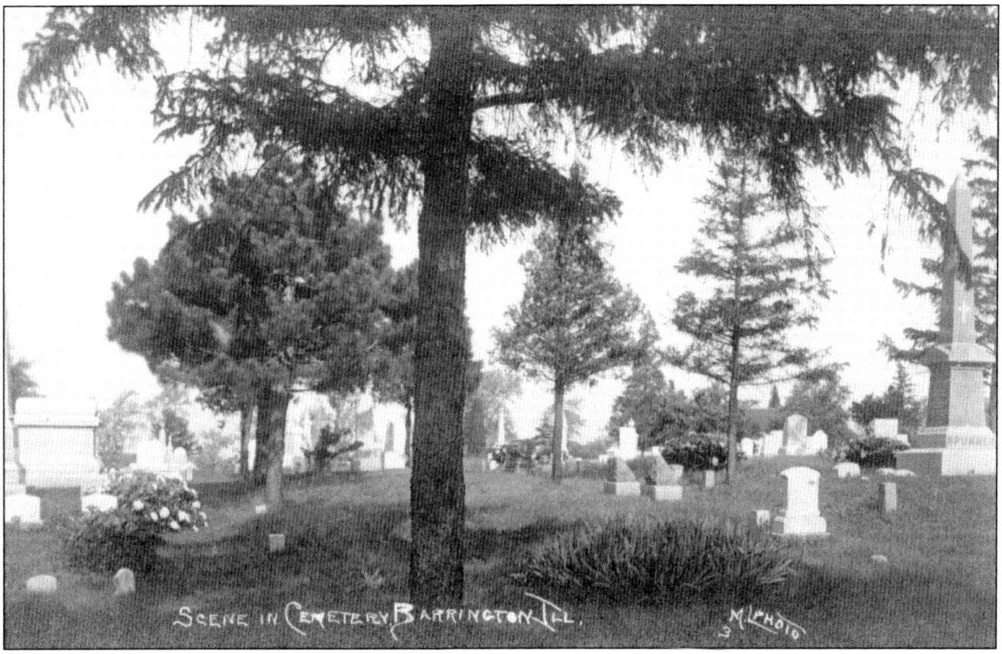

M.L. Photo Company recorded this image looking northwest in one of the oldest parts of Evergreen Cemetery. This view included gravestones of some of the earliest Barrington settlers. The actual date of the photograph is unknown, but based on the size of the evergreens (which still stand) it was taken at least 70 years ago.

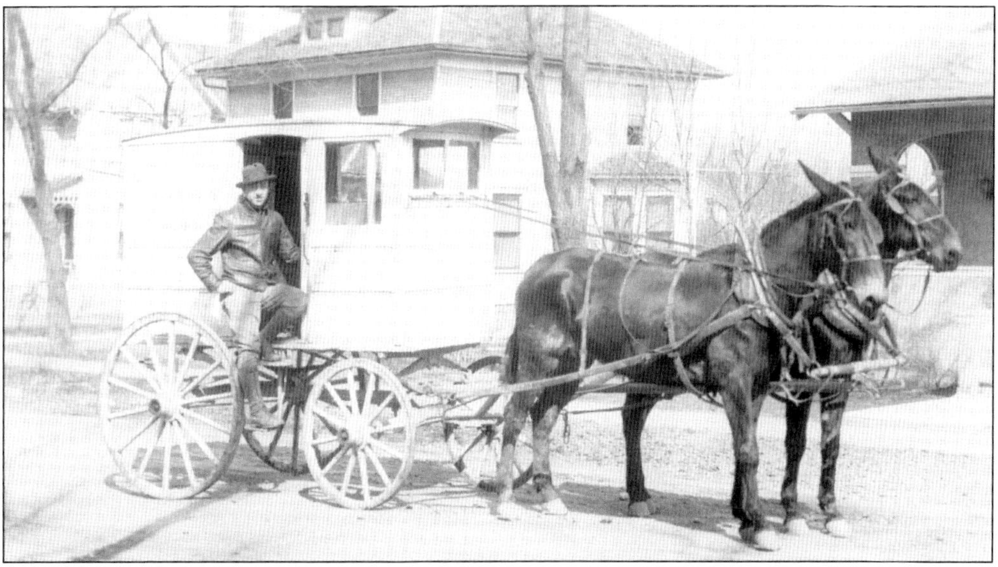

An unidentified photographer snapped this image of the Castle Knoll Dairy Farm delivery team and wagon. Fresh milk and eggs were delivered to local residents daily. It is noted on the card that this image may have been taken on Lake Street.

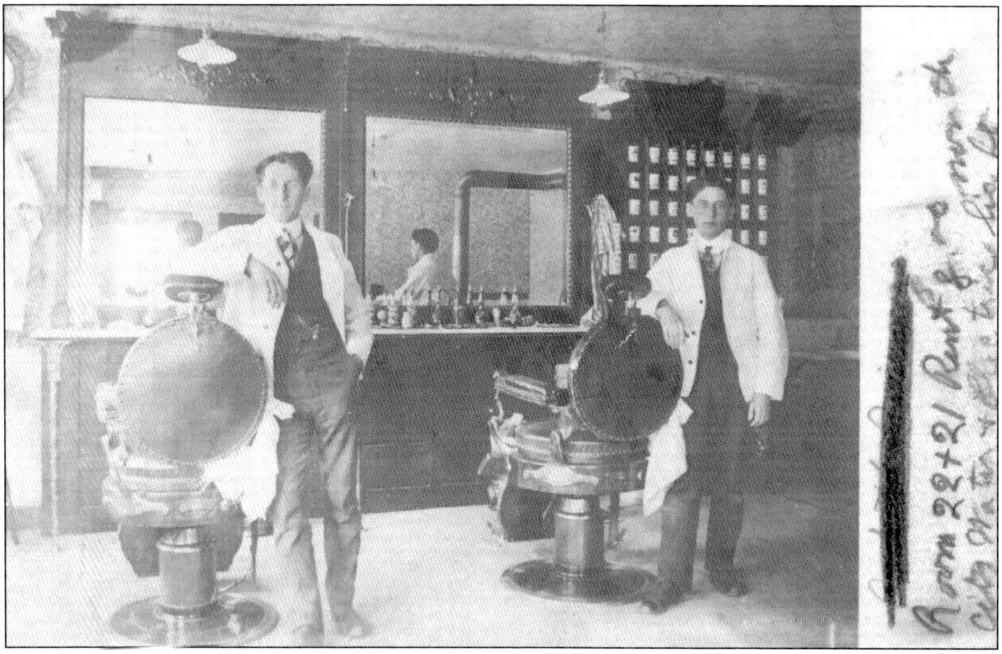

In this interior view of Thies Barber Shop, the barber chairs are shown with barbers ready to serve the customers. A notation on the border of the card indicates that rent for rooms 21 and 22 is $8 per month, with city water and electric light included. Note the interesting bottles on the counter and the shaving mug rack immediately behind the barber on the right. Customers brought in their own personal shaving mugs and placed them in one of the small compartments within the rack. When a customer requested a shave, the barber could take down the customer's personal shaving mug.

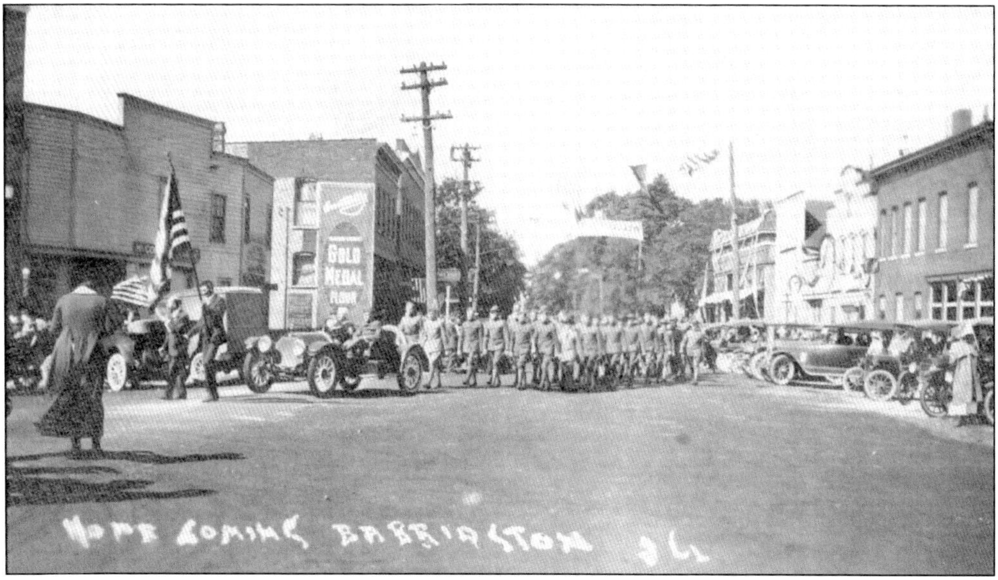

P.L. Huckins captured this image of soldiers returned from World War I parading down Main Street in downtown Barrington. The businesses are decorated in a patriotic theme and flags are visible both in the parade and mounted on the front of the buildings.

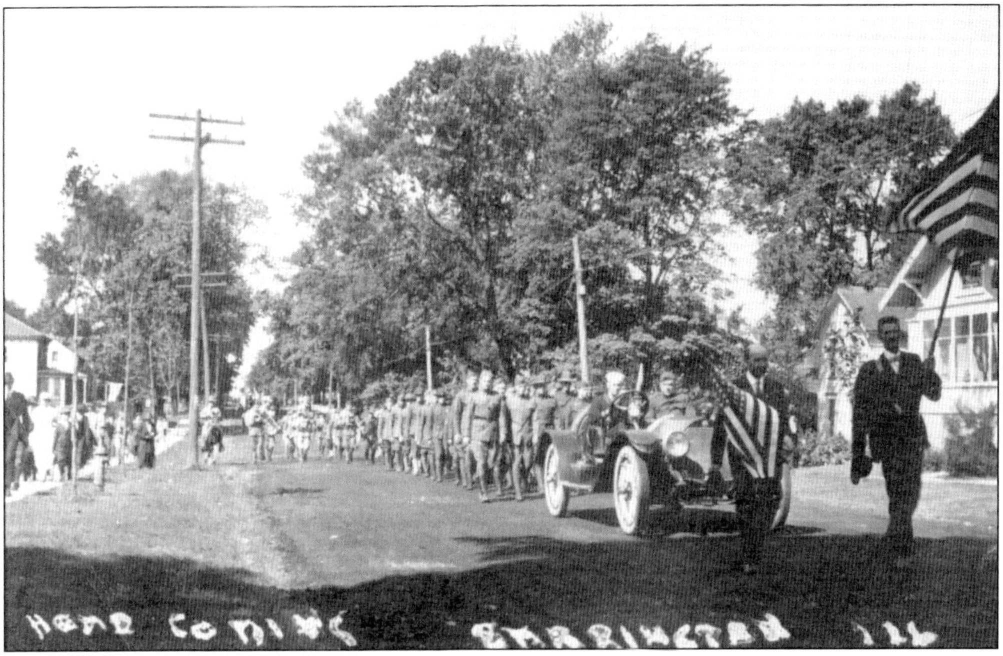

A band follows World War I soldiers in a parade down Station Street; immediately behind the band is a float (not visible in the picture) elaborately decorated with American flags.

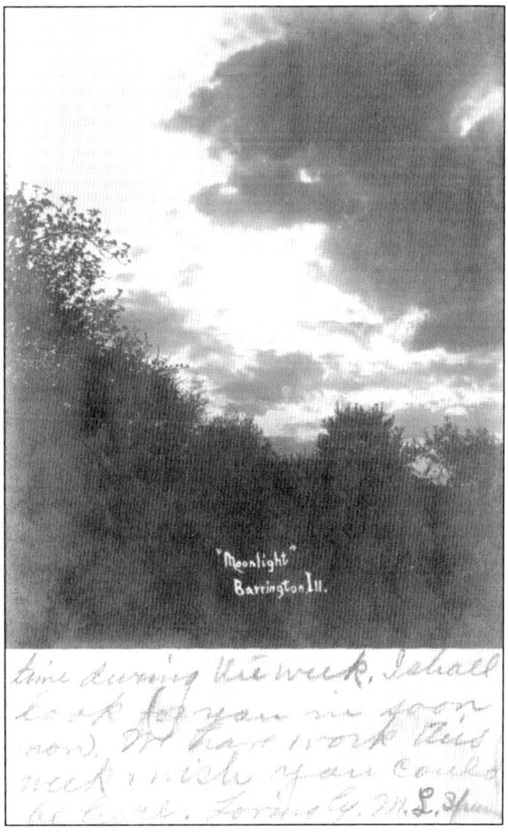

This postcard is attributed to George Froelich Jr. who experimented with different images of both woodland areas and evening sunsets. This card is simply titled "Moonlight."

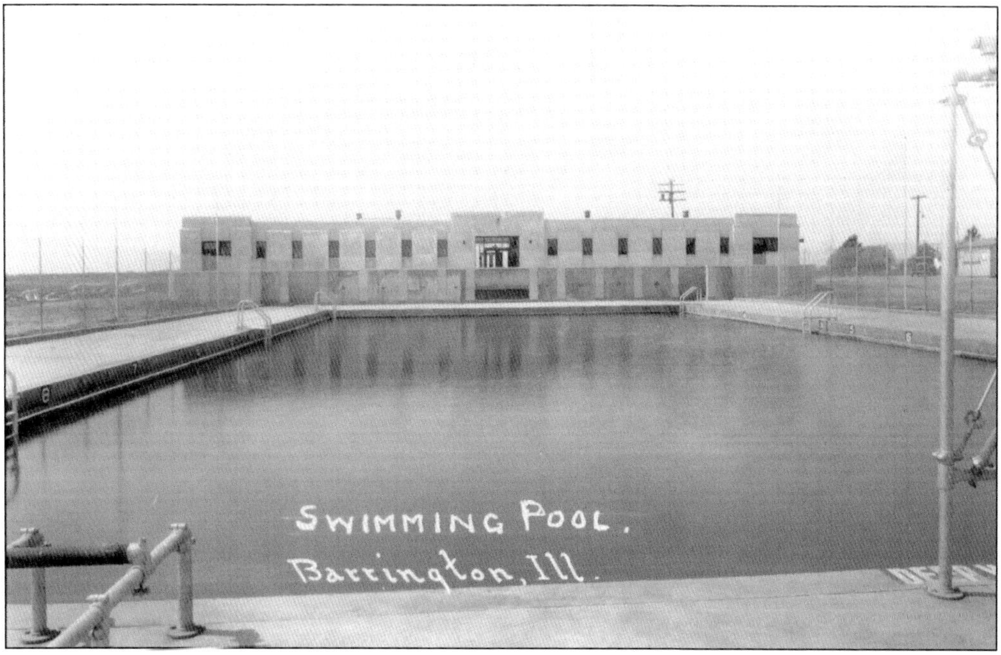

In 1930, the Barrington Park District Board acquired a parcel of land west of Hough Street and south of Northwest Highway and constructed a shelter house and swimming pool. This is one of the earliest-known images of the pool and building.

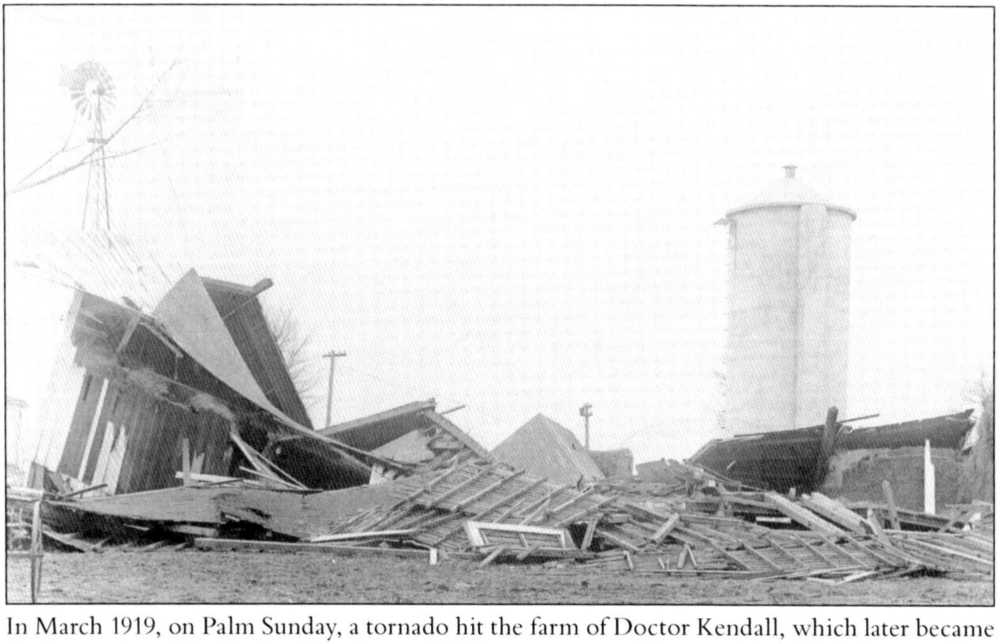

In March 1919, on Palm Sunday, a tornado hit the farm of Doctor Kendall, which later became the future site of the Quaker Oats Farm. This image, captured by an unidentified photographer, shows the impact of that tornado. On the message side of the card, the sender noted: "My Dear Friend: This is the way our barn looked after the tornado passed over Palm Sunday. So you see how impossible it would be for me to come Easter much as I would like to! We are busy hunting for wreckers, masons, carpenters etc."

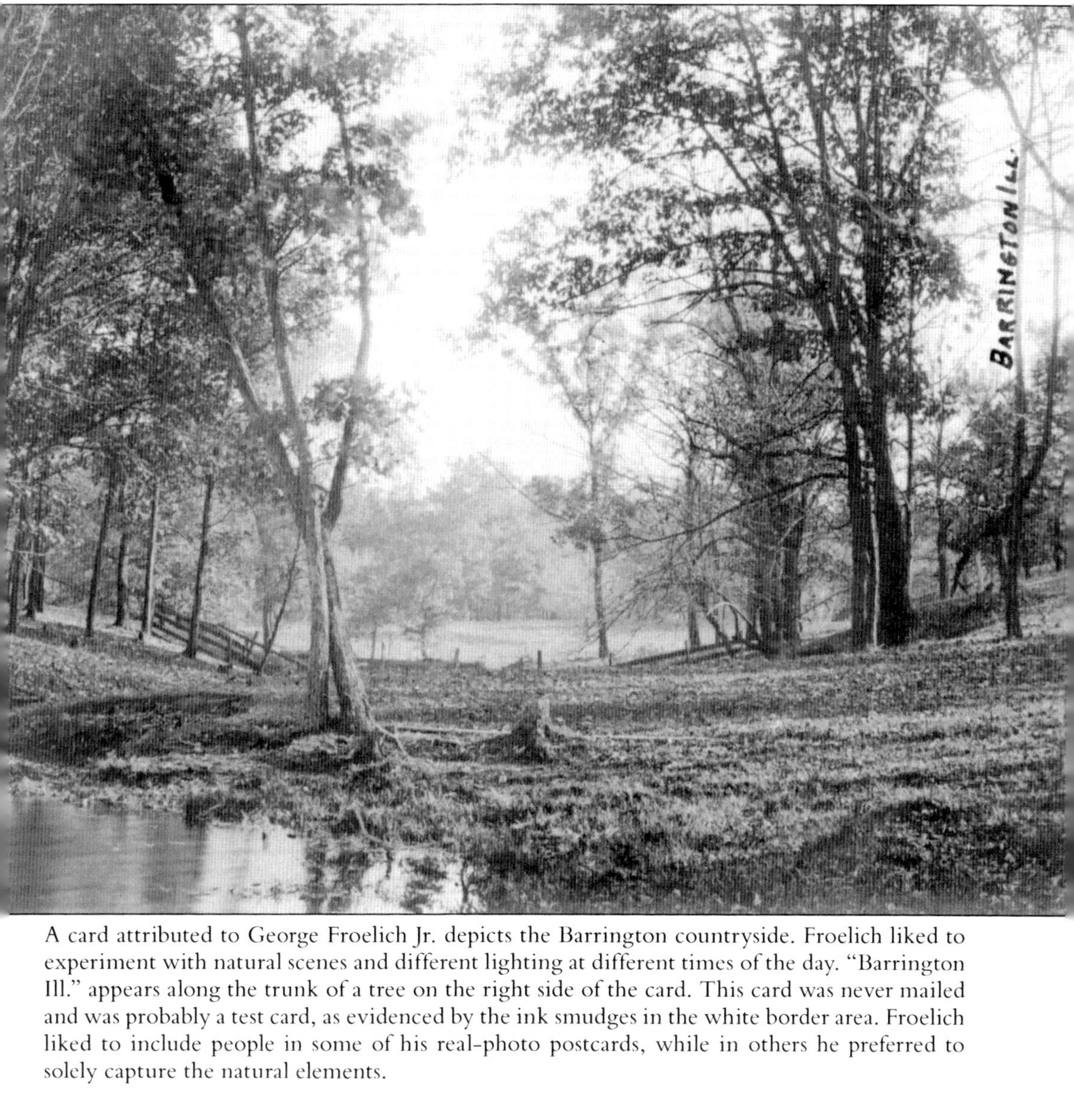

A card attributed to George Froelich Jr. depicts the Barrington countryside. Froelich liked to experiment with natural scenes and different lighting at different times of the day. "Barrington Ill." appears along the trunk of a tree on the right side of the card. This card was never mailed and was probably a test card, as evidenced by the ink smudges in the white border area. Froelich liked to include people in some of his real-photo postcards, while in others he preferred to solely capture the natural elements.

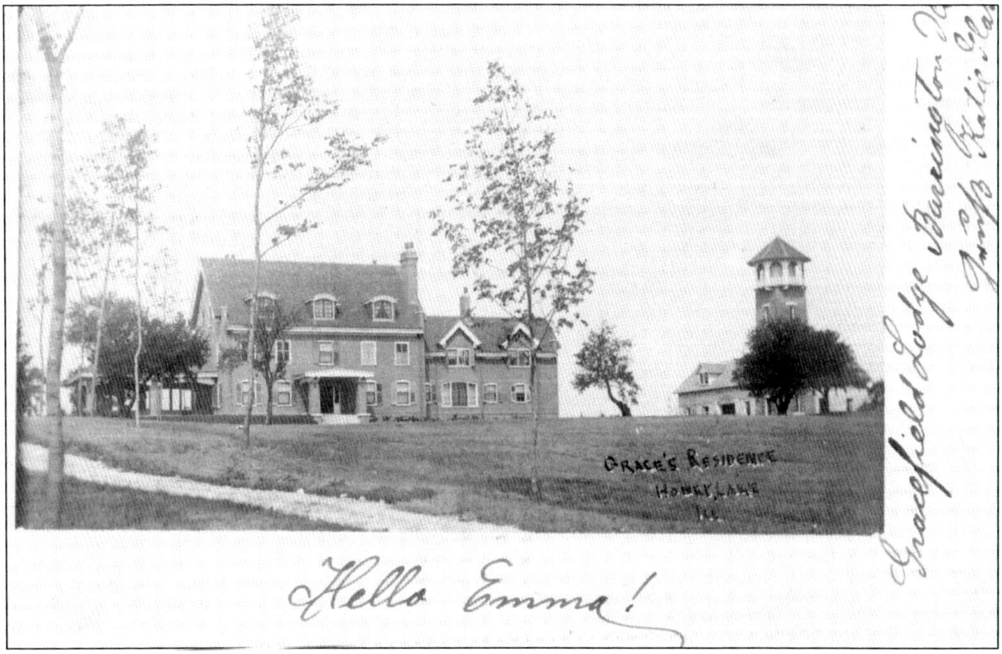

William Grace, of William Grace Company, purchased the William Sandman farm and built Gracefield Lodge or "Gracefield," which became Grace's country home. The William Grace Company of Chicago was located at 1408 Wabash Avenue. After Grace died, this became the Biltmore Club and Biltmore community. This 1906 image shows the grounds of the estate with newly planted trees.

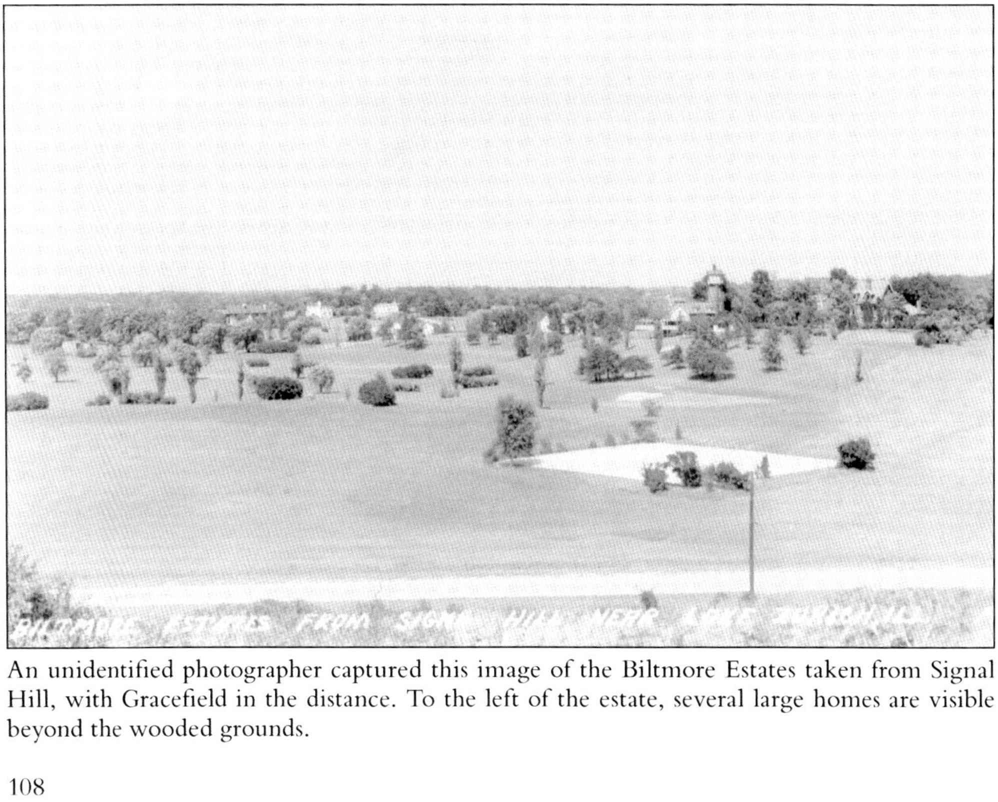

An unidentified photographer captured this image of the Biltmore Estates taken from Signal Hill, with Gracefield in the distance. To the left of the estate, several large homes are visible beyond the wooded grounds.

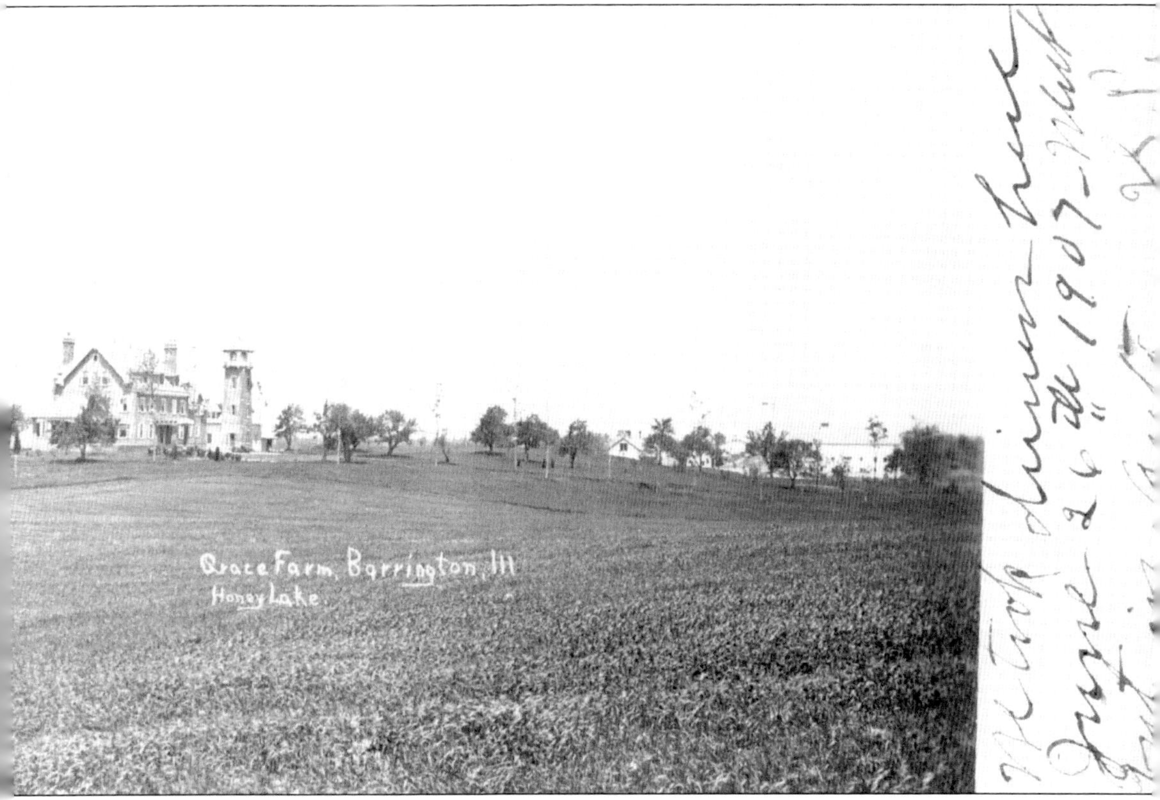

This 1906 image of Grace Farm is attributed to photographer George Froelich Jr. It offers a wide perspective of the entire farm, including several buildings located a good distance from the main house. Many new trees have been planted on the gently rolling hills of the estate. The sender of the card noted: "We took dinner here June 26th 1907 and went out in auto. J.S.P."

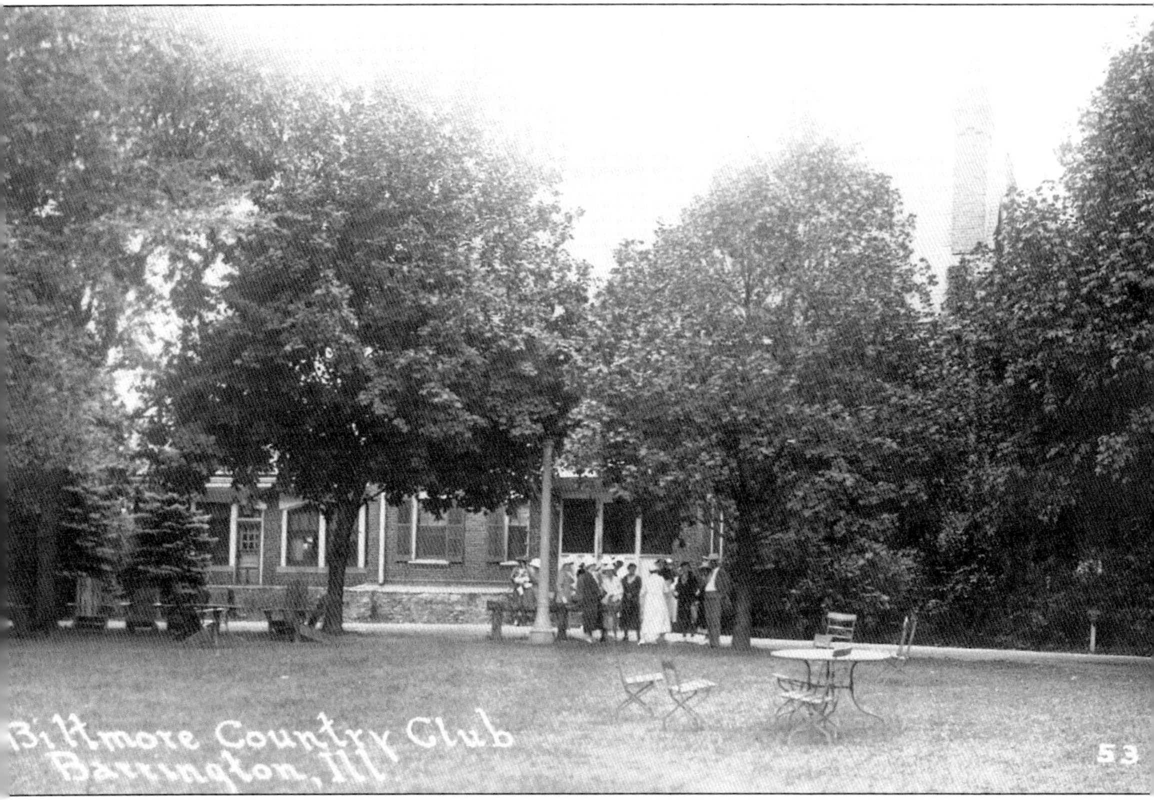

This unidentified photographer captured a closer view of the house and grounds of the Biltmore Country Club (recognized as the Grace Farm before 1926) with guests visiting on the shaded lawn.

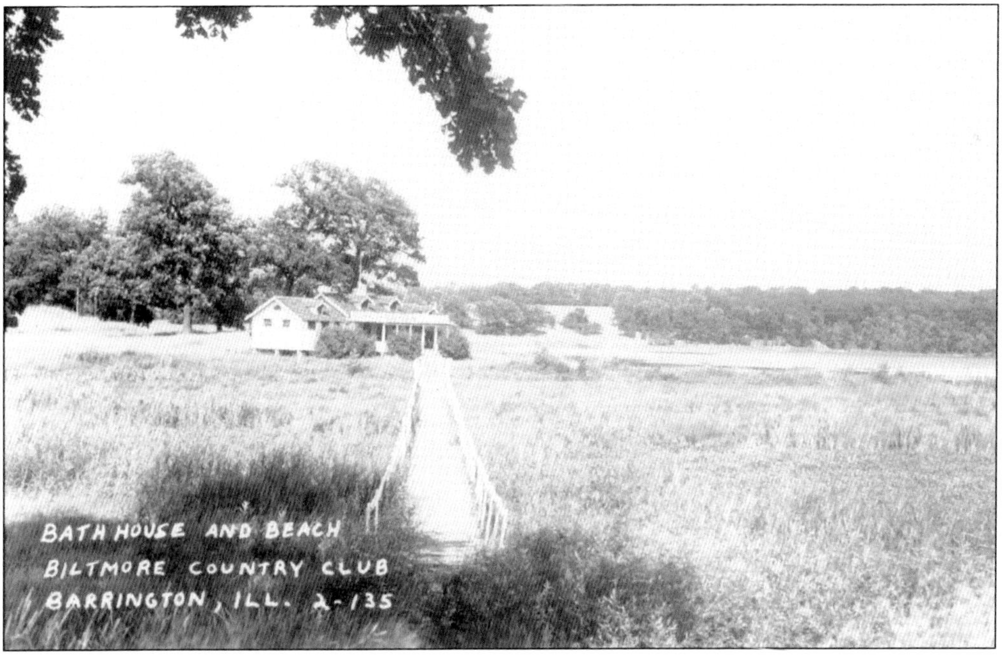

An unidentified photographer captured this landscape photograph of the bathhouse and beach at the Biltmore Country Club. Honey Lake is to the right of the buildings.

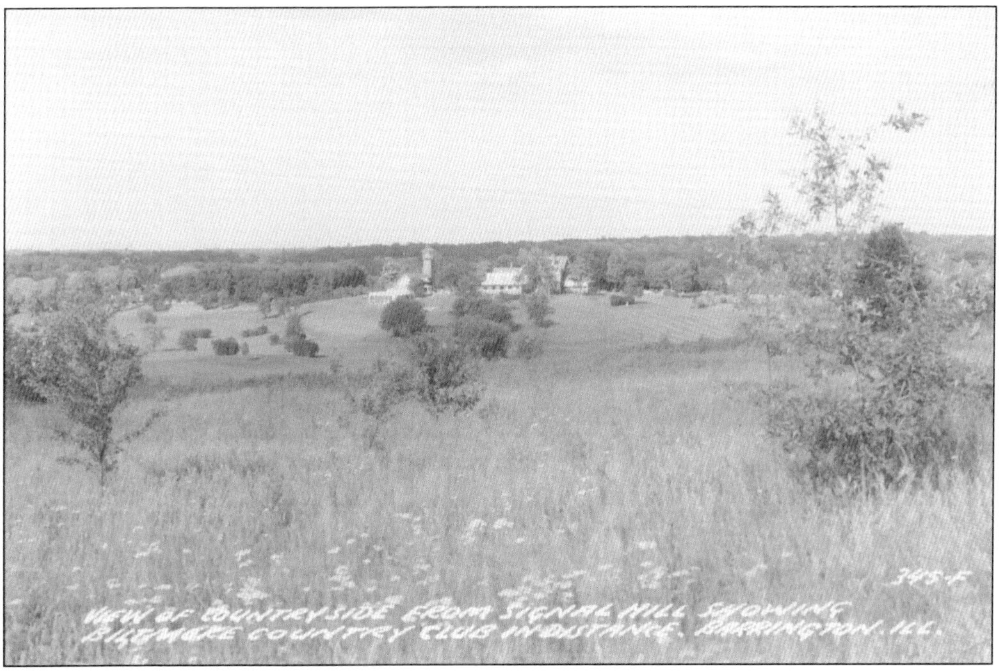

The trees and ground plantings have matured in this 1950s photograph of the Biltmore countryside from Signal Hill. The Biltmore Country Club is located in the center of the card.

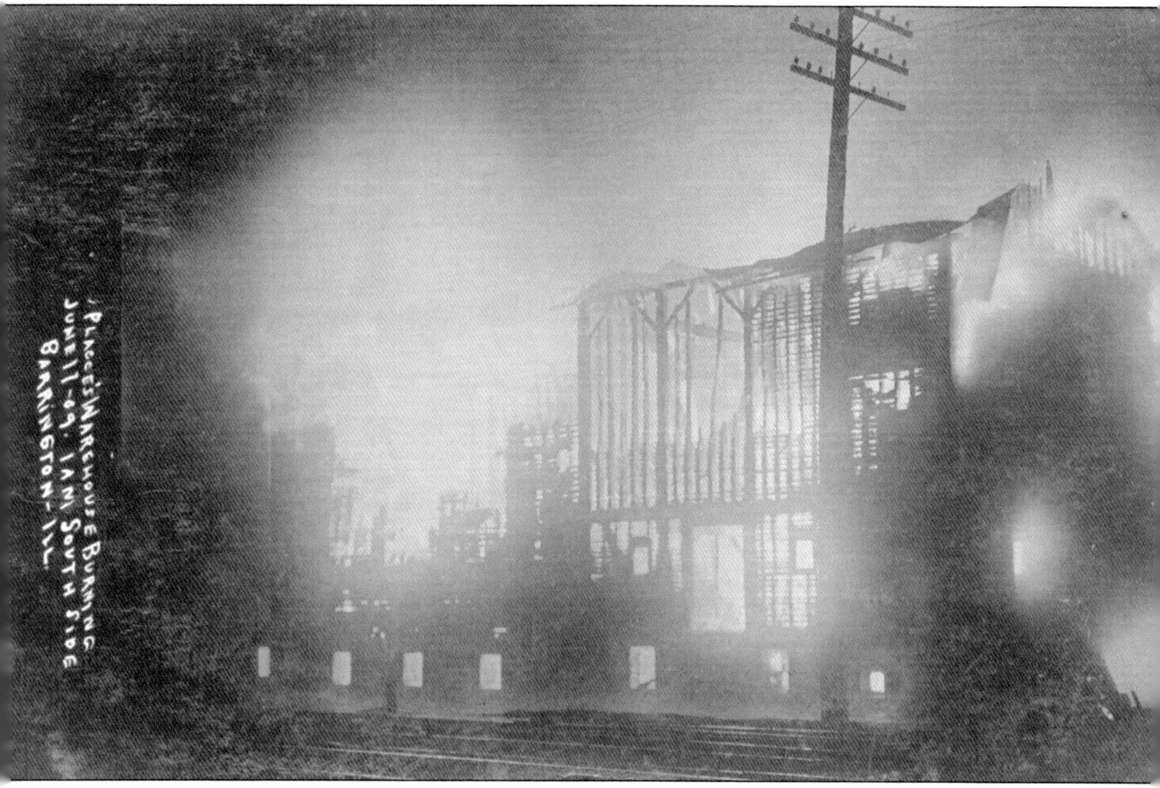

Barrington has had its share of downtown fires. Some of the buildings that burned included the C&NW roundhouse, the Lamey Review Building in 1904, Bowman Dairy in 1904, the J.F. Gieske Laundry in 1906 and 1907, and the Dan Lamey store in 1908. This postcard pictures Plagge's warehouse, located on the south side of town, burning down on June 11, 1909. This late-night photograph is attributed to George Froelich Jr., who experimented with capturing real-photo postcards under all kinds of conditions.

Americans increasingly enjoyed the new hobby of creating their own real-photo postcards. This image from November 1907 shows Justine Lydia Spunner of Barrington at one year of age. The message on the reverse side of the card reads: "Well, what do you think of me? My momma says I am a terror, but what good are girls if you don't know things. Lovingly Justine."

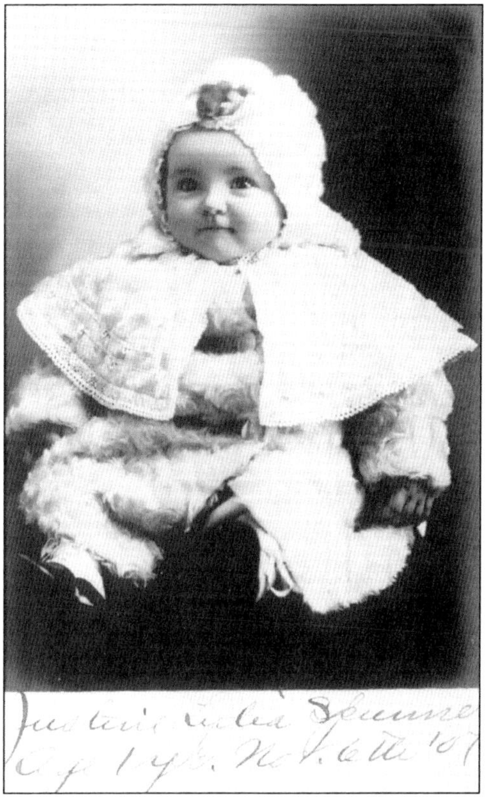

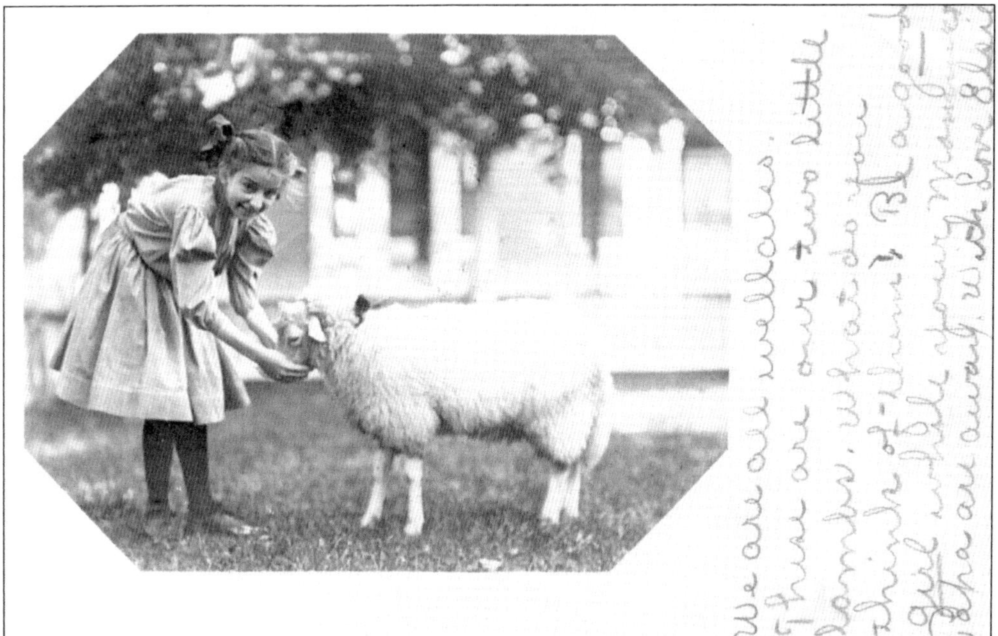

A local photographer captured this image of a young girl with her lamb in 1923. The note on the card reads: "We are all well also. These are our two little lambs. What do you think of them? Be a good girl while your momma and papa are away. With Love, Elsie."

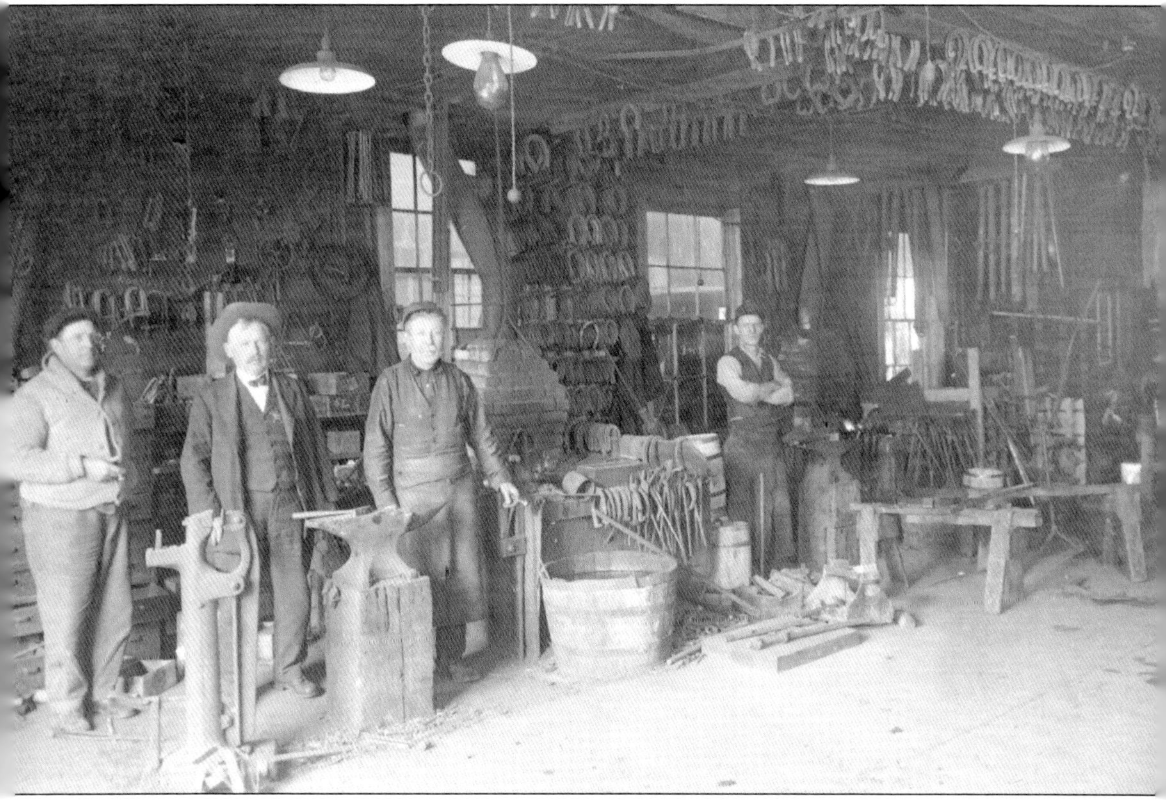

Blacksmithing and horseshoeing were hard and hot work, essential to the community when a horse needed new shoes or a wagon needed repair. Barrington had several blacksmiths. This image features a large assortment of horseshoes hanging from the beams and next to the forge. Unfortunately, the shop's exact location and the pictured individuals are not identified.

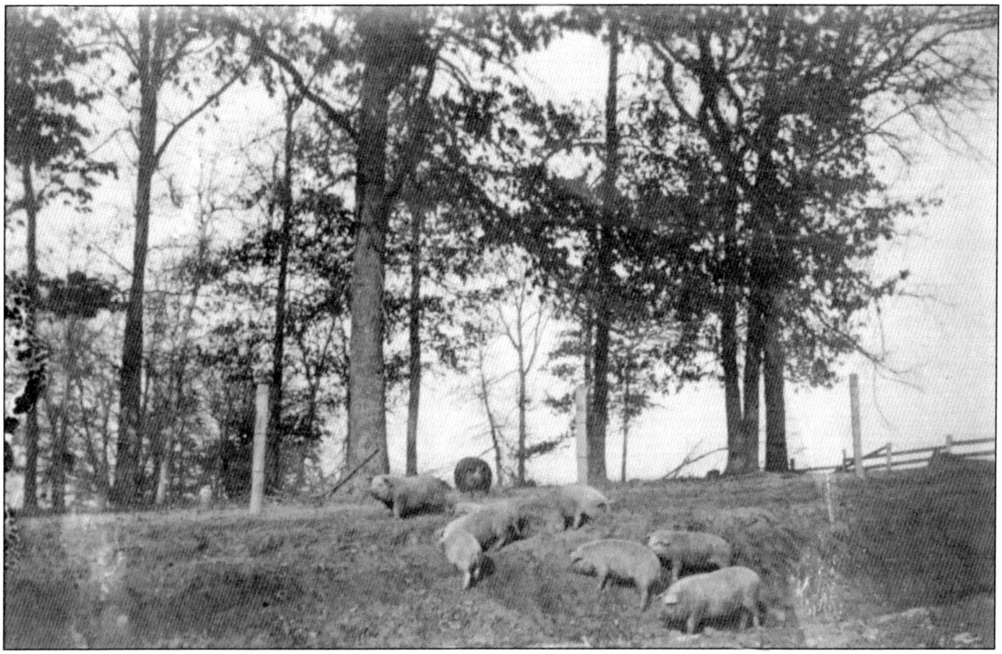

Photographer George Froelich Jr. captured this country scene of pigs moving about wooded acreage in 1907. The community had dairy farms and a butter factory; many residents raised their own livestock for food, with some bound for the Chicago livestock markets.

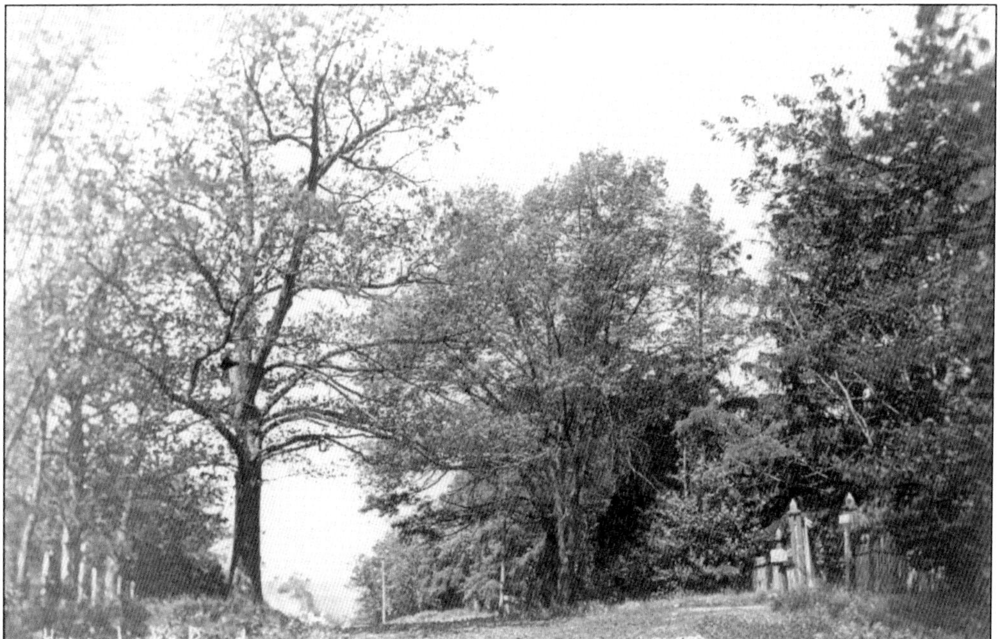

This clear and detailed photograph was captured along Honey Lake Road by George Froelich Jr. A mailbox and fence stand on the right side of the dirt road, leading to what was probably a farmhouse.

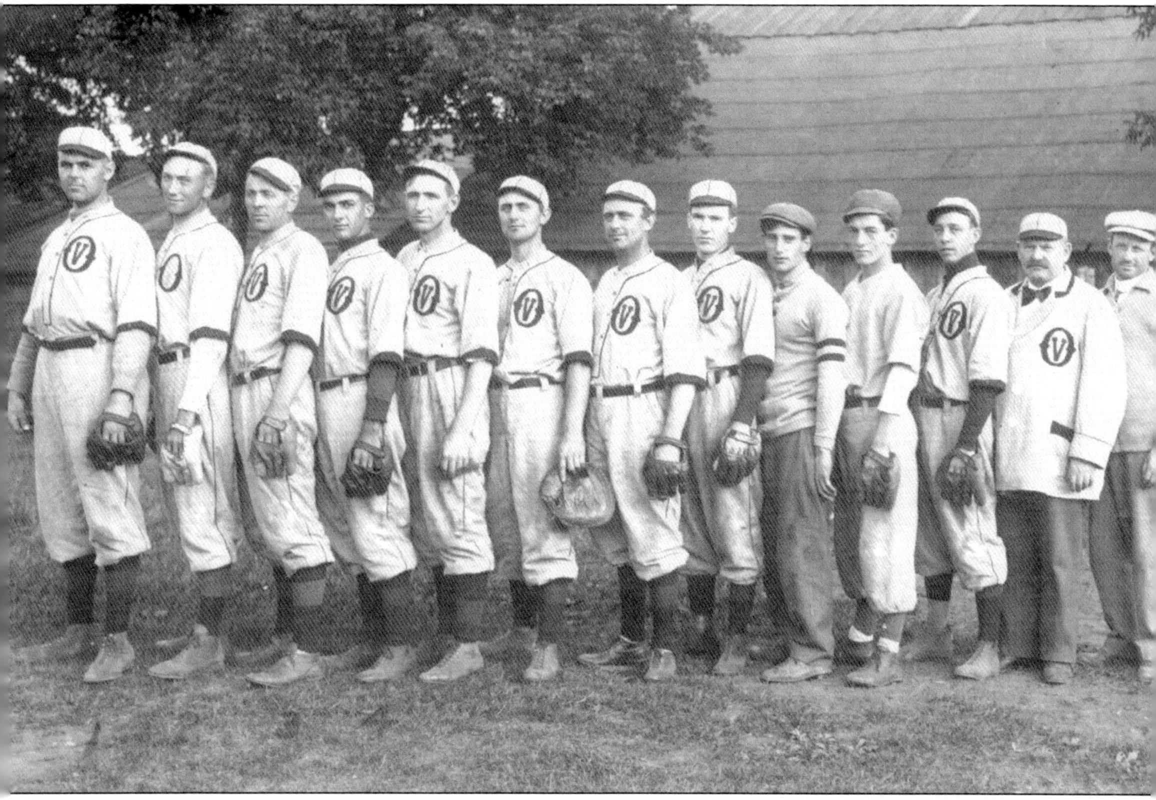

Max Lines captured this photograph of Barrington's O.V. baseball team in 1913. It is not known what the "O.V." on the uniforms stood for. Perhaps they were the initials of a local merchant or store underwriting the uniforms. The team members pictured here include well-known Barrington family names such as Waterman, Pomeroy, Loggie, Plagge, Shearer, Landwer, Francis, Brown, Banks, Carr, Blocks, and Lines.

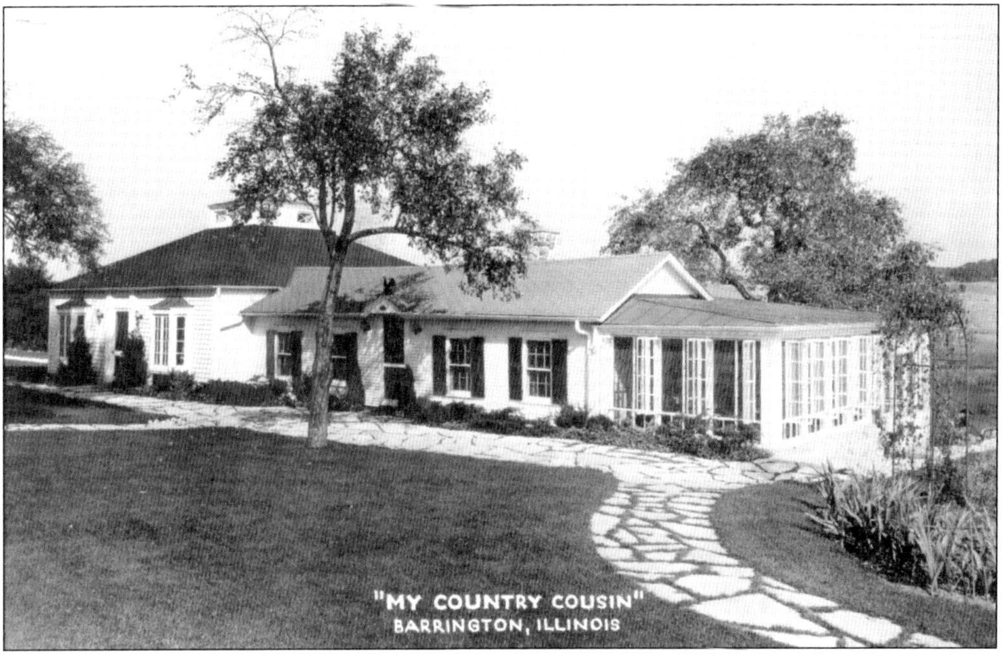

"My Country Cousin," on Sutton Road, was a favorite retreat for Barrington and Chicago residents, offering a refreshing country experience away from busy city life. My Country Cousin was owned by Frank Payne and was especially popular in the 1940s for one-day getaways.

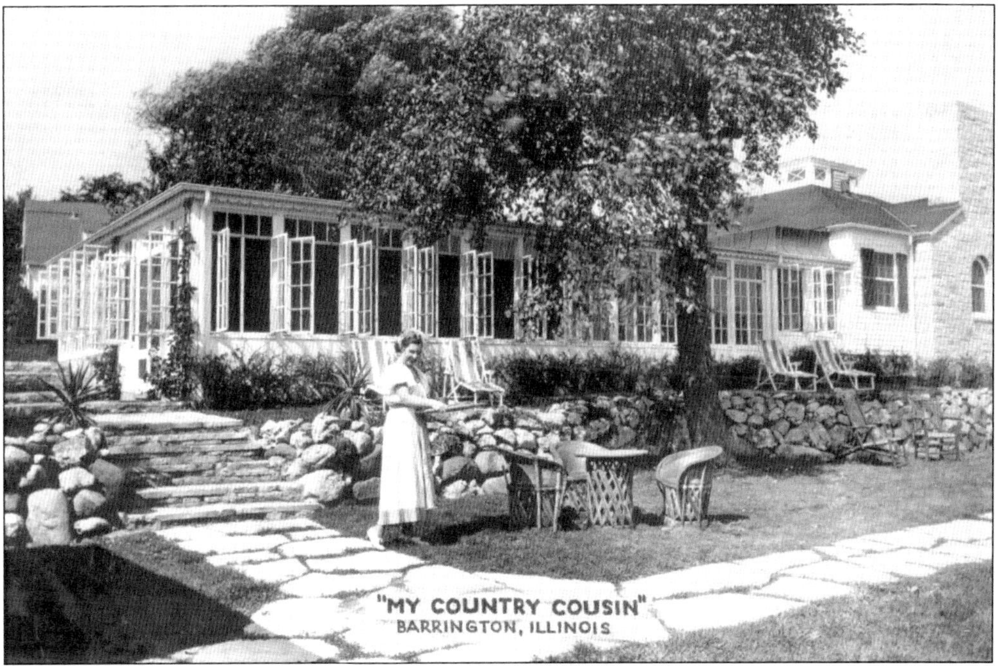

Visitors and guests to "My Country Cousin" could enjoy the beautiful countryside of Barrington while having tea and light refreshments. A note on the reverse side of this card states: "Here with Betty Grace, Payne and Specks Tilden on Saturday, May 4, 1940." My Country Cousin used this postcard and the previous one for marketing purposes.

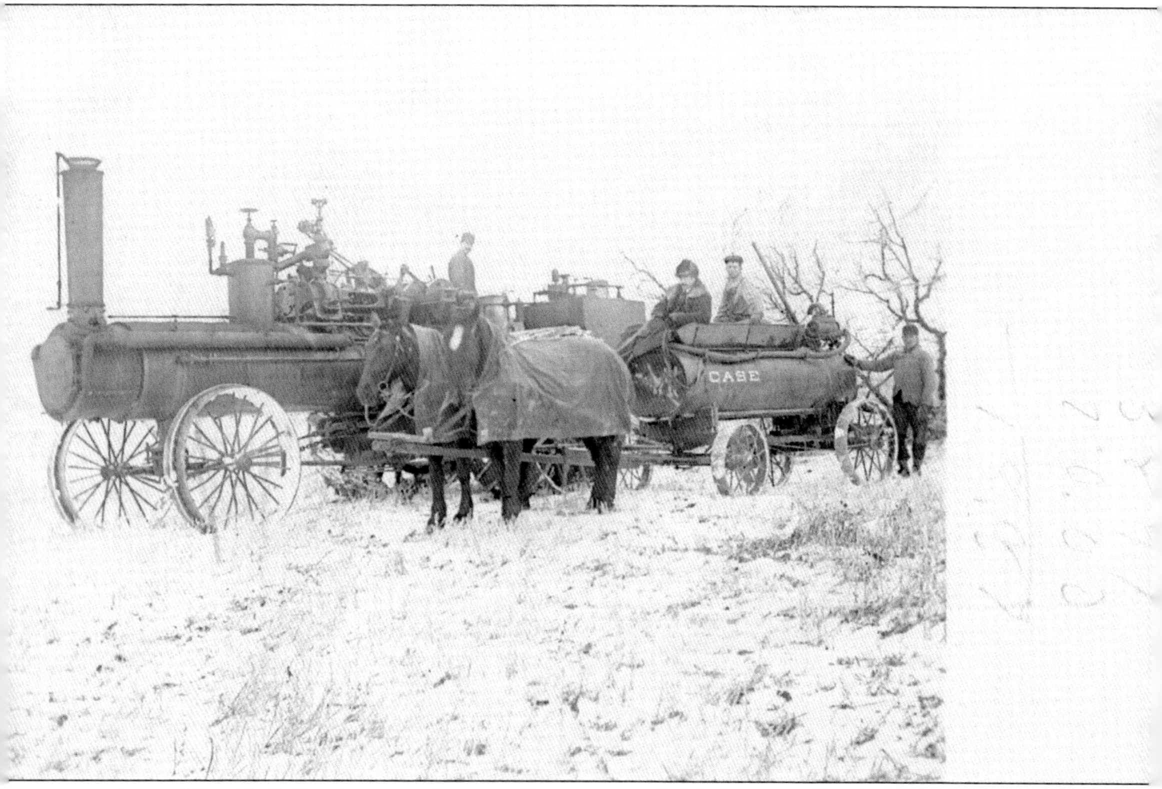

An unidentified Barrington photographer captured this image of a Case steam engine and horse-drawn water wagon. This equipment was used in the late 1800s for moving houses, cornhusking, operating sawmills, filling silos, and also as a threshing machine. In cold weather, the horses were covered to help keep the chill and snow off of them.

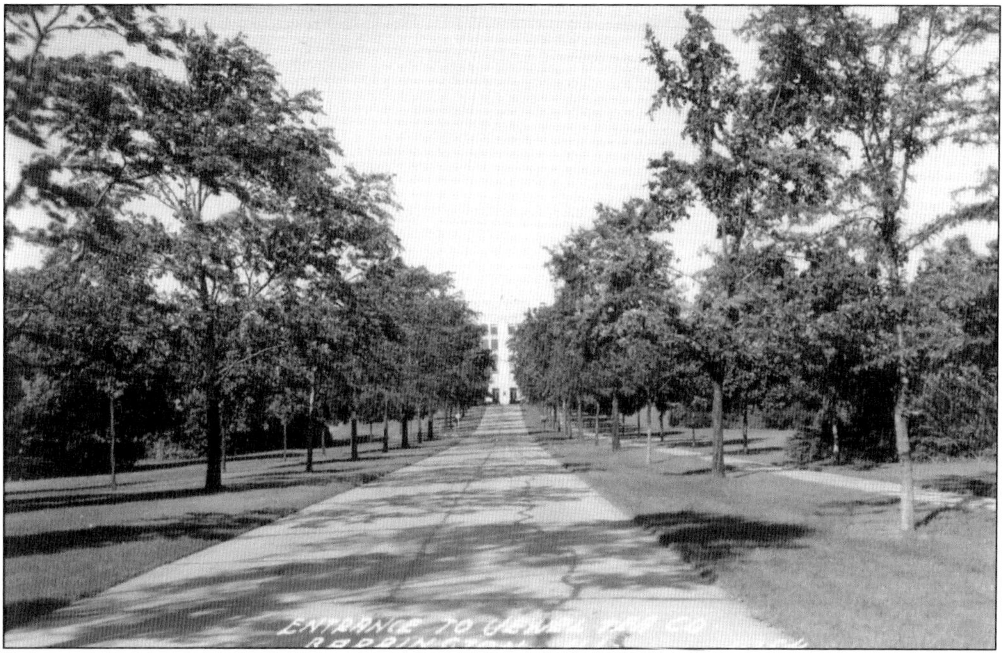

In 1928, the Jewel Tea Company purchased 211 acres of farmland in Barrington, and in 1929 it officially broke ground to construct a building on the site. In 1930, Jewel announced that it was moving the company's new general headquarters office and Midwest plant to Barrington. This image depicts the main entrance to the Jewel Tea Company.

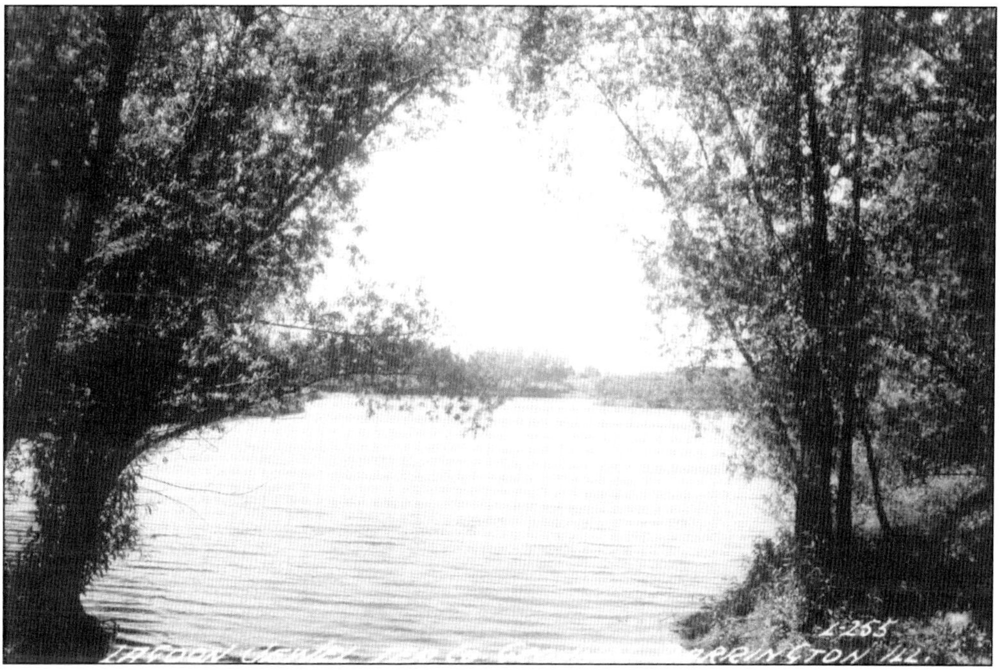

This real-photo postcard shows the lagoon on the Jewel Tea Company grounds, where employees could fish in the stocked lake.

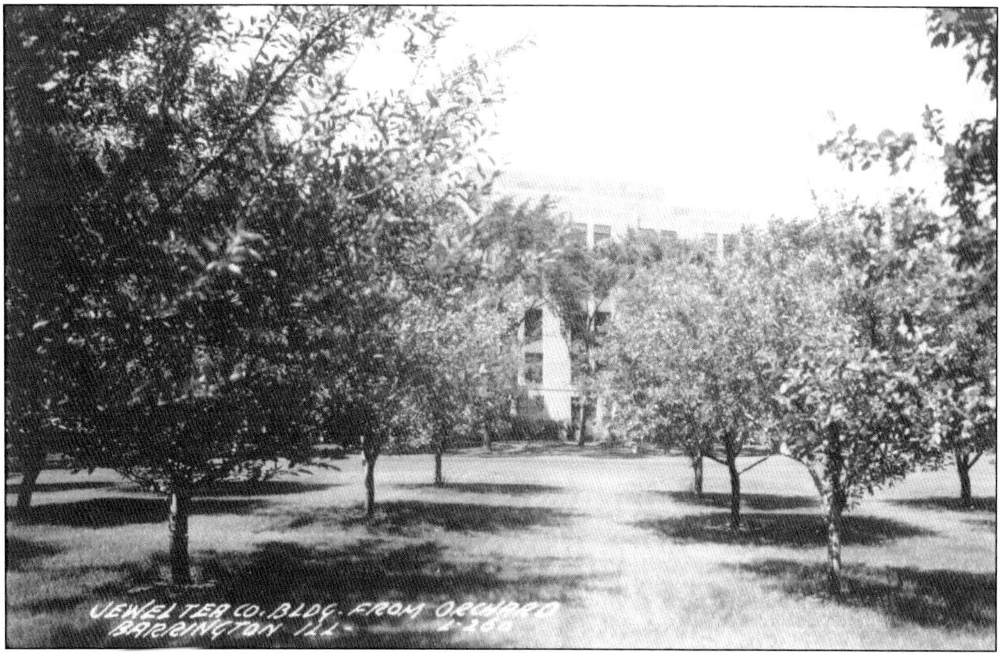

In this black-and-white real-photo postcard of the orchard on the grounds of the Jewel Tea Company, the main office building can be seen in the background.

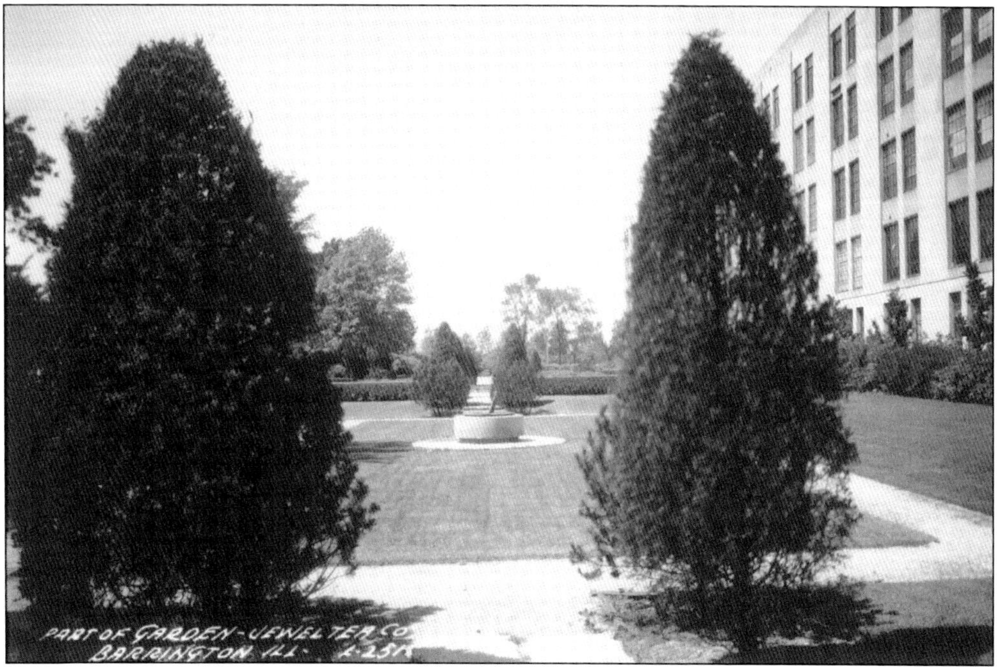

The Jewel Tea Company grounds were beautifully landscaped with 55,000 trees, shrubs, and bushes. Jewel made an announcement to its customers that the plant was located in "clean, sunshine, light, and air" in the village of Barrington.

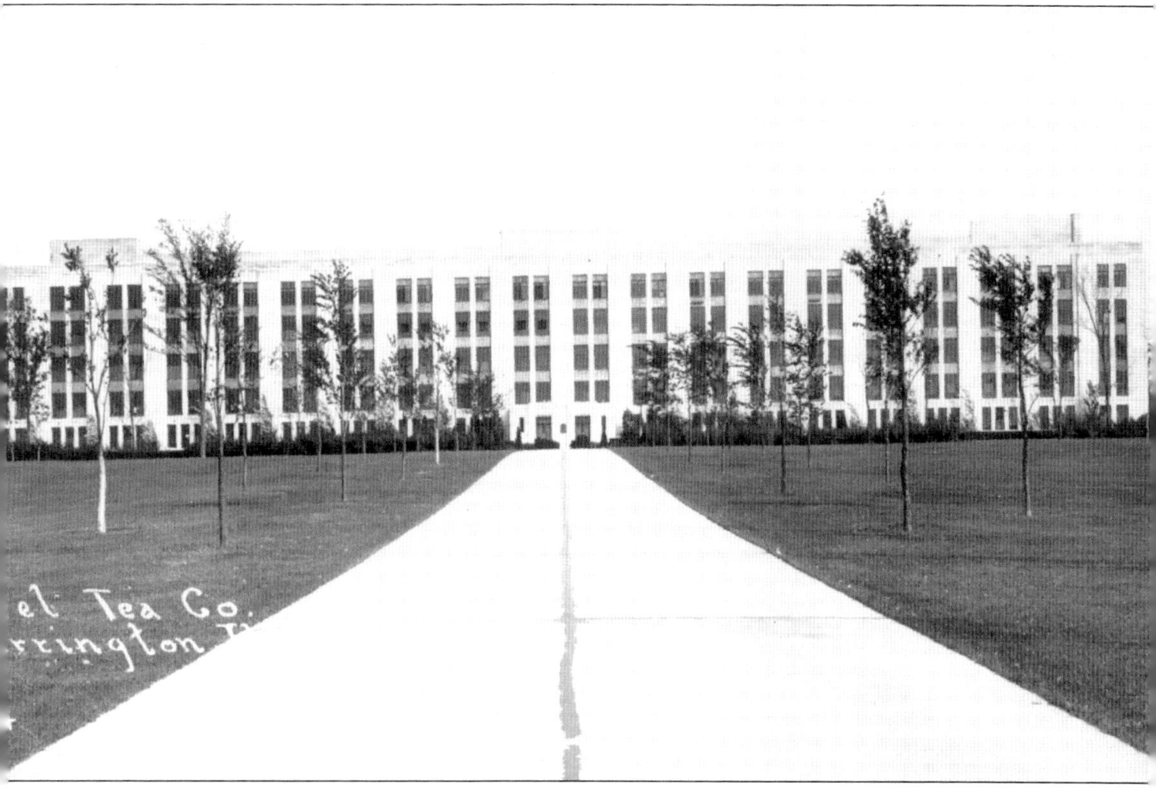

An unidentified photographer captured this image of the Jewel Tea Company headquarters, constructed of marble, limestone, and brass. In 1899, the Jewel Tea Company was primarily a home-delivery service offering tea, coffee, spices, and premiums.

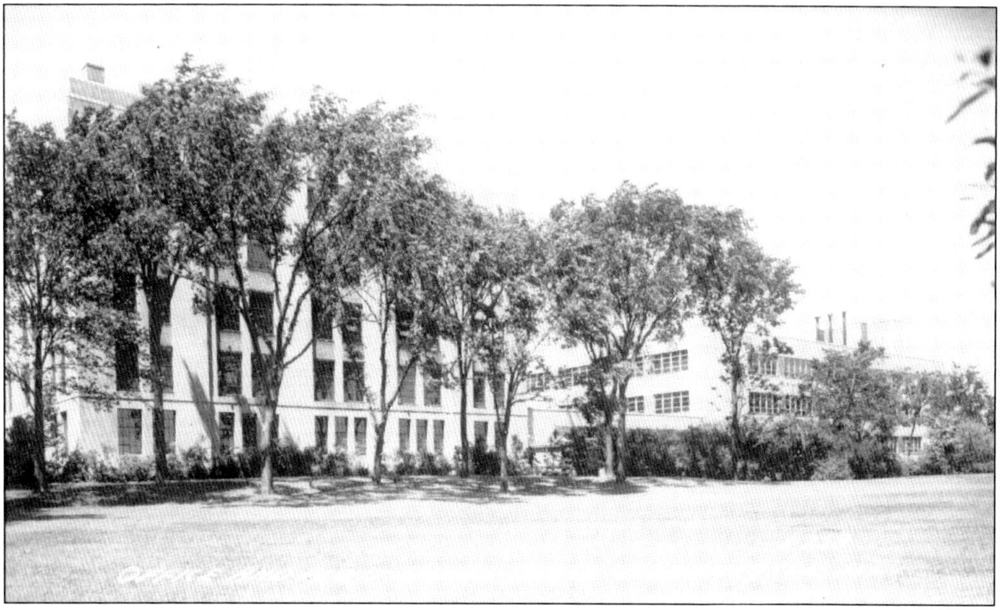

This image captures a view of both the office and plant of the Jewel Tea Company. The plantings around the buildings are maturing and the grounds are well maintained. On coffee-roasting days at Jewel, the smell of freshly roasted coffee would spread from the plant across the entire community.

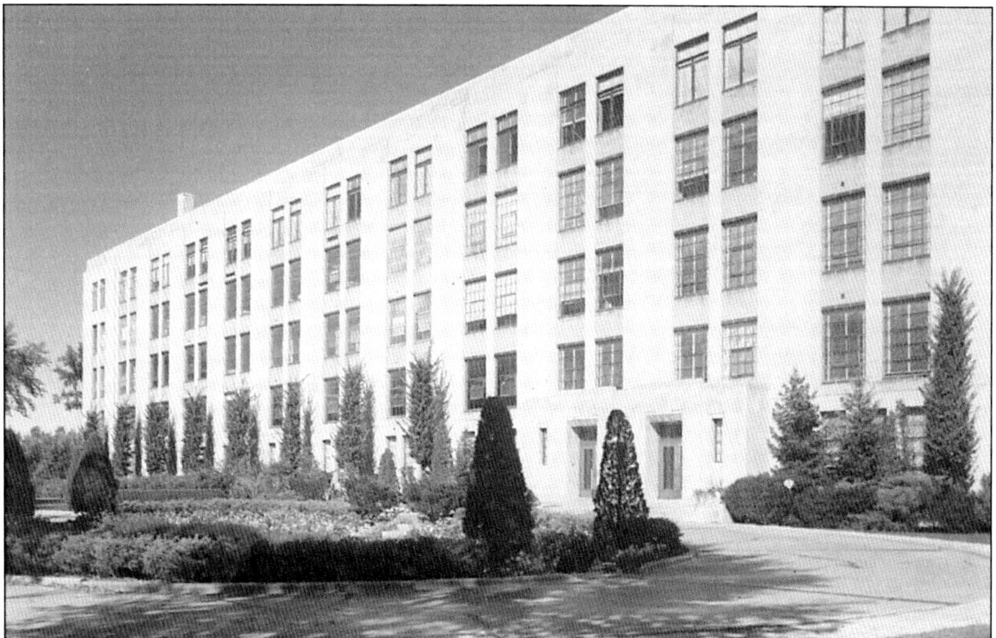

This color image of the Jewel Tea Company corporate headquarters in the mid-1950s includes a circular flower garden in the foreground of the photograph.

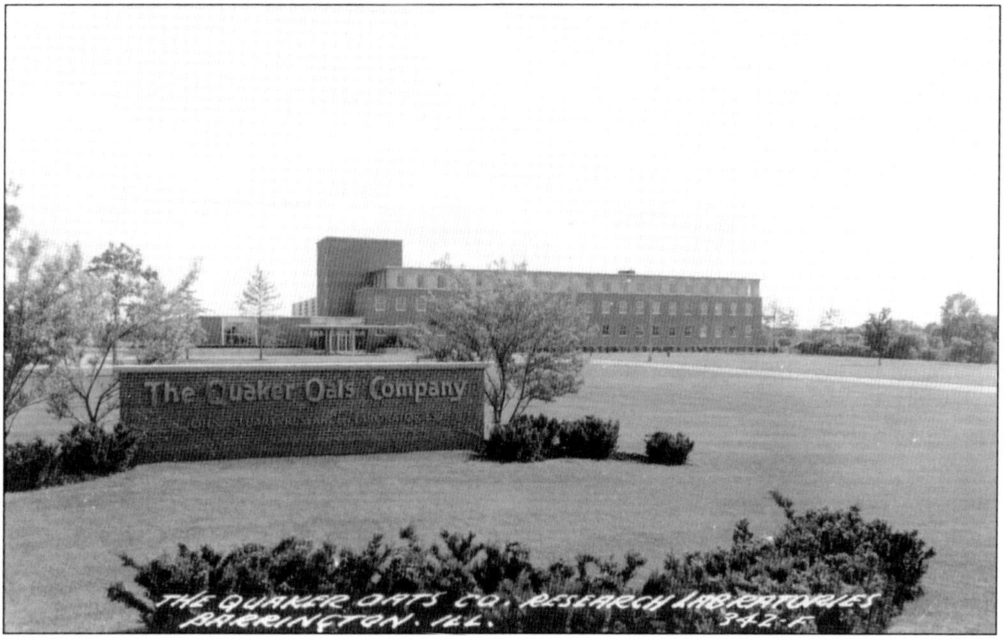

Barrington was also home to the Quaker Oats Company Research Laboratories. Quaker Oats is now a unit of PepsiCo, one of the world's largest consumer packaged goods companies. This image shows the company's facility on West Main Street, across from Barrington High School.

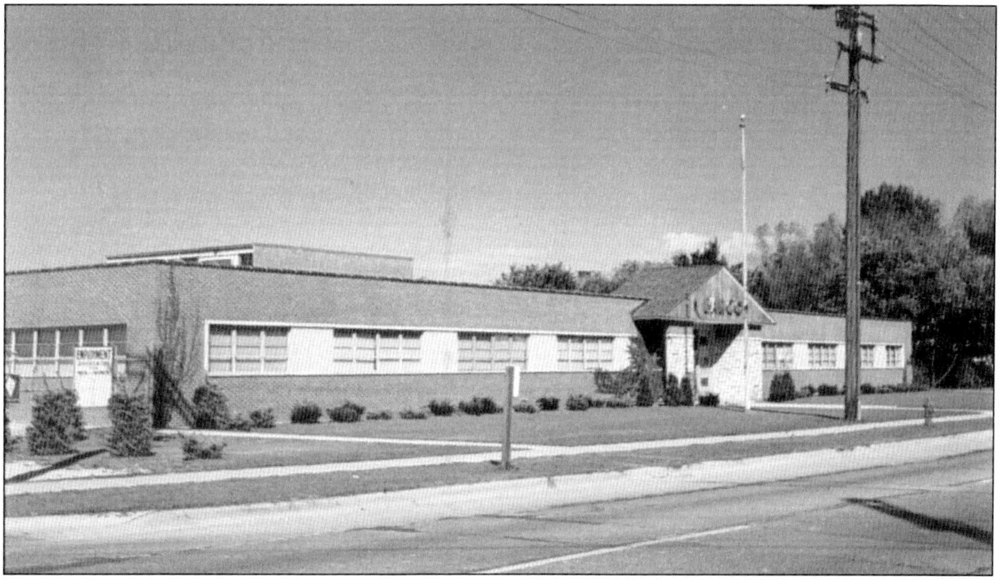
The Barco Plant is shown in this color photograph postcard from the mid-1950s. Barco manufactured plane swivels for single and multiplane movement for loading arms, high-pressure self-aligning swivels for aircraft, and rotary unions for water and steam on continuous rotating machinery. Barco was purchased by Aeroquip Corporation in 1961, but the Barrington plant remained the production facility until 1988, when Marison Industries purchased Barco Products and a new facility was built in Cary, Illinois, to house the corporate headquarters and manufacturing.

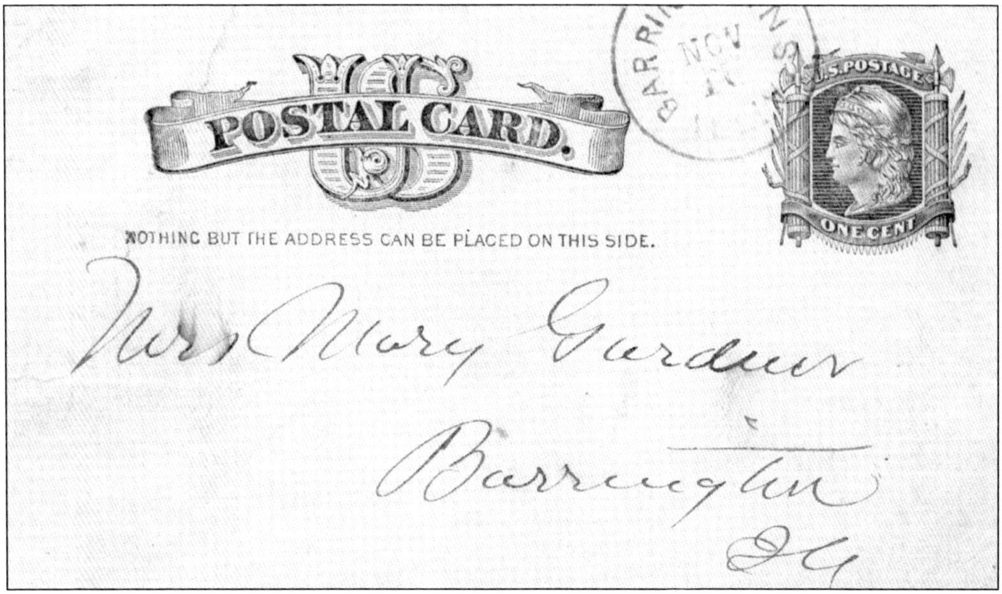

The US Post Office also offered postcards for individual and business use. This card is postmarked from Barrington Station, with the preprinted 1¢ postage imprint. The post office was established as Barrington Station in 1856, and this card was sent to Mary Gardner in 1883.

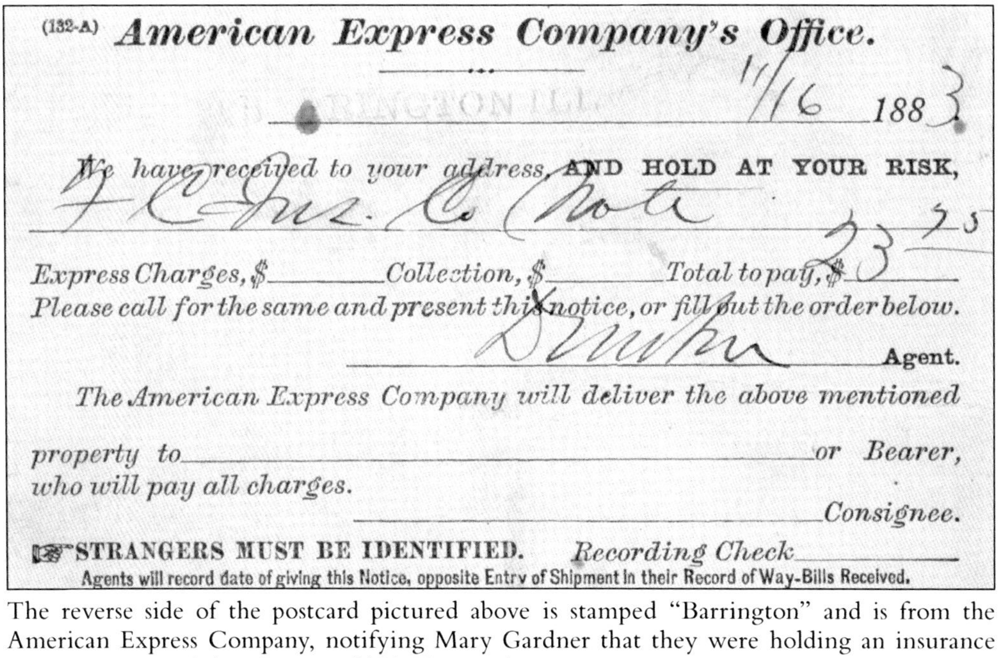
(132-A) **American Express Company's Office.**

BARRINGTON ILL. 11/16 1883

We have received to your address, **AND HOLD AT YOUR RISK,**

Express Charges, $ ___ Collection, $ ___ Total to pay, $ 23 75

Please call for the same and present this notice, or fill out the order below.

__________ **Agent.**

The American Express Company will deliver the above mentioned property to __________ *or Bearer, who will pay all charges.*

__________ *Consignee.*

STRANGERS MUST BE IDENTIFIED. *Recording Check* ______

Agents will record date of giving this Notice, opposite Entry of Shipment in their Record of Way-Bills Received.

The reverse side of the postcard pictured above is stamped "Barrington" and is from the American Express Company, notifying Mary Gardner that they were holding an insurance company note and that charges of $23.75 were due.

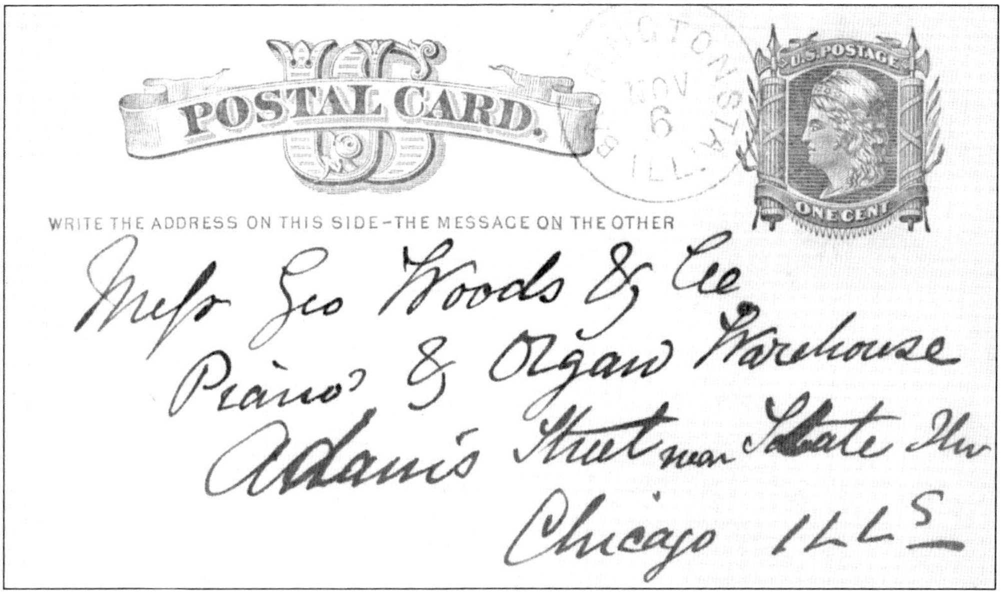
POSTAL CARD.
U.S. POSTAGE
ONE CENT
WRITE THE ADDRESS ON THIS SIDE—THE MESSAGE ON THE OTHER
Messrs Geo Woods & Co
Pianos & Organ Warehouse
Adams Street near State Str
Chicago ILLS

This US Postal Service card is also postmarked at Barrington Station and was addressed to the George Woods and Company Piano and Organ Warehouse on Adams Street in Chicago. It probably dates from the middle to late 1880s.

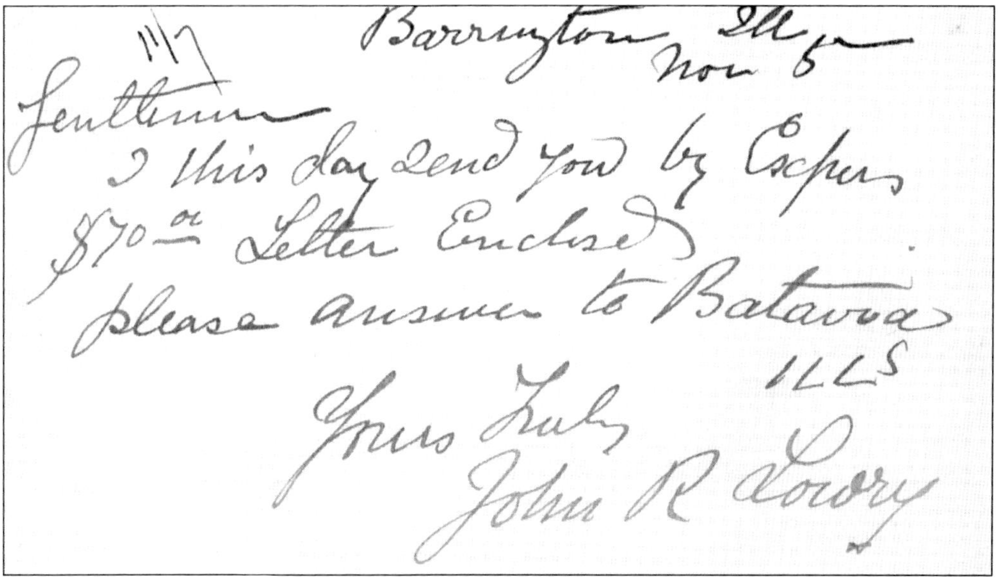
11/7
Barrington Ill
Nov 6
Gentlemen
I this day send you by Express
$70.00 Letter Enclosed
please answer to Batavia
ILLS
Yours Truly
John R Lowry

The message contained on this card notifies George Wood that John Lowry was sending $70 with a letter enclosed by express. He asks Wood to respond to him at the Batavia, Illinois, address. The Barrington post office was established as a money-order office in June 1875 and became a postal savings depository in February 1912.

Bibliography

Andreas, A.T. *History of Cook County, Illinois*. Self-published, 1884.

Barrington Area Bicentennial Commission. *Tales of Old Barrington*. Barrington, IL: Barrington Press, 1976.

Cumins, A.W. *Directory of McHenry County, Illinois,* Chicago, IL: Culver, Page Hoyne and Company, 1877.

Daniels, Daisy Paddock. *Prairieville U.S.A.* Arlington Heights, IL: Historical Society and Museum, 1971.

Froelich, George Jr. *Personal Diary of George Froelich Jr.* Barrington, IL: 1909.

Goodspeed, Weston A. and Daniel D. Healy. *History of Cook County, Illinois in Two Volumes.* Chicago, IL: The Goodspeed Historical Association, 1909.

Lines, Arnett C. Notes and discussions with Lines and photograph postcards compiled by Ken Munson. Barrington, IL: 1966–1969.

———. *Echoes of a Century 1847–1947.* The First Baptist Church of Barrington, Barrington, IL: publisher unknown, 1947.

Lines, Roy Max. Notes and discussions with Lines compiled by Ken Munson and photograph album. Barrington, IL: 1967–1969.

Miller, Arthur. Postcards, photographs, and notes from conversations with Miller compiled by Ken Munson. 1972–1977.

Munson, Ruth, Archivist, Barrington Area Historical Society. Research notes, writings and photograph album. Barrington, IL: 1968–2000.

Newhall, Beaumont. *The History of Photography.* New York, NY: Doubleday and Company, 1964.

Nye, Lowell Albert. *McHenry County Illinois 1832–1968.* Woodstock, IL: McHenry County Board of Supervisors, 1968.

Partridge, Charles A. *Historical Encyclopedia of Illinois and History of Lake County.* Chicago, Illinois Munsell Publishing Company, 1902.

Index